ON MY OWN

ON MY OWN

KOREAN BUSINESSES

AND RACE RELATIONS

IN AMERICA

IN-JIN YOON

The University of Chicago Press / Chicago & London

In-Jin Yoon is assistant professor in the Department of Sociology at
Korea University.

The University of Chicago Press, Chicago 60637
The University of Chicago Press, Ltd., London
© 1997 by The University of Chicago
All rights reserved. Published 1997
Printed in the United States of America
06 05 04 03 02 01 00 99 98 97   5 4 3 2 1

ISBN (cloth): 0-226-95927-9
ISBN (paper): 0-226-95928-7

Library of Congress Cataloging-in-Publication Data

Yoon, In-Jin, 1963–
    On my own : Korean businesses and race relations in America / In-
Jin Yoon.
        p.   cm.
    Includes bibliographical references and index.
    ISBN 0-226-95927-9. — ISBN 0-226-95928-7 (pbk.)
    1. Minority business enterprises—United States.   2. Korean Amer-
ican businesspeople.   3. Afro-Americans—Relations with Korean
Americans.   4. Small business—United States.   5. Entrepreneurship—United States.   6. Korea (South)—Emigration and immigration.
    I. Title.
HD2346.U5Y66   1997
338.6′422′089957073—dc21   96-39395
                                                                 CIP

♾ The paper used in this publication meets the minimum requirements
of the American National Standard for Information Sciences—Perma-
nence of Paper for Printed Library Materials, ANSI Z39.48-1984.

I dedicate this book to my parents and my wife,
who have sustained me with their constant love, faith, and prayer.

CONTENTS

While I was writing this book, I felt I was self-employed like the Korean immigrant merchants whom I chose to write about. I spent most of my time in a small office, working alone and late, as most Korean merchants do in their small stores. Because of limited funding, I had to conduct fieldwork and numerous interviews on my own, just as many Korean merchants depend on their own labor and that of family members. Husband and wife are the basic unit of operation in Korean immigrant businesses, and this book too is truly a product of teamwork. My wife helped me in numerous ways while I was conducting a survey in Los Angeles, and she also provided me with ideas, suggestions, and encouragement whenever I confronted problems in my research. Finally, because English is my second language, I had to work much harder at my writing than did my American colleagues, just as Korean merchants who are not fluent in English have difficulty in communication and often are mistreated and cheated as a result. Because of these and many other resemblances, I could sympathize with the feelings and experiences—such as social isolation, humiliation, and marginality—that Korean immigrant merchants and their families must endure in their businesses and personal lives.

This book, entitled *On My Own*, is a study of why Korean immigrants want to run their own businesses, how they realize their dreams, and what consequences they create and encounter in their lives and relations with their neighbors and society at large. The title *On My Own* has a double meaning. On the one hand, it represents Korean immigrants' strong motivations to become economically and socially independent through self-employment. On the other hand, it illustrates their social, economic, and political isolation from mainstream society, particularly in times of political crisis. During the civil unrest in Los Angeles in April

1992, for example, Koreans were left unprotected from rioters and opportunistic looters. The police let Koreatown burn down and no politicians came forward to defend the merchants, so the Koreans armed themselves to protect their lives and properties. After the unrest, they realized that they could not live in isolation, and they made greater efforts to improve relations with their neighbors of different colors and races.

This book is the outcome of my ten years of research on Korean immigrants in Chicago and Los Angeles. It originated from my M.A. thesis, written in 1985 at the University of Chicago, which examined Korean immigrant businesses in Chicago's black neighborhoods. I then developed this work into a Ph.D. thesis, including more detailed analyses of Korean immigration to the United States and a comparative analysis of self-employment among various racial and ethnic groups.

The turmoil in Los Angeles occurred shortly after the completion of the thesis in December 1991. At the time, I happened to be staying in Santa Barbara for a job interview with the Asian American Studies Program at the University of California, Santa Barbara, and I watched the burning and looting on TV at the program chair's residence. These events and the enormous financial and psychological toll they took on the Korean merchants required me to undertake a significant revision of my thesis before it could be published. I needed to explain why Korean merchants became the biggest victims of the destruction and why inner-city blacks and Latinos channeled their frustration and anger toward Koreans instead of toward whites. After I joined the faculty at Santa Barbara in July 1992, I started a two-year research project to examine Korean–black–Latino relations in Los Angeles. As a result, this book became a comprehensive study of Korean immigration, immigrant entrepreneurship, and Korean–black relations in Chicago and Los Angeles.

This project would not have been possible without the help of the following people. Professor Gerald Suttles at the University of Chicago, who was my adviser and the chair of my dissertation committee, inspired my work on Korean immigrant businesses in Chicago and guided me with constant encouragement, intellectual insights, and kind advice. He has been an example of modesty, sincere scholarship, and caring for students. I also wish to extend my appreciation to Professors Douglas Massey, William Parish, William Wilson, and Marta Tienda for their encouragement and helpful suggestions. In particular, Professor Wilson offered me a yearlong postdoctoral position in the Center for the Study of Urban Inequality, which provided me with valuable time for writing as well as for learning about urban poverty and public policy.

Professor Sucheng Chan, a leading scholar in Asian American studies, helped me acquire deeper insights into and knowledge about Koreans and other Asian Americans. As the chair of the Asian American Studies Department at Santa Barbara, she also played an instrumental role in helping me acquire equipment and funds for my research. The fellowship I had with other colleagues at the University of California, Santa Barbara—to name a few, Nolan Zane, Jay Chan, Xiajian Xao, Jon Cruz, Harvey Molotch, Mitchell Denier, and Richard Appelbaum—helped me refine my thinking and analysis on issues of race relations and entrepreneurship.

Professors Pyong Gap Min and Steve Gold read earlier drafts of this book and provided helpful comments and suggestions for revision. Their candid and objective evaluations helped this book become more coherent in its themes and broader and more comparative in its perspectives.

I am greatly indebted to the Population Research Center at the National Opinion Research Center, which provided me with a Hewelett Demographic Training Fellowship during my graduate studies at the University of Chicago. My appreciation is also extended to Allen Holden, Yun-Ji Qian, Natsumi Aratame, and other fellows at the Population Research Center Computer Room, NORC, who provided me with kind and professional assistance in computation and statistical analysis. Mark Schildhauer, Jane Murdock, and Steve Velasco at the Social Science Computing Facility of the University of California, Santa Barbara, provided me with similar assistance in computation and technical support.

Many undergraduate and graduate students participated as research assistants in my research projects in Chicago and Los Angeles. David Engstrom and Carolyn Lim worked as interviewers for the Chicago survey, and Jung-Hwa Lee, Sung-Hwan Kim, Haeng-Ja Chung, Dal-Seok Yang, and Soo-Ik Chung worked as interviewers for the Los Angeles survey. I also greatly appreciated the research assistance of Bora Rhim, Sun-A Lee, and Jane Song, who painstakingly searched for and photocopied newspaper and journal articles on Korean businesses and relations between Koreans and members of other races.

I have to express my appreciation to the Korean merchants and to the directors and staffs of various Korean associations in Chicago and Los Angeles who agreed to be interviewed and provided me with candid answers to my questions and valuable insights into the Korean community. They participated in the interviews with the belief that I could represent their feelings, views, and voices, which are often too foreign to be heard in the mainstream media. I hope they will read this book in order to better understand and improve their current conditions.

I am fortunate to have my parents, who constantly pray for my health and my studies and always teach me to build scholarship on faith in God. Without their emotional, financial, and spiritual support, this book would not have been possible. My wife, Hyang-Ju Lee, is also a continuing source of encouragement and faith. She helped me enormously with the Los Angeles survey and waited patiently for the final revision. She called and made appointments with Korean merchants on my behalf and provided me with ideas and suggestions whenever I confronted problems in my study. She is a true partner in my intellectual journey.

On April 29, 1992, four white officers from the Los Angeles Police Department were acquitted on charges of excessive use of force against Rodney King. The 25-year-old black motorist had been chased by the police for a speed violation on the evening of March 3, 1991, and severely beaten when he refused to comply with their order to surrender. The beating scene was coincidentally captured on videotape by George Holiday, an amateur cameraman, and played repeatedly as evidence of police brutality against minorities. No one suspected that the officers would escape punishment, but the predominantly white jury in Simi Valley, a bedroom town that houses large numbers of police, delivered a not-guilty verdict. Soon after the announcement of the verdict, Los Angeles experienced an eruption of violence and racial hatred that claimed sixty lives and caused nearly $1 billion in property damage. One of the casualties was Edward Jae Sung Lee, an 18-year-old Korean American who was accidentally shot in Koreatown by a Korean vigilante who mistook him for a looter.

A Mother Still Waits

Ninety days later, Edward's mother, Jung Hui Lee, calmly reflected on the death of her only son during an interview for *Sa-I-Gu*, a documentary film about a group of Korean American women shopkeepers victimized by the civil unrest: "At the time, I thought one man shot my son. I was so resentful at that person. But thinking broadly about what happened to my son, it wasn't that individual who shot him. The LAPD did not act soon enough. When the National Guard came, they were nowhere in sight of Koreatown. . . . Something was drastically wrong."[1]

Mrs. Lee and her husband had arrived in the United States in April

1972 to start a better life for themselves and their future children. Not once had she hired a baby-sitter for her son, concerned that he might not receive good care in the hands of a stranger. Instead, she worked in a sewing factory in the morning and came home by four in the afternoon; her husband left for his night-shift cleaning job at six in the evening.[2] So they raised their son as if they were passing a marathon baton.

"I still feel pain in my chest when I think of those times," continued Mrs. Lee. "I am embarrassed, but I used to have a cleaning job at night. I took my son with me. He was a junior high school student. He had a strong body and vacuumed for me. He was at the age to study and play, but he went from one place to another with a heavy vacuum cleaner. When I think of that, my chest feels tight—it hurts," she tearfully recalled. But through their hard work and frugality, the Lees eventually managed to open their own luggage retail store in Koreatown.

Then came the events of April 29, 1992. After the not-guilty verdict was announced, signs of protest appeared first at the intersection of Florence and Normandie. Members of the crowd gathered there began to throw stones at passing cars and pedestrians. They set fire to and looted Tom's Liquor Store, a Japanese-owned business, and such acts of arson and looting soon spread. Roughly twenty-five police officers tried to restrain the angry crowd but made a fatal retreat after their attempt to make arrests prompted shouting, rock throwing, and pushing. Lieutenant Mike Moulin, the field commander who ordered the retreat, later defended his decision: "I didn't want [the officers] killed" (Curry and McDowell 1992, 39). The police did not move back in for two hours, awaiting orders from their superiors. During this critical time, L.A.P.D. Chief Daryl Gates was in affluent Brentwood attending a small party to raise funds to oppose a Los Angeles ballot measure that would have made the police chief more accountable to elected officials. His absence created a vacuum in command at the highest echelon of the police department.

The failure of the police to react more quickly and decisively to the rioting caused great casualties and property damage that could have been prevented. Immediately after the retreat of the police, a Japanese American was pulled out of his car and beaten by the mob. Reginald Denny, a white truck driver who stopped at the besieged intersection, was pulled from his truck and hit and kicked on the head, knee, and elbow by four young black men. This brutal scene was captured by a TV crew on a helicopter and broadcast numerous times, as if to mitigate the guilt whites might have felt toward blacks after watching the beating of Rodney King on videotape. As reported in the front-page story of the *Los Angeles Times* at the peak of the burning and looting, the beating of Reginald Denny represented "the face on the flip side of the Rodney King coin, the unofficial black-on-white response to the official white-on-black beating."

The precipitating cause of the civil unrest was a wrong verdict biased against a black man, and the initial disturbances were acts of protest against antiblack racism among white people and in the American judicial system.[3] But the disturbances became more violent and destructive as members of black gangs started burning stores in South Central Los Angeles. Thousands of poor inner-city residents from different racial backgrounds joined in a widespread looting rampage that continued for three days, until the National Guard started arresting looters on May 1. The unrest was a truly multiracial and multiethnic event in which members of various groups were both victims and victimizers. An analysis of police records shows that a total of 12,127 people were arrested during these three days. Of these, 43 percent were Latinos, 34 percent blacks, and 14 percent whites (Ong and Hee 1993, 10). However, among those who committed serious crimes such as battery and arson, 38 percent were blacks, 28 percent Latinos, and 17 percent whites. Black store owners in South Central marked the windows of their stores with signs reading "Black-Owned," but that did not save many of them.

An analysis of damage patterns tells us that blacks and Latinos behaved differently during the unrest. Korean stores in South Central, a solidly black neighborhood, sustained more fire damage but less looting than those elsewhere in Los Angeles (Light, Har-Chvi, and Kan 1994, 80). If we assume that the motives for arson are hatred and revenge and the motive for looting is acquisition, we might conclude that blacks who set fire to Korean stores did so out of hatred and revenge against these merchants, whereas Latinos who looted Korean stores did so for the acquisition of material goods.[4]

Koreans became the major victims of the unrest partly because of the heavy concentration of Korean businesses in South Central and partly because of the escalating tensions between Korean store owners and black customers in the area (Ong and Hee 1993). Of a total of 4,500 stores that were either burned down or looted, 2,300 were Korean-owned, and of a total of $1 billion in property damages, $400 million was borne by Koreans.

Mrs. Lee continued her story about her son's death. "As he listened to Radio Korea that reported Korean stores were being looted, he became excited," she explained. "'It has been twenty years since Koreans came here. Everything we have worked for is now in flames. It disappeared in one morning,' he said. 'How can we just sit here and watch it happen? We Koreans should go out and protect our own,' he said. How could I send my only son into the riots? So I pleaded with him to stay and protect the family. 'Mother, because of people like you, we Koreans have been stricken. If Koreans are all like you, it will happen again in ten years. We can't sit still,' he said.

"At the moment the radio was telling the Haengju San Sung story.[5] He asked what that meant. I explained that during a Japanese invasion [in 1592] women fought, carrying stones in their aprons. 'Haengju' meaning apron. 'How can you sit still and tell such a story? Mother, you, too, must go out and fight,' he said and went out.

"In the evening, my daughter said, 'Mom, something has happened to my brother.' Then she started crying. I urged her to tell me what had happened. 'I think the victim yesterday might have been Eddie,' she said. My husband and I went to the *Korea Times*. I glanced at that day's paper. The headline read 'First Korean Victim.' There was one thread of hope. When my son went out, he wore a white shirt and blue jeans. The man in the picture wore a black T-shirt. This couldn't be my son. I was clutching at straws. His face was my son's, but his clothes were not. He could not possibly have changed them. I asked the man at the newspaper where my son was. I was told he was in the morgue. I went there. I discovered they had nothing to confirm my son's identity. Then he brought out a pair of glasses, two dimes, and a pen. That was all he had when he was sacrificed. About that T-shirt . . . in the *L.A. Times*, the picture was in color. What looked black in the Korean newspaper was my son's blood."

At the time of the interview, Mrs. Lee had not yet comprehended these events. "It's exactly three months, ninety days since my son died. As I told you before, even though I saw the body at the funeral, I don't remember it. My mind just won't accept it. I know people think it strange that I wait for my son after seeing his body. He just went out and did not come back yet."

Korean American Blues

Mrs. Lee lost her beloved son and more than two thousand Korean shopkeepers lost their lifetime investment in that one day in 1992. What they lost was not only property, which can be regained sooner or later, but also dreams, sweat, and tears, which cannot be easily recovered. For many Koreans, as for Mrs. Lee, April 29—in Korean, *Sa-I-Gu*—marked the shattering of a naive belief in the American Dream and American law enforcement.[6] It was an awakening to their minority status and unfair treatment in a country that they believed to be a land of opportunity for all. It was also a painful lesson about the fragility of their economic base, which depends on the impoverished, oppressed, and rebellious classes of society. It reminded them that they could not survive in isolation in a multiracial society such as the United States and that they needed political power in order to sustain their economic prosperity.

Beginning in 1970, five years after the United States opened its doors to all immigrants regardless of their national origin, about 30,000 Koreans had crossed the Pacific Ocean annually to start a new life in the United States. A high percentage of these immigrants were college-educated, white-collar, and middle-class people in South Korea who immigrated to the United States seeking the upward social and economic mobility that was denied them in their homeland. Ironically, they faced the same limited opportunities for upward mobility once they arrived. The language barrier, a mismatch between Korean education and American occupations, unfamiliarity with American customs and institutions, and prejudice and discrimination against immigrants and racial minorities all contributed to their difficulty in finding white-collar and professional employment in the American job market. The positions initially available to them were low-level, low-paying, and dead-end jobs in either the Korean ethnic economy or the secondary labor market of the general economy. Under these conditions, self-employment in small businesses became the most attractive alternative to unrewarding positions in the labor market.

As a growing number of Korean immigrants turned to small business as their second career in the United States, a complex web of social networks based on kinship, friendship, church membership, and school ties slowly formed in the immigrant community. In formal and informal meetings, running a small business became a common topic of conversation. Success stories of Korean business owners spread within the community and offered role models to other immigrants. Financial assistance and business advice were exchanged among family members, friends, and church members. Information about certain business opportunities circulated exclusively within the Korean community. In this manner, small business became an ethnic matter, not simply an individual initiative.

Once the networks of entrepreneurship were firmly established, Korean immigrants began to arrive in the United States with capital and entrepreneurial skills in hand. They could therefore start their businesses within several years of their arrival, without the long tour of duty in the secondary labor market required of their predecessors. As the Korean ethnic economy expanded substantially in the 1980s, South Korean export firms and financial institutions started establishing more branch offices, exporting more goods, investing more capital, and hiring more Korean immigrant employees in large American cities with a heavy concentration of Koreans and Korean businesses. Consequently, the ethnic economy continued to expand. Now small business is the most important livelihood for immigrants and the backbone of the Korean American community. Two-thirds of the adult Korean immigrants in Los Angeles find their employment in small businesses, as owners, employees, or unpaid family workers (Min 1993).

Their concentration in small business does not, however, demonstrate that they are wholehearted advocates of entrepreneurship. Small business is not entirely a symbol of success for Koreans, as conservative theorists usually envision. Nor is it simply a disguised form of cheap labor and exploitation of oneself and one's family members, as Marxist theorists claim. On balance, it is a bittersweet livelihood, entailing enormous physical, psychological, familial, and social costs to generate a moderate income. Many Korean business owners contract incurable illnesses and mental disorders from years of long hours and enormous stress. Their children cry for their time, attention, and love while they strive to make enough money for the children's education. A significant number of Korean business owners are injured or lose their lives every year at the hands of robbers, their American Dream unfulfilled. It is not worth risking one's life for small monetary gains. But in the absence of other economic alternatives, small business remains the most viable means for Korean immigrants to secure an economic foothold in the United States.

The concentration of Koreans in small business also entails social costs that threaten the survival of these businesses. One such cost is tension between Korean store owners and black and Latino customers in the inner-city neighborhoods of large American cities.[7] In particular, Korean–black relations reached a level of conflict when some black nationalist activists in New York City and Los Angeles organized boycotts against Korean stores, forcing several of them to close. In reaction, Koreans from all walks of life donated money to the stores under attack and marched in mass demonstrations calling for adequate police protection and racial harmony.

Korean–black relations have been prone to conflict because Korean businesses flourish in low-income black neighborhoods where most of the residents cannot even make a start in business. For Koreans, such neighborhoods represent a dangerous but very affordable place to establish a business. But from the viewpoint of many blacks, Koreans—like their Jewish and Italian predecessors—are interested only in making money without contributing to the economic well-being of the local residents. They are viewed as part of the white system that oppresses black people. As the economic conditions of inner-city blacks deteriorate, Koreans, Latinos, and other immigrants are likely to be viewed as competitors for jobs, housing, education, and public assistance programs.

Language barriers, cultural misunderstandings, and frequent over-the-counter disputes have also led black customers to believe that they are being disrespected and mistreated by Korean store owners. Some black nationalist activists have turned individual blacks' bad feelings toward individual Korean stores into a collective opinion against Korean businesses as a group. They have also transformed store-level disputes into an essentially political phenomenon, using boycotts of Korean businesses to gain economic autonomy in their communities. Thus, Koreans and blacks fail to acknowledge their common minority status in a white-dominated society and to take collective action to challenge the status quo that created and maintains racial injustice and discrimination against minorities.

The Organization of the Book

This book is a thorough and systematic analysis of why Koreans immigrated to the United States, why and how they started small businesses, how they interpret their businesses and immigrant lives, and how their entrepreneurial activity causes tensions and conflicts between them and members of other minority groups. After analyzing the nature and patterns of such conflicts, the book discusses and recommends programs and policies that can improve race relations at the individual, community, and governmental levels.

This is not the first scholarly study of immigration, entrepreneurship, and race relations among Korean Americans. Several books have already investigated extensively the characteristics of Korean immigrant business owners and their businesses (I. Kim 1981; Hurh and Kim 1984; Min 1988; Light and Bonacich 1988), but they have become outdated as new aspects and dimensions of Korean immigrant entrepreneurship continue to surface and call for new explanations.

For instance, Illsoo Kim's *New Urban Immigrants*, the groundbreaking work on contemporary Korean immigrants and their community that motivated me to study the subject when I was a graduate student at the University of Chicago, was based on his long ethnographic study of the New York Korean community in the 1970s. Ivan Light and Edna Bonacich's *Immigrant Entrepreneurs*, which investigates Korean immigrant entrepreneurship from various angles, had as one of its primary sources of data a telephone survey of 204 Korean business owners in Los Angeles that was conducted in 1977. Although these earlier studies set the direction of research on the subject, dynamic changes in Korean immigration, community life, immigrant entrepreneurship, and race relations call for more up-to-date empirical research and more creative theoretical explanations.

One exception to the general pattern is Pyong Gap Min's recent book on Korean businesses and Korean–black relations in New York and Los Angeles (1996). In his study, which is the crystallization of almost two decades of research on the Korean immigrant community, he claims that the concentration of members of an immigrant or ethnic group in small businesses intensifies conflicts with out-group members, which in turn enhances ethnic solidarity among in-group members. Although the same idea had already been proposed by Bonacich and Modell (1980) and applied to Japanese American agricultural businesses on the West Coast before World War II, Min's study is significant because it examines in detail the procedures by which a group's economic position in society (in his case, a middleman minority) enhances its ethnic solidarity.

Although Min and I deal with the same topics, our approaches to them differ in some important respects. First, Min starts with middleman minority theory to explain the concentration of Korean immigrants in small business and the consequent racial conflicts with minority customers. I think this theory is too restrictive to be applied to Korean businesses. Following Light and Bonacich (1988), I argue that Korean immigrant entrepreneurship consists of various types of businesses: ethnic-oriented in Koreatown, majority-oriented in white neighborhoods, minority-oriented in minority neighborhoods. Although some types of Korean establishments can be characterized as middleman minority businesses, I think that the intermediary role of Koreans has been grossly exaggerated. By not defining them simply as middlemen, I try to avoid the danger of holding Korean business owners largely responsible for the economic problems and consequent hostility of inner-city minorities toward Korean businesses.

Second, the concentration of Korean immigrants in small business can enhance their internal solidarity in relations with non-Koreans, but it can simultaneously increase their internal conflicts and class divisions. In other words, this pattern of employment creates two contradictory forces—the centripetal force at the ethnic group level and the centrifugal force at the individual level—a situation that has not been seriously considered in Min's work. Thus, my study focuses on how the interplay of class and ethnicity, the two organizing principles of human association, affects internal solidarity and division in Korean immigrant entrepreneurship and the Korean American community. By so doing, I want to examine the conditions under which ethnic solidarity emerges, strengthens, weakens, and becomes irrelevant.

The organization of this book is as follows. Chapter 1 is a historical and comparative analysis of the state of small business in the U.S. economy. I explain why immigrants are still heavily concentrated in small business, which was once thought to be in decline in the capitalist economy, and why certain immigrant and ethnic groups participate in small businesses at high rates while others do not. I also critique existing theories of immigrant and ethnic entrepreneurship and propose a synthetic model that can explain more adequately aspects that were overlooked by previous studies.

Chapter 2 is a historical and sociological explanation of the causes and mechanisms of Korean immigration to the United States from 1903 to the present. It provides information about the social, economic, and political conditions of Korea and the United States that initiated and still maintain such immigration. It also provides information about the characteristics of Korean immigrants, their motivations for emigrating, and their economic and social adaptation in the United States. These kinds of information are essential for understanding why many Korean immigrants became self-employed business owners in the United States.

Chapter 3 is a survey of the growth of Korean immigrant entrepreneurship in Chicago and Los Angeles. It explains how demographic changes in American cities (such as the outmigration of whites and their businesses from central cities) and export-oriented economic development in South Korea combined to enable Korean immigrants to establish businesses in inner-city neighborhoods. It also analyzes the characteristics of Korean business owners, their positions in the American labor market, their motivations for becoming entrepreneurs, and the resources they have used to establish and maintain their businesses.

As discussed in this introduction, racial tensions between Korean store owners and minority customers now threaten the very survival of such businesses. Thus, any discussion of Korean immigrant entrepreneurship inevitably leads to a discussion of the racial conflict between Koreans and members of other minority groups. It is the intriguing interrelationship of immigration, entrepreneurship, and race relations that makes Korean Americans a unique American ethnic group, worthy of a thorough and systematic study.

Chapter 4 provides a multivariate analysis of the causes, patterns, and consequences of the Korean–black conflict. I first survey major incidents in Chicago, New York City, and Los Angeles to help explain how such conflict starts, progresses, and ends. Next I introduce a theoretical framework that explains the Korean–black conflict from a broad racial/ethnic stratification system perspective. This model goes beyond cultural and psychological explanations that attribute the causes of conflicts to minorities themselves. It is based on the idea that the ways in which groups look at and relate to one another are significantly affected by their relative positions in the American racial/ethnic stratification system, independent of their cultural backgrounds and personal attributes. I then analyze how personal and psychological factors (such as prejudice, language barriers, and cultural misunderstanding), economic factors (deteriorating economic conditions of inner-city black residents and competition from Korean businesses), and political factors (black nationalism and boycotts) turn Korean–black relations into Korean–black conflicts. A special effort is made to explain why Korean businesses experience greater hostility and rejection from the black community than from the Latino community. I also propose and discuss public policies and programs that could help Koreans and other minorities improve their relations.

Finally, in chapter 5, I summarize my major findings and predict future directions in Korean immigration, entrepreneurship, and race relations.

ONE

THE STATE OF IMMIGRANT AND ETHNIC ENTREPRENEURSHIP IN AMERICA

Small business has been a persistent avenue of economic mobility for some immigrant and ethnic groups in the United States, including Jewish, Greek, Italian, Chinese, and Japanese Americans. The first generation of each of these groups faced limited opportunities in the labor market, and many individuals turned to small businesses. In the typical pattern, immigrants earned modest incomes by virtue of hard work and thrift to educate their children, who in turn often became professionals or white-collar workers. Even when economic mobility could not be achieved within the first generation, succeeding generations could enter the mainstream of society to compete for social prestige and wealth.[1]

In contrast, blacks, Mexicans, and Puerto Ricans have participated in small businesses at lower rates than the members of these minority groups. The low economic mobility of blacks has often been attributed to the absence of such an entrepreneurial class (Frazier 1957; Glazer and Moynihan 1970; Light 1972; Sowell 1975). Similarly, the absence of an enclave economy is said to trap Mexicans in the secondary labor market, whereas the existence of an enclave economy in Miami provides Cubans with employment and business opportunities that are not easily available in the general economy (Portes and Bach 1985).

Some of the immigrant groups that have arrived in the United States since the passage of the 1965 Immigration and Nationality Act seem to have followed the historic path of self-employment in small businesses. Korean immigrants, for example, have concentrated in small businesses at very high rates. According to the 1980 U.S. census, about 12 percent of Korean Americans were self-employed in 1979, compared to less than 7 percent of the general population (U.S. Bureau of the Census 1983, 47, 159). As a matter of fact, Korean immigrants showed the highest rate of self-employment among seventeen groups that arrived in the United

States between 1970 and 1980 (U.S. Bureau of the Census 1984, 12). By 1990, this rate had jumped to 17 percent, whereas the corresponding rate for the general population increased moderately to 9.7 percent (U.S. Bureau of the Census 1993a, 22, 113).[2]

The concentration of members of some immigrant groups in small businesses may seem puzzling because self-employment had been losing ground in the U.S. economy for decades before the mid-1970s. Many sociologists had concluded that it was incompatible with capitalist economic concentration and would become an economic anachronism in the future (Mills 1951, 24; Bottomore 1966, 50; O'Connor 1973, 29–30; Horvat 1982, 11–15). Karl Marx himself ([1867] 1977, 776–81) had predicted that the expansion of capitalism would destroy all precapitalist forms of commodity production, such as those practiced by peasants, artisans, and small shopkeepers. The concentration and centralization of capital, according to Marx, would also drive out small firms, which could not compete with larger ones that could take advantage of economies of scale.

Why, then, do some immigrant groups continue to concentrate in small businesses? Why do some groups participate in them at high rates while others do not? Do small businesses facilitate upward economic mobility of immigrants and their descendants? These three questions are the central issues I want to explore in this chapter. First I provide some background information on trends of self-employment in the United States. Then I examine the degree of variation in self-employment rates among various racial and ethnic groups and investigate the relationship between an ethnic group's self-employment rate and its overall economic status (as measured by average personal income, family income, and the degree of labor utilization). This historical overview is followed by a survey of major theories of immigrant and ethnic entrepreneurship. In this review of the literature, I critically examine the strengths and weaknesses of each theory and propose an approach that accounts for the new dimensions of immigrant and ethnic business.

Trends of Self-Employment in the United States

Recently, a growing body of research has rejected the prediction of an inevitable decline in small businesses in the postmodern economy (Ray 1975; Fain 1980; Birch 1981; 1987; Boissevain 1984; Becker 1984; Light and Sanchez 1987; Haber et al. 1987; Steinmetz and Wright 1989). As

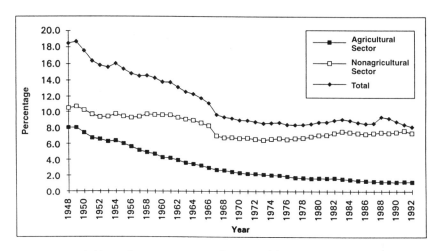

Figure 1.1. Self-Employment Rates in the United States, 1948–92
Sources: U.S. Bureau of Labor Statistics, *Handbook of Labor Statistics*, 1989, 112; U.S. Bureau of the Census, *Employment and Earnings*, January issues of 1989–92. Labor statistics are derived from the annual *Current Population Survey* conducted by the U.S. Bureau of the Census.
Note: The total employed refers to the members of the civilian noninstitutional population aged 16 years and over who worked during the period.

figure 1.1 illustrates, the decline of self-employment slowed down during the late 1960s, and signs of recovery began to appear in the late 1970s. In 1950, 17.6 percent of the civilian population aged 16 years and over had been self-employed. This rate declined to 13.8 percent in 1960 and to 8.9 percent in 1970. It began to rise in 1978 from 8.4 percent and reached a peak in 1988 at 9.4 percent before dropping slightly in 1990 to 8.8 percent (U.S. Bureau of Labor Statistics 1989; 1992).

The recovery of self-employment was faster and more robust in the nonagricultural sector than in the agricultural sector, which experienced a monotonic decrease in the proportion of self-employed workers among the total employed. In 1948, such workers accounted for 8 percent of the total, a figure that dropped to 4.2 percent in 1960, 2.3 percent in 1970, 1.7 percent in 1980, and 1.2 percent in 1990. Although the self-employment rate within the agricultural sector actually declined rather slowly, the rapid reduction in the number of agricultural workers between 1950 and 1967 was responsible for the shrinking proportion of self-employed farmers in the workforce as a whole. As the agricultural industry became smaller and smaller from the 1970s on, it had less effect on changes in the overall self-employment rates.

Researchers offer different explanations for the recovery of self-employment in the 1970s and 1980s. Some think that it is a response to growing unemployment during the economic recessions of the late 1970s. According to these scholars, recessions often provide the impetus for new individuals to venture into the precarious world of independent businesses (Bregger 1963; Ray 1975; Bechhofer and Elliott 1985). To support their argument, they have correlated the unemployment rate and the self-employment rate during specific time periods, but their findings generally do not support their hypothesis (Ray 1975; Steinmetz and Wright 1989). One obvious problem with their approach is the fact that people do not turn to self-employment simply because they have lost their jobs. Self-employed workers are generally more educated and more highly motivated than those who are most vulnerable to unemployment. In his study of Soviet Jewish and Vietnamese refugees in San Francisco, Gold (1988, 418) claims that there is little evidence to indicate that small business is a direct alternative to unemployment. Businesses that were started solely for the purpose of creating a job for oneself were very likely to fail. Similarly, Light and Rosenstein (1995, 152) state that it is the underemployed, not the unemployed, who have a higher chance of turning to small business in the face of labor market disadvantages.

An alternative explanation attributes the recent rise of self-employment to the structural transformation of the American economy (Birch 1981; Bechhofer and Elliott 1985; Solomon 1986; Steinmetz and Wright 1989). This transformation is said to accompany the sharp decline in large-scale manufacturing and the expansion of various forms of service businesses in which self-employment has always been prevalent (Wilson 1978; Waldinger, Aldrich, and Ward 1990). As table 1.1 shows, the manufacturing industry employed 28.2 percent of all U.S. workers in 1960, but its share of the workforce dropped to 22.4 percent in 1980 and 17.7 percent in 1990. In contrast, postindustrial sectors such as finance, insurance, real estate, and professional services expanded rapidly, from 26.1 percent in 1960 to 34.7 percent in 1980 and 39.6 percent in 1990.

In addition to these changes in industrial distribution, changes in self-employment within industries—what Steinmetz and Wright (1989) have called "class shift effect"—were partly responsible for the recent rise (see table 1.2). Although this trend was most noticeable in construction, which posted about a 30 percent increase between 1972 and 1987, even the traditional manufacturing sector experienced a modest rise. In

Table 1.1. Industrial Distribution in the United States, 1940–90 (Percentages)

Industry	1940	1950	1960	1970	1980	1990
Agriculture, forestry, and fisheries	19.2	12.7	7.0	3.7	3.0	2.7
Mining	2.1	1.7	1.1	0.8	1.1	0.6
Construction	4.7	6.2	6.2	6.0	5.9	6.2
Manufacturing	23.9	26.4	28.2	26.2	22.4	17.7
Transportation and public utilities	7.0	8.0	7.2	7.7	7.3	7.1
Wholesale and retail trade	17.7	18.9	19.0	20.1	20.4	21.2
Finance, insurance, and real estate	3.3	3.5	4.3	5.0	6.0	6.9
Service	19.4	18.2	21.8	26.0	28.7	32.7
Personal	9.0	6.2	6.2	4.5	3.2	3.2
Business and repair	2.0	2.4	2.6	3.3	4.2	4.8
Entertainment	1.0	0.9	0.8	0.8	1.0	1.4
Professional	7.4	8.7	12.2	17.4	20.3	23.3
Public administration	3.2	4.5	5.2	4.7	5.3	4.8
Total employed[a]	44,160	55,592	62,031	76,553	97,639	115,681

Source: U.S. Bureau of the Census, *1950 Census of Population*, 1953, 285; *1960 Census of Population*, 1964, 565; *1970 Census of Population*, 1973, 806–9; *1980 Census of Population*, 1983, 47–48; *1990 Census of Population*, 1993, 21–22.

a. The total employed is expressed in thousands. This total included workers aged 14 years and older until the 1960 census; it changed to include those 16 years and older beginning with the 1970 census.

1972, only 1.2 percent of manufacturing workers were self-employed, but that figure increased steadily to 1.6 percent in 1980 and 1.7 percent in 1990. The growth of self-employment in manufacturing is attributed to trends toward decentralization and subcontracting to bypass unions and reduce wages, trends that favor many small businesses.

Still other researchers draw our attention to an easily neglected cause, the influx of new immigrants into the labor market (Light and Sanchez 1987). Because immigrants are generally more likely to be self-employed than the native-born, they claim, this influx has raised the overall self-employment rate. Allowing for the difference between the self-employment rate of immigrants (9.2 percent) and that of the native-born (7.1 percent), Light and Sanchez estimated that between 16 and 52 percent of the increase in the rate of nonagricultural self-employment between 1970 and 1980 could be attributed to immigration. Their argument is quite plausible, since immigrants not only adapt to the U.S. economy but more importantly create business opportunities either in their own ethnic communities or in low-income minority neighbor-

Table 1.2. Self-Employment Rates Within Industries, 1972–87 (Percentages)

Industry	1972	1975	1980	1982	1985	1987
Agriculture, forestry, and fisheries	50.4	49.8	47.8	47.1	44.9	43.6
Mining	2.1	2.1	2.9	3.3	2.1	3.3
Construction	14.1	16.5	18.9	19.4	18.6	18.6
Manufacturing	1.2	1.4	1.6	1.7	1.7	1.7
Transportation and public utilities	3.7	3.9	4.3	4.6	4.2	4.3
Wholesale and retail trade	10.2	9.6	9.4	9.0	8.0	7.9
Finance, insurance, and real estate	6.0	7.1	7.6	7.8	8.0	7.7
Service	10.0	9.6	9.8	10.2	10.4	10.2
Personal	18.6	19.6	21.8	21.3	20.4	19.4
Business and repair	19.3	20.3	19.2	20.4	19.9	19.2
Entertainment	13.4	12.7	13.2	13.9	12.9	12.7
Professional	5.8	5.2	5.3	5.5	5.6	5.5
Public administration	0.0	0.0	0.0	0.0	0.0	0.0
Overall self-employment rate	8.7	8.7	8.7	8.9	8.7	8.6

Source: U.S. Bureau of Labor Statistics, *Labor Force Statistics Derived from the Current Population Survey, 1948–87*, 1988, 628–54.

Note: A self-employment rate is calculated as the number of self-employed persons divided by the total number of employed persons aged 16 years and over.

hoods (Ong, Bonacich, and Cheng 1994, ch. 1). For instance, the influx of Korean immigrants into large cities after 1965 brought a mushrooming of small businesses in minority neighborhoods (I. Kim 1981).

However, Light and Sanchez's estimate seems to be somewhat overstated for the following reason. The self-employment rate among immigrants in 1980 covers all immigrants, both recent and earlier arrivals. If we are interested in the hypothetical relationship between the rise of self-employment and the influx of new immigrants, we should use cohort-specific rates.[3] Since self-employment rates among immigrants increase along with the length of residence in the United States, recent immigrants tend to have lower rates than their predecessors. Using the overall rate instead of cohort-specific rates is thus likely to inflate the role of immigration in the rise of self-employment during the period from 1970 to 1980.

In summary, although scholars have not yet reached a consensus on what caused the trend, the recovery of self-employment has been robust during the past two decades, and it is safe to conclude that the prospects of small businesses in the capitalist economy are not so bleak as previously predicted. On the contrary, the very nature of the postindustrial economy, which requires flexible production methods as well as mobility of workers and information, seems to provide expanding opportunities for small firms that can adapt more efficiently than larger ones to heterogeneous and unstable segments of the market. For these reasons, it is not surprising that immigrants continue to engage in small businesses at high rates.

Intergroup Differences in Self-Employment Rates

The fall and rise of self-employment in the general economy seem to have had little impact on immigrant and ethnic businesses. As noted earlier, self-employment rates among the members of certain minority groups have always been high. Moreover, differences in these rates among various racial and ethnic groups have been widespread and persistent for decades, regardless of trends in the general population (Goldscheider and Kobrin 1980). Tables 1.3 and 1.4 illustrate such differences among U.S. ancestry groups in 1980 and 1990.

In 1980, Palestinians, Jordanians, Iraqis, Russians, and Israelis were the most likely to be self-employed among one hundred ancestry groups, whereas blacks (African Americans), Puerto Ricans, West Indians, Eskimos, and Laotians were the least likely.[4] Generally speaking, persons of Arab ancestry were clustered near the top of this distribution, persons of European and East Asian ancestry were above the national average, and persons of South American or African ancestry were clustered near the low end. The same pattern of intergroup differences was observed in the 1990 census.

In 1990, Korean Americans ranked the highest in self-employment rates, with a quarter of their civilian workers self-employed. This was more than twice the national average. The next highest groups included Israelis and Russians, whose exceptionally high rates of self-employment seem to be due to the high proportion of Jews, who are well known for their entrepreneurial tradition, among them.[5] Palestinians, Iranians, Lebanese, and other Arab Americans were also clustered near the top of the distribution. Among Asian Americans, Taiwanese, Pakistanis, Asian Indians, Chinese (from mainland China), and Thais recorded self-employment rates above the national average, but Japanese, Filipinos, and Southeast Asians were below the national average. Hispanic Americans generally did not fare well in the rankings (eighteen out of twenty-

Table 1.3. Self-Employment Rates Among U.S. Ancestry Groups, 1980
(Ranked Highest to Lowest)

Ancestry Group	Rate	Ancestry Group	Rate
1. Palestinian	24.4	46. Dutch West Indian	9.3
2. Jordanian	21.4	47. British	9.2
3. Iraqi	18.1	48. Cuban	9.1
4. Russian	17.9	49. Asian Indian	9.0
5. Israeli	17.5	**National average**	**9.0**
6. Iranian	17.5		
7. Lebanese	16.5	50. Ukrainian	8.9
8. Korean	16.1	51. French	8.8
9. Romanian	16.0	52. Canadian	8.6
10. Greek	15.0	53. Yugoslavian	8.6
11. Armenian	14.9	54. Spanish	8.4
12. Swiss	14.6	55. Brazilian	8.4
13. Austrian	14.5	56. Finnish	8.3
14. Luxemburger	14.1	57. Indonesian	8.2
15. Syrian	14.1	58. Ethiopian	8.2
16. Australian	13.7	59. Irish	8.1
17. Turkish	13.5	60. Polish	8.1
18. Danish	12.9	61. Bolivian	8.0
19. Latvian	12.7	62. Serbian	7.6
20. Basque	12.4	63. Slav	7.5
21. Norwegian	12.4	64. Thai	7.5
22. Taiwanese	12.2	65. Estonian	7.5
23. Argentinean	12.0	66. Croatian	7.2
24. Scandinavian	12.0	67. French Canadian	7.2
25. Flemish	11.9	68. Chilean	7.2
26. Icelander	11.5	69. Portuguese	7.1
27. Sicilian	11.5	70. American Indian	7.0
28. Albanian	11.3	71. Maltese	7.0
29. Bohemian	11.2	72. Peruvian	6.2
30. Swedish	11.1	73. Venezuelan	5.9
31. Czechoslovakian	11.0	74. Slovene	5.9
32. Scottish	10.9	75. Nicaraguan	5.6
33. Welsh	10.9	76. Colombian	5.6
34. Bulgarian	10.7	77. Slovak	5.6
35. English	10.7	78. Filipino	4.4
36. Hungarian	10.6	79. Mexican	4.2
37. Lithuanian	10.6	80. Costa Rican	4.0
38. Belgian	10.5	81. Ecuadorian	4.0
39. Japanese	10.4	82. Hawaiian	3.8
40. German	10.4	83. Malaysian	3.8
41. Dutch	10.3	84. Nigerian	3.7
42. Chinese	10.2	85. Jamaican	3.5
43. Pakistani	10.0	86. Salvadoran	3.4
44. Egyptian	9.8	87. Panamanian	3.4
45. Italian	9.3	88. Dominican	3.4

Table 1.3. *continued*

Ancestry Group	Rate	Ancestry Group	Rate
89. Vietnamese	3.1	97. Eskimo	2.6
90. Honduran	3.0	98. Guyanese	2.6
91. Haitian	2.9	99. Trinidadian/Tobagonian	2.0
92. African-American	2.9	100. Laotian	1.6
93. Guatemalan	2.8		
94. Puerto Rican	2.8		
95. Guamanian	2.7		
96. West Indian	2.7		

Source: U.S. Bureau of the Census, 5 percent Public Use Microdata Sample of the 1980 census.

Note: Only civilian employed workers aged 16 years and older were included. The first entry listing a person's ancestry was used to determine his or her classification. To make the ancestry codes of the 1980 and 1990 censuses compatible, subancestry codes were aggregated to create commonly recognized national groupings.

two ancestry groups from Latin America were below the national average), but Cubans were a notable exception to this pattern, indicating the importance of the ethnic enclave economy in the Miami area (Wilson and Portes 1980). Blacks and Puerto Ricans increased their self-employment rates from 2.9 percent and 2.8 percent respectively in 1980 to 3.7 percent in 1990, but they were still at the low end of the distribution. Overall, most economically disadvantaged groups, such as Puerto Ricans, blacks, and Southeast Asian refugee groups, were clustered near the bottom of the rankings. This pattern suggests a positive association between an ethnic group's self-employment rate and its overall economic status.

Table 1.5 provides evidence in support of such an association. An ethnic group's economic status is measured in terms of its average family and personal income, percentage of full-time workers, and percentage of unemployed persons out of the total labor force. As indicated by the coefficient of correlation, which was 0.68 and was statistically significant at the 0.01 level, there was a strong, positive association between a group's self-employment rate and its average family income. Similarly, the self-employment rate was strongly and positively associated with average personal income and the percentage of full-time workers but negatively correlated with the percentage of unemployed persons. These associations tend to show that ethnic groups with higher self-employment rates achieve higher economic status and more adequate labor utilization than those with lower rates.

Table 1.4. Self-Employment Rates Among U.S. Ancestry Groups, 1990
(Ranked Highest to Lowest)

Ancestry Group	Rate	Ancestry Group	Rate
1. Korean	24.3	46. Maltese	11.4
2. Israeli	22.0	47. German	11.3
3. Palestinian	20.1	48. Ukranian	11.1
4. Russian	19.8	49. Finnish	10.9
5. Egyptian	19.4	50. Chinese	10.8
6. Iranian	18.7	51. Italian	10.8
7. Armenian	17.6	52. Canadian	10.6
8. Austrian	17.3	53. French	10.6
9. Romanian	17.2	54. Venezuelan	10.4
10. Lebanese	16.7	55. Thai	10.3
11. Icelander	16.7	56. Basque	10.2
12. Greek	16.6		
13. Taiwanese	16.5	**National average**	**10.2**
14. Swiss	16.4		
15. United Arab Emirates	16.1	57. French Canadian	10.1
16. Syrian	16.0	58. Irish	9.8
17. Turkish	16.0	59. Japanese	9.7
18. Celtic	15.6	60. Sicilian	9.5
19. Argentinean	14.7	61. Polish	9.3
20. Luxemberger	14.7	62. Albanian	9.2
21. Latvian	14.4	63. Slavic	9.2
22. Norwegian	14.3	64. Dutch West Indian	9.2
23. Bulgarian	14.0	65. Croatian	9.2
24. Danish	13.9	66. Colombian	8.9
25. Scandinavian	13.7	67. Chilean	8.8
26. Belgian	13.7	68. Slovak	8.6
27. Czech	13.6	69. Slovene	8.3
28. Pakistani	13.3	70. American Indian	8.3
29. Australian	13.3	71. Bolivian	8.2
30. Swedish	13.2	72. Portuguese	8.1
31. Asian Indian	13.0	73. Vietnamese	8.0
32. English	12.7	74. Ethiopian	7.2
33. Scotch-Irish	12.6	75. Honduran	7.0
34. Lithuanian	12.4	76. Brazilian	6.7
35. Scottish	12.3	77. Trinidadian/Tobagonian	6.7
36. British	12.3	78. Cambodian	6.0
37. Czechoslovakian	12.2	79. Dominican	6.0
38. Welsh	12.2	80. Jamaican	5.9
39. Hungarian	12.1	81. Guatemalan	5.7
40. Serbian	11.9	82. Mexican	5.6
41. Yugoslavian	11.9	83. Salvadoran	5.5
42. Dutch	11.6	84. Hawaiian	5.1
43. Costa Rican	11.5	85. Nigerian	5.0
44. Spanish	11.5	86. Ecuadorian	5.0
45. Cuban	11.4	87. Eskimo	4.9
		88. Nicaraguan	4.9

Table 1.4. *continued*

Ancestry Group	Rate	Ancestry Group	Rate
89. Panamanian	4.8	96. Laotian	2.8
90. Filipino	4.7	97. Guamanian	2.8
91. Haitian	4.6	98. Samoan	2.8
92. Guyanese	3.9	99. Malaysian	2.7
93. West Indian	3.8		
94. Puerto Rican	3.7		
95. African-American	3.7		

Source: U.S. Bureau of the Census, 1 percent Public Use Microdata Sample of the 1980 census.

Note: Only civilian employed workers aged 16 years and older were included. The first entry listing a person's ancestry was used to determine his or her classification. For more information on the definitions of ancestry groups, techniques for handling multiple ancestries, and problems with the census ancestry question, see Lieberson and Walters 1988, McKenney and Cresce 1990, Cresce et al. 1992, and Fairlie and Meyer 1994.

Such strong associations do not, however, prove that higher rates of self-employment lead to higher economic status. This is because the marks of a group's higher economic status, such as greater wealth, may be a cause rather than a consequence of its higher self-employment rate. In other words, wealthier people have greater capital at their disposal that can be used for business if they have a strong entrepreneurial motivation. In order to establish whether such a causal relationship exists at the individual level, we would need to measure a person's wealth at one point in time (time 1) and his or her likelihood of being self-employed at a later point (time 2).[6] At a collective level, we would need to determine to what degree group differences in the amount of assets at time 1 explain group differences in self-employment rates at time 2.

Determining the nature of the relationship between an ethnic group's average wealth and its average self-employment rate is a difficult task, primarily because of the dearth of longitudinal data on these issues. However, existing sociological literature on immigrant and ethnic entrepreneurship suggests that business ownership often initiates upward economic mobility. It shows that immigrants start their businesses with only a small amount of capital, the substantial portion of it coming from personal savings, loans from family members and friends, and such informal financial institutions as rotating credit associations (Light 1972; Lovell-Troy 1981; Waldinger 1986; Kim and Hurh 1985; Yoon 1991b; Portes and Zhou 1992; Fairlie 1994). The amount of the assets is not as important as the person's motivation for business ownership and his or her

Table 1.5. Economic Indicators of U.S. Ancestry Groups, 1990
(Ranked Highest to Lowest by the Average Family Income)

Ancestry Group	Family Income	Personal Income	% Full-Time[a]	% Unemployed	Sample Size
1. Russian	68,463	28,738	38.9	2.1	20,164
2. Asian Indian	65,945	18,514	34.6	2.6	5,044
3. Egyptian	64,337	20,741	36.4	3.2	689
4. Syrian	56,791	19,548	36.0	2.0	955
5. Israeli	56,579	18,555	31.0	2.1	662
6. Australian	56,419	22,829	40.6	4.4	318
7. Austrian	56,355	25,854	37.5	2.0	5,162
8. Latvian	55,779	24,203	37.7	1.1	727
9. Japanese	55,200	18,545	37.8	1.3	8,696
10. Filipino	53,566	12,870	35.0	2.6	12,643
11. Romanian	53,444	23,172	37.0	2.5	2,246
12. Icelander	52,724	16,241	30.4	2.6	303
13. British	52,221	21,301	39.8	2.1	8,281
14. Taiwanese	51,760	14,473	28.8	1.9	1,701
15. Celtic	51,676	18,135	44.4	3.7	214
16. Lithuanian	50,990	21,545	38.0	2.5	5,196
17. Maltese	50,804	17,228	39.1	0.4	279
18. Turkish	50,776	18,297	34.1	4.4	592
19. Greek	50,592	17,841	36.6	2.7	8,737
20. Chinese	50,233	14,689	34.3	2.3	13,591
21. Hungarian	48,957	19,640	37.4	2.4	9,455
22. Guyanese	48,910	12,285	40.6	3.7	699
23. Serbian	48,291	18,350	35.6	2.8	793
24. Armenian	48,177	17,398	31.1	4.4	2,529
25. Iranian	48,031	16,117	33.4	3.1	1,932
26. Italian	47,954	16,808	37.5	2.6	109,254
27. Lebanese	47,659	17,264	37.9	2.5	2,743
28. Scottish	46,721	19,824	38.7	2.2	32,879
29. Ukrainian	46,466	18,857	35.4	2.8	4,868
30. Yugoslavian	46,450	16,798	35.3	3.7	1,784
31. Pakistani	46,336	13,019	30.9	4.6	805
32. Korean	46,307	10,473	25.5	2.4	7,369
33. Polish	46,178	16,854	37.6	2.6	62,919
34. Albanian	45,773	15,019	37.2	1.5	411
35. Bulgarian	45,702	16,523	38.1	3.3	210
36. Canadian	45,695	17,462	33.3	2.3	3,604
37. Welsh	45,588	19,951	40.0	2.1	10,596
38. Swiss	45,548	18,732	37.5	1.9	6,352
39. English	45,162	17,274	35.5	2.2	224,832
40. Palestinian	45,102	13,136	28.7	3.3	456
41. Belgian	45,015	16,740	38.6	2.0	2,415
42. Thai	44,497	9,879	30.7	3.1	1,008
43. Slovene	44,444	17,100	32.2	1.6	804
44. Basque	44,401	16,094	36.2	2.5	279

Table 1.5. *continued*

Ancestry Group	Family Income	Personal Income	% Full-Time[a]	% Unemployed	Sample Size
45. Danish	44,198	17,038	36.1	1.9	10,313
46. Hawaiian	44,111	11,112	32.3	2.8	2,096
47. Slovak	44,033	16,744	37.1	2.3	11,707
48. Swedish	44,000	17,000	37.4	2.0	28,872
49. Sicilian	43,777	18,981	44.4	3.2	347
50. Scandinavian	43,647	15,235	35.3	2.5	4,455
51. Scotch-Irish	43,594	17,514	34.8	2.1	44,389
52. Luxemburger	43,532	17,256	33.8	2.1	281
53. Czechoslovakian	43,224	21,206	42.6	2.1	2,325
54. United Arab Emirates	42,728	13,733	33.9	4.1	292
55. Irish	42,722	15,225	36.2	2.7	228,634
56. Portuguese	42,405	14,372	36.9	3.2	8,749
57. West Indian	41,958	13,409	37.6	4.5	1,141
58. Brazilian	41,697	10,396	35.0	3.5	480
59. Czech	41,472	15,571	37.5	2.3	8,065
60. German	41,250	15,043	37.5	2.3	464,819
61. Norwegian	41,182	15,805	36.6	2.5	25,108
62. French Canadian	40,951	15,896	39.9	3.2	16,680
63. Croatian	40,766	15,782	35.8	2.3	3,882
64. Chilean	40,279	10,891	30.1	2.9	554
65. Slavic	40,210	15,040	38.3	0.8	399
66. French	40,146	14,107	35.8	3.1	63,912
67. Cuban	40,049	12,806	35.4	3.7	7,778
68. Jamaican	39,879	13,315	38.4	4.9	3,294
69. Argentinean	39,850	11,420	31.7	2.6	505
70. Trinidadian	39,558	13,770	41.3	4.9	549
71. Finnish	39,433	14,676	34.5	3.1	4,769
72. Dutch	39,112	14,630	35.3	2.4	35,585
73. Vietnamese	38,864	8,742	26.8	4.4	5,126
74. Bolivian	38,843	9,907	30.2	2.2	268
75. Panamanian	38,820	11,198	34.0	6.2	632
76. Ecuadorian	38,762	9,947	30.2	4.9	1,803
77. Spanish	38,663	14,201	34.6	3.9	3,042
78. Venezuelan	37,845	10,470	27.6	2.5	315
79. Costa Rican	37,746	10,008	31.1	4.1	389
80. Colombian	36,296	9,856	31.4	4.5	2,849
81. Eskimo	35,722	7,006	9.9	6.6	994
82. Malaysian	35,370	10,848	27.6	3.1	261
83. Nigerian	35,273	12,749	30.2	6.0	600
84. Samoan	33,988	6,076	22.2	3.7	508
85. Guamanian	33,010	9,482	32.2	4.2	354
86. Dutch West Indian	31,776	12,586	37.2	3.9	333
87. Nicaraguan	31,736	7,263	26.2	4.7	1,571
88. Haitian	31,292	8,504	30.7	7.1	2,326
89. Ethiopian	30,923	10,936	31.8	6.7	239

Table 1.5. *continued*

Ancestry Group	Family Income	Personal Income	% Full-Time[a]	% Unemployed	Sample Size
90. Guatemalan	30,263	7,524	28.8	4.9	2,047
91. Honduran	29,794	7,529	25.3	6.6	964
92. American Indian	29,248	9,610	29.6	4.9	51,772
93. Mexican	29,231	7,276	23.6	4.8	110,540
94. Salvadorian	28,998	6,716	28.6	5.0	4,296
95. Puerto Rican	27,982	8,355	25.1	5.2	15,872
96. Laotian	27,754	5,331	19.1	3.3	1,286
97. Dominican	27,138	7,142	23.7	6.8	3,852
98. African-American	26,849	8,622	26.5	5.4	204,453
99. Cambodian	25,342	4,782	13.2	3.1	1,300

Source: Same as for table 1.4.

Note: Coefficients of correlation (all = significant at the 0.01 level):
    self-employment rate*average family income = 0.68
    self-employment rate*average personal income = 0.66
    self-employment rate*percent of full-time workers = 0.34
    self-employment rate*percent of the unemployed = −0.49

a. The percentage of those who worked 50 to 52 weeks out of those who were 16 years and older and who worked in 1989.

ability to mobilize resources such as capital, information, and workers. The experiences of immigrant Jews, Chinese, and Japanese before World War II clearly indicate that familiarity with small businesses in their home countries, a strong work ethic and family ties, and cooperative social and economic relations among coethnics enabled members of the three groups to overcome their shortage of seed capital in starting small businesses. Once the parents had established a solid economic foothold in America via small business, the younger generations of these groups achieved higher socioeconomic status than the corresponding generations of other ethnic groups. This pattern of intergenerational economic mobility demonstrates the importance of small business as a vehicle of upward social and economic mobility for America's disadvantaged immigrant and ethnic groups.

Given these facts, why don't all minority groups participate in small business at high rates? In the remaining section of this chapter, I examine which factors lead individuals to become self-employed and how differences in these factors across ethnic groups can explain differences in self-employment rates.

Theories of Immigrant and Ethnic Entrepreneurship

Large numbers of scholars from many disciplines have attempted to explain the widespread and persistent group differences in self-employment rates. Their approaches to this question can be grouped into four basic categories: cultural theory, middleman minority theory, disadvantage theory, and opportunity structures theory.

Cultural Theory

According to cultural theory, the propensity of some immigrant and ethnic groups toward small business can be explained by their cultural attributes. As described previously, these attributes include a tradition of buying and selling in their home country, a reliance on cultural institutions such as rotating credit associations, and a spirit of cooperation among coethnics. Cultural theory is divided into orthodox and reactive versions, depending on which attributes are emphasized.

The orthodox version regards the cultural tradition of buying and selling as the major factor in the success of some immigrant and ethnic groups in business. According to this theory, immigrants who were raised in a society with such a tradition are more likely to pursue entrepreneurial careers than those who lack such a cultural background (Frazier 1957; Freedman 1959; Glazer and Moynihan 1970; Loewen 1971; Light 1972; Sowell 1975). A tradition of entrepreneurship is thought to endow individuals with familiarity with and some knowledge of business transactions, financial management, and—most important—a conception of an entrepreneurial career as a respectable vocation (Freedman 1959; Lai 1980). Freedman explains the success of Chinese emigrants in commerce as follows:

> Shrewdness in handling money was an important part of the equipment which ordinary Chinese took with them when they went overseas in search of a livelihood. Their financial skill rested above all on three characteristics of the society in which they were raised: the respectability of the pursuit of riches, the relative immunity of surplus wealth from confiscation by political superiors, and the legitimacy of careful and interested financial dealings between neighbors and even close kinsmen. The Chinese were economically successful in South-East Asia not simply because they were energetic immigrants, but

more fundamentally because in their quest for riches they knew how
to handle money and organize men in relation to money. (64–65)

Similarly, the low rate of participation in business among blacks is
often attributed to the absence of an entrepreneurial tradition in their
cultural repertoire (Frazier 1957; Glazer and Moynihan 1970; Light
1972; Caplovitz 1973; Sowell 1975), although this cultural explanation
has been challenged by several black scholars.[7] The slavery experience
of American blacks is said to have wiped out their cultural heritage, and
their total dependence on whites for their livelihood is thought to have
denied them opportunities to develop an entrepreneurial tradition
within white-dominated American society. Frazier (1957) explains the
legacy of slavery as follows:[8]

> The Negro lacks a business tradition or the experience of people who,
> over generations, have engaged in buying and selling. . . . The Negro
> slave sloughed off almost completely his African heritage. The Afri-
> can family system was destroyed and the slave was separated from his
> kinsmen and friends. Moreover, in the U.S.A. there was little chance
> that he could reknit the ties of kinship and associations. (165, 187)

While orthodox cultural theory was initially developed to explain
why certain ethnic groups are more successful in business than others, it
is now increasingly used to explain why subgroups within a single ethnic
group differ from one another in self-employment rates. Gold (1988)
and Halter (1995) explain the overrepresentation of Soviet Jewish refugees from the Ukraine in small businesses in terms of their strong commercial orientation. Soviet Jews from the port city of Odessa are well
known for a "hustling mentality" that is said to inspire them to go into
business at a higher rate than Soviet Jews from other parts of Russia.
Gold (1988; 1994) finds that the Chinese-Vietnamese dominate ethnic
businesses in Little Saigon in Orange County, California, as they used
to do in Vietnam as a middleman minority. In their analysis of intragroup
differences in business, Kim, Hurh, and Fernandez (1989) divide Asian
Indians into Gujeratis and non-Gujeratis because the former have been
known for their entrepreneurship in India and the former British colo-
nies. They find that after controlling for age, gender, year of immigration, English proficiency, and education, Gujeratis still exceed non-
Gujeratis significantly in self-employment rates, evidence of a legacy of
entrepreneurial culture.

One limitation of orthodox cultural theory is, however, its underestimation or neglect of structural factors such as discrimination against racial minorities in the labor market and in financial institutions. Although a tradition of entrepreneurship facilitates business participation among some immigrant groups, most immigrants turn to self-employment as an adaptation to limited opportunities. If they did not face disadvantages and discrimination, they would not necessarily choose self-employment in small businesses. Another problem with orthodox theory is that it is invoked only after a particular group has shown a strong propensity toward small business. As Portes and Zhou (1992, 513) point out, such an explanation is tautological because a certain minority's success in business is explained by its possession of the cultural attributes necessary for success.

As an alternative to the orthodox version, reactive cultural theory views the concentration of immigrants in small businesses as an adaptation to the circumstances of limited opportunity in a host society. The disadvantages and discrimination faced by immigrant workers in the general labor market are regarded as the primary causes of their high rates of participation in small businesses. According to this theory, such obstacles enhance ethnic solidarity and cooperation among group members, and this kind of collective approach gives them an edge in competition with other groups.[9] In short, they respond to social discrimination by creating their own exclusive boundaries to match those they face. Thus immigrant businesses represent a group response to a hostile social environment, and they depend on the capacity of group members to mobilize resources collectively and to maintain cooperative social and economic relations. For this reason, reactive cultural theory focuses on the conditions under which group solidarity emerges and the ways in which it promotes collective action in the face of discrimination (Bonacich and Modell 1980; Portes and Zhou 1992). Light (1980) summarizes this position as follows:

> The reactive version is that alien status releases latent *facilitators*
> which promote entrepreneurship. The *facilitators* emerge from the
> minority situation rather than the cultural baggage of a particular
> group. An example is enhanced social solidarity attendant upon minority status. Insofar as enhanced solidarity encourages entrepreneurship,
> a situation has brought out a collective response which is not cultural
> in the orthodox sense. A collective propensity endows a minority with

ambitions, motivations, institutions, skills, and so on, which distinguish members from nonmembers. These constitute entrepreneurial
resources [emphasis added]. (34–36)

Reactive cultural theory usefully incorporates situational factors into
its theoretical framework, but it tends to overemphasize group solidarity
and cooperation while downplaying intragroup class divisions and conflicts. By highlighting the situational character of ethnic solidarity, it also
downplays the importance of individual backgrounds and of cultural and
economic ties between the countries of origin and destination in the
growth of immigrant entrepreneurship. We need to recognize that group
solidarity does not emerge out of a cultural vacuum and that the common
origin and culture (including both mental and instrumental aspects)
shared by members of an ethnic group provide important ingredients
out of which solidarity and trust grow.

Another problem with this theory is that it defines a cultural tradition of entrepreneurship more narrowly than was intended by previous
researchers. Measuring the proportion of immigrants with business skills
and backgrounds is often considered sufficient to establish whether such
a tradition exists within a particular group, and when a group does not
include a sizable number of people with entrepreneurial backgrounds,
researchers conclude that it does not have a cultural tradition of entrepreneurship. The concentration of group members in businesses is instead seen as a purely situational adaptation. This narrow definition has
led some theorists to exactly such a conclusion about contemporary Korean immigrants, since only a small proportion of them had actually
managed their own businesses in Korea (Bonacich, Light, and Wong
1980; Light and Bonacich 1988; Waldinger 1989).

The counterpoint I want to make is that entrepreneurship is not an
unfamiliar experience for many Korean immigrants. Small business is
quite viable in the contemporary South Korean economy, and self-
employment is still proportionately higher in Korea than in many other
countries (Hong and Surh 1985; Yee 1990). Table 1.6 shows that although the proportions of self-employed and unpaid family workers
among all Korean workers have declined during the last three decades,
more than 40 percent of Koreans still engaged in small businesses in
1988.

Peddling is still regarded as a quick and easy way of making a living
in Korea, one that allows a poor and disadvantaged person to begin with

Table 1.6. Self-Employed and Unpaid Family Workers in South Korea, 1965–88 (in Thousands)

Year	Self-Employed Workers		Unpaid Family Workers	
	N	%	N	%
1965	3,019	36.8	2,552	31.1
1970	3,331	34.2	2,628	27.0
1975	4,012	33.9	3,015	25.5
1980	4,645	33.8	2,577	18.8
1985	4,679	31.3	2,187	14.6
1988	5,093	30.2	2,167	12.9

Source: Korean Ministry of Labor, *Yearbook of Labor Statistics,* 1975, 1980, 1985, 1988, 1989.

limited capital (I. Kim 1981). Having grown up in a society in which self-employment is so prevalent, many Koreans are likely to develop some familiarity with and knowledge of small business, at least through family members and friends who are engaged in such businesses. When Korean immigrants began coming to the United States only to find limited opportunities in the wage labor market, their prior socialization prepared many of them to regard small businesses as a feasible alternative.

A cultural tradition of entrepreneurship, then, does not have to involve specific business skills and training. It can be more meaningfully conceived of as a general socialization in and exposure to business transactions and financial management, which facilitate the development of a concept of small business as a respectable career.[10] Thus, it is quite conceivable that immigrants who have not engaged in businesses as owners or managers in their home countries but who were socialized in a milieu of entrepreneurship have a higher likelihood of being self-employed in the United States than others who lack this experience. The prevalence of self-employment in the home country (empirically measured by the proportion of self-employed workers in the labor force) is therefore a more accurate measurement of a cultural tradition of entrepreneurship than the proportion of immigrants with a business background.[11]

Middleman Minority Theory

Middleman minority theory defines certain groups concentrated in trades as middlemen, who distribute the products of the elite to the masses and serve the interests of both the elite and themselves. Middle-man minorities are thought to emerge in societies with rigid stratification systems that create a status gap between the elite and the masses, thus necessitating a third group to perform intermediate, often despised roles in trades and in services such as tax collection and money lending (Rinder 1958–59; Stryker 1958; Blalock 1967; Kourvetaris 1988). The status gap as well as negative attitudes toward commerce, which requires extensive interaction with the masses, discourage elites from entering smaller trades. The masses, who possess neither the resources nor the experience to perform entrepreneurial roles and who share the same negative attitudes toward trades, cannot or will not enter these trades. Thus, intermediate entrepreneurial positions are filled by middleman minorities.

Such minorities are said to perform better in the marketplace than members of majority groups partly because of their adaptive capacity, which may be the product of cultural heritage (Freedman 1959; Bona-cich 1973; Lai 1980; O'Brien and Fugita 1982), and partly because of their marginal status in society, which enables them to deal more objectively and indifferently with local customers than members of majority groups (Becker 1956; Blalock 1967; Sway 1980). Their marginal status, however, makes their position precarious because they are numerically weak and their economic success is dependent on the goodwill and toler-ance of the elite. In times of political stress, middleman minorities be-come easy targets for the frustration and anger of the masses for several reasons: they are the masses' primary channel of contact with the elite; they are more accessible than the elite, who are too powerful to chal-lenge; and they have acquired some of the social and economic status of the elite (Blalock 1967, 81). Because of their vulnerable position as middlemen, they are often the objects of pejorative stereotypes ("para-sites" or persons with dual identity) and are subject to hostility and fre-quent persecution.

Middleman minority theory was initially developed to analyze mi-nority–majority relations in peasant and colonial societies. These socie-ties were characterized by rigid stratification, negative attitudes toward certain trades, and a refusal to allow the assimilation of minority mem-bers into mainstream society. Middleman minority groups in preindus-trial societies included the Jews in medieval Europe, the Armenian Christians in late nineteenth- and early twentieth-century Turkey (Stryker 1958), the Greeks in Asia Minor and Egypt (Kourvetaris 1988), and the Chinese in Southeast Asia (Cator 1936; Furnivall 1956; Willmott 1966; Thompson and Adloff 1955).

Some scholars have attempted to extend middleman minority theory to modern industrialized societies such as the United States. Rinder (1958–59), for example, has proposed that

> within American society stratification is tremendously diversified, and class or strata boundaries are highly flexible as well as continuous. Nevertheless, a status gap is apparent on the margin of white–Negro relations. In the urban Negro ghettoes, Jews have been prominent in venturing into this gap. (257)

Bonacich has been the leading middleman minority theorist and has strenuously maintained the applicability of the theory to modern industrialized societies. In her original formulation of this theory, Bonacich (1973) emphasized the sojourning orientation of certain immigrant groups over their economic function ("functional requisites," to use her term) as the primary criterion for defining a middleman minority. A sojourning orientation, according to Bonacich, promotes a tendency toward concentration in portable and easily liquidated lines of self-employment, which will not tie up immigrants' assets in land if they decide to go back home. Since such immigrants do hope to return to their homelands, they tend to maintain their culture and restrict their social interactions with members of other groups by living in segregated communities.

The resistance to assimilation and the economic competitiveness demonstrated by certain middleman minority groups, as this theory goes, arouse the hostility of the host people, which in turn increases their incentive for stronger ethnic solidarity. Such solidarity promotes immigrant small businesses in two forms. First, it provides prospective immigrant entrepreneurs with resources such as capital, training, and information essential to start businesses. Second, it restricts internal competition. Primordial ties based on extended kinship and region of origin help control the competition between coethnics.

In addition to a sojourning orientation, Bonacich's theory proposed three key criteria for identifying middleman minority groups: the retention of a separate and distinctive minority culture and community; a concentration in trades and small businesses; and the hostility of the surrounding society (Bonacich and Modell 1980). Thus, the criteria for

middleman minority groups have shifted from economic and social functions to descriptive characteristics (E. Wong 1985).

That Chinese and Japanese Americans before World War II exhib-
ited such characteristics led Bonacich to label them middleman minorities. This identification has met with a series of criticisms on both theoretical and empirical grounds. Portes and Bach (1985), Waldinger
(1986), and Cherry (1990) have questioned the linkage between a sojourning orientation and the development of ethnic small businesses, ar-
guing that permanent immigrants are more likely to engage in businesses
than sojourning immigrants. O'Brien and Fugita (1982) and E. Wong
(1985) have argued that the concentration of the prewar Chinese and
Japanese in small businesses was caused not by a sojourning orientation
but by anti-Asian racism and discrimination that limited job opportunities in the general labor market:

> Because of discrimination, they did not . . . have the chance to pursue
> higher paying opportunities in the urban labor markets, which had
> drawn so many white workers from the fields. In addition, the Japa-
> nese were generally excluded from participation in any sort of broad-
> based working-class movement because of the discriminatory policies
> of American labor unions at the time. . . . One of the few remaining
> options open to the immigrants was to become involved in small-scale
> intensive farming. (O'Brien and Fugita 1982, 191)

O'Brien and Fugita also challenge Bonacich's sojourning theory on the
empirical ground that Japanese farmers were not middlemen between
white capitalists and the masses but direct producers whose clientele
consisted of the general population.

Middleman minority theorists themselves acknowledge such problems with the theory, noting the lack of empirical evidence and the ambi-
guities in defining the boundaries of middleman groups. Bonacich and
Modell (1980) have questioned the validity of the theory with respect to
the Japanese American experience by noting that the enterprises of this
group were concentrated in agriculture, a line of work very different
from those of trading and commerce. They have also acknowledged the
complete lack of evidence for the middleman role that such farmers were
thought to play between white capitalists and subordinated minority
groups (252).

Having met with such criticisms, Bonacich and her colleagues have nonetheless turned to Koreans as new candidates for middleman minority status.[12] They suggest that

> in a sense Korean small enterprises were akin to the middlemen of colonial regions. . . . The ghetto and barrio are especially interesting from this point of view, in that locating there gave Koreans the appearance of a classic middleman minority. They acted as the interface between big capital and depressed minorities, providing the latter with the goods sold by the former and bearing some of the hostilities toward Anglo America. (Light and Bonacich 1988, 393)

Some Korean-American scholars agree with Bonacich and her colleagues. Pyong Gap Min (1990), for example, argues that middleman minority theory is useful for understanding Korean immigrants' entrepreneurship on the grounds that

> Korean entrepreneurs serve a much larger proportion of low income, minority customers than the chance factor allows and that much of the merchandise Korean merchants distribute to minority customers is produced by corporations. Korean entrepreneurs' problems have much to do with their dependence upon minority customers and non-Koreans, white wholesalers and manufacturers. Thus, the middleman minority seems to be the most useful theoretical perspective in analyzing problems of Korean immigrant entrepreneurs. (438)

In order to test whether or not Korean business owners play the middleman role between the capitalist and the oppressed minority member, one important thing we need to know is what proportion of the products and services sold in Korean businesses located in minority areas are those of U.S. capitalists. On this matter, Light and Bonacich (1988) provide evidence that contradicts the middleman minority argument: products of large American corporations account for a smaller proportion of their sales than those imported from several developing Asian countries, such as Taiwan and South Korea. Their study also reveals that the majority of suppliers for Korean businesses in minority areas are themselves Korean, not Anglo-American.

My own study of Korean immigrant businesses in Chicago's black neighborhoods shows that the majority of products sold there are cheap consumer goods that are manufactured in several Asian countries and imported and distributed by Korean suppliers (Yoon 1991a). In South Central Los Angeles, products made in the United States account for a higher proportion of sales in Korean stores. This is because grocery and liquor stores and auto parts and repair stores are prevalent in South Central, whereas they are almost absent in Chicago's black neighborhoods. Still, products made in South Korea and other Asian countries are important, particularly in Korean indoor swap meets in black and Latino neighborhoods (Chang 1990). In both Chicago and Los Angeles, Korean retailers rely more heavily on Korean suppliers than on American suppliers, who themselves are racially and ethnically heterogeneous. Undoubtedly, some types of Korean businesses, such as liquor stores, play the middleman role, but this pattern has been exaggerated out of proportion to their numbers in the total Korean business community in South Central. The competitive advantages of Korean immigrant businesses do not derive mainly from a middleman role but from the strong vertical integration between Korean suppliers and retailers (Yoon 1991a; Chin, Yoon, and Smith 1996).

Another reason why I oppose middleman minority theory is that it has unnecessarily harmful political implications on Korean–black relations. It pits blacks and Koreans against each other by defining Korean merchants in black neighborhoods as economic exploiters on behalf of white capitalists. But there is little empirical evidence that such capitalists assist Koreans to function as middlemen; Koreans are simply filling a vacuum neglected by large businesses. Thus it is false to single out Koreans as a cause of the economic plight of inner-city blacks. Their problems are caused more by larger socioeconomic forces, such as massive job losses and sharp cuts in welfare programs, than by Korean merchants. Radical black leaders criticize Koreans for being interested only in money and for not contributing to the communities where they make this money, but as Abelmann and Lie (1995, 155) succinctly point out, it would be a feat of ethnic romanticism to believe that black merchants would return their profit to the black community.

Disadvantage Theory

Disadvantage theory explains the high business participation rates of immigrants in terms of the disadvantages they experience in the American labor market. Language barriers, less transferable skills and education, and discrimination against immigrants are said to drive such workers into the more autonomous and secure self-employment sector.[13]

Theorists have proposed two competing explanations for the causes of these disadvantages. One approach, known as human capital theory, focuses on immigrants' lack of transferable skills and education, limited proficiency in English, and unfamiliarity with American culture and society. For example, Chiswick (1982, 123) explains the earnings differential between foreign-born and native-born workers in terms of the difficulty the former encounter in applying skills acquired in school and on the job in their country of origin to the American labor market. According to this view, the best way for an individual to improve his or her position is to invest in human capital: more schooling, job training, English language training, and stronger attachment or commitment to work. Thus from the human capital perspective, the individual, not society, is to blame for his or her misfortune.

The other approach, termed segmented labor market theory or split labor market theory, challenges this perspective on the grounds that regardless of their investments in human capital, minority workers (including racial minorities, females, and immigrants) are systematically excluded from employment that offers high income, job security, and promotion (Doeringer and Piore 1971; Bonacich 1972; Edwards, Reich, and Gordon 1975). Minority workers are said to earn lower wages than dominant workers (in the United States, white males) even when human capital resources are held constant (Li 1980; M. Wong 1982). This radical approach views the American labor market as sharply segmented by race, gender, and nativity. Dominant workers are said to exclude minority workers from preferred employment positions in order to protect their own privileges and leave the undesirable jobs to minorities.

The experience of Chinese and Japanese immigrants in the American labor market before World War II can be explained by segmented labor market theory. These immigrants were initially welcomed when they came to fill the labor shortages on Hawaii's sugar plantations and in the mines and railroad construction camps on the West Coast. But when labor competition developed during economic depressions, they became the targets of anti-Oriental campaigns and institutional discrimination (Nishi 1979; Boswell 1986). Working-class whites, the primary source of these protests, felt their job security and standard of living were being threatened by the Asian immigrants, who would work for less money than they would (Hilton 1979). Racial discrimination excluded the Chinese and Japanese from skilled occupations and pushed them into petty businesses catering to their own ethnic groups or providing services such as laundering and cooking to working-class whites (Boswell 1986).

Whites did not oppose such Chinese businesses as laundromats and restaurants, which offered at a cheap price services they were reluctant to provide.

Even today, Asian Americans are not exempt from discriminatory practices in the segmented American labor market. Although they fare well in terms of unemployment and family income, they are reported to be troubled by underemployment and limited mobility. Asian Americans with educational backgrounds comparable to those of whites receive lower monetary returns on their education (Chung 1979; Li 1980; M. Wong 1982; Kim and Hurh 1983; Hsia 1988). In addition, they are generally excluded from positions of power and influence. According to a report from the U.S. Commission on Civil Rights (1988, 74), American-born Chinese, Filipino, and Japanese men aged 25 to 64 in 1980 were 7 to 11 percent less likely to become managers than comparable Anglo-Americans. Because of their superior educational attainment and English proficiency, labor market disadvantage cannot be a major cause of their underrepresentation in management positions. Artificial barriers based on attitudinal and organizational bias have prevented qualified Asian Americans from advancing into such positions (Hsia 1988; U.S. Commission on Civil Rights 1992, ch. 6).

The underutilization of human capital is particularly severe for recent Asian immigrants who, though well educated and of middle-class origin, cannot find appropriate employment. What is generally available to them are marginal or peripheral jobs characterized by low wages, hard physical labor, long hours of work, and little job security or opportunities for promotion (Kim, Hurh, and Fernandez 1989, 77). Such stark employment opportunities eventually drive many Asian immigrants toward self-employment in the small business sector.

The concentration of immigrants in this sector is thus a situational adaptation to the American labor market. From the perspective of disadvantage theory, self-employment is not a mark of success but an alternative to underemployment and low wages (Chung 1979; Bonacich 1988). Persistent high participation in small businesses is a symptom of their disadvantaged position. For most Asian Americans, small business is a "matter of economic necessity" in the struggle to establish a solid economic base in the United States (Kim and Hurh 1983, 14).

Although disadvantage theory explains fairly accurately why immigrants become self-employed at higher rates than the native-born, it still does not explain why members of some disadvantaged groups participate in businesses at high rates while others do not. For instance, blacks have been the victims of more severe discrimination than any other racial or ethnic group in the United States, and their current social and economic position remains the most disadvantaged. Despite these facts, they have not shown much involvement in entrepreneurship. Thus, disadvantages can provide a strong motivation for self-employment, but they do not automatically transform workers into owners of their own businesses.[14]

There is no question that the kinds of disadvantages blacks face cannot be compared with those of immigrants who have come to the United States voluntarily to advance their economic standing. Segregation and racial discrimination have clearly hindered the development of black entrepreneurship (Bates 1991; Butler 1991; Green and Pryde 1991). One of the hurdles potential black entrepreneurs face is the practice of discriminatory lending. Grown and Bates (1992) examined random nationwide samples of construction companies and found that black firms are treated differently by commercial banks than are nonminority companies with otherwise identical traits. They are less likely to have their business loan applications approved than other applicants, and when they do receive loans, the amounts are smaller than those given to others. Similarly, Portes and Stepick (1993, 46) revealed that between 1968 and 1980, 46 percent ($47.7 million) of SBA loans in Dade County, Florida, went to Cuban and other Latino businesses and only 6 percent ($6.5 million) to black firms. Undercapitalization of such firms, in turn, is shown to increase the likelihood of firm discontinuance.

Because of a lack of capital, training, and experience in business as well as a generally low level of education, black entrepreneurs are likely to own businesses that are smaller in size, lower in prestige, and higher in insolvency rates than those owned by other racial groups. This, in turn, reduces opportunities for potential black entrepreneurs to acquire role models as well as technical and managerial training and experience. And these factors diminish blacks' motivation to become self-employed. Green and Pryde (1991) find that among both lower- and middle-class native blacks runs a uniformly negative perception of black entrepreneurs. They believe that "although black individuals may occasionally succeed as entrepreneurs, blacks as a group have few prospects for success in business because they lack the step-by-step concrete understanding of how entrepreneurial goals are achieved" (114). Thus, without resources—whether role models or money—disadvantages in the general labor market only reduce individuals' chance of business ownership.[15]

Opportunity Structures Theory

Unlike the previous theories, which emphasize the supply side of immigrant and ethnic entrepreneurship, opportunity structures theory focuses on the demand side. According to this theory, the growth of immigrant and ethnic businesses is inconceivable without opportunities conducive to such businesses, including ethnic markets, minority neighborhoods, the peripheral sector of open markets, and the import–export trade between immigrants' countries of origin and destination (Waldinger 1986; Waldinger, Aldrich, and Ward 1990; Chin, Yoon, and Smith 1996).

Ethnic markets. Ethnic markets develop from the demands of individuals for their own cultural products (such as ethnic foods and newspapers). Such demands create protected markets for ethnic business owners, who know about the things their coethnics want (Light 1972; Portes and Zhou 1992). When immigrants have difficulty speaking English or are unaccustomed to the bureaucratic procedures and formal institutions of the United States, business opportunities arise for immigrant professionals (such as accountants, lawyers, or health specialists), who can deliver more personalized service than members of other racial or ethnic groups (Waldinger 1986, 19). At the turn of the century, for example, most initial business opportunities for Chinese and Japanese immigrants involved catering to their fellow immigrants (Boswell 1986). Both groups soon engaged heavily in agricultural businesses, such as truck farming, and gradually expanded their markets to white clients (Bloom and Riemer 1949; Bonacich and Modell 1980; Chan 1986).

While the demand for cultural products has played a key role in the growth of most immigrant and ethnic businesses, such community support has not been forthcoming for black entrepreneurs. Unlike immigrants, who come from a foreign culture and have special needs that might give rise to a market, blacks, who share the same language and many of the same tastes for cultural products as whites, are easily served by white-owned businesses. Unprotected by exclusive patronage from blacks or the claim of a self-contained community, neophyte black business owners have to compete with them, even in predominantly black communities. The concentration of black entrepreneurs in selected personal service trades (such as barber and beauty shops) results from the absence of white competition in these lines of business (Glazer and Moynihan 1970; Light 1972; Yancy 1974).

Minority neighborhoods. Low-income minority neighborhoods in large cities such as New York, Los Angeles, and Chicago have provided business opportunities for recent immigrant groups, such as Koreans and Arabs (Bonacich, Light, and Wong 1980; Blackistone 1981; I. Kim 1981; Kim and Hurh 1985; Yoon 1995). Ethnic residential succession—the transformation of predominantly white areas into predominantly black areas—created replacement business opportunities in these racially transitional areas, not because whites deserted their businesses but because they failed to replace those that closed. (Aldrich and Reiss, Jr. 1976). Businesses in these neighborhoods had been dominated by first-generation European immigrants (many of them Jews or Italians), who kept their declining businesses until they became too old to run them or died out. Subsequent immigrants from these groups did not replace the businesses because of the dropping market value of the stores, the shrinking base of coethnic customers, and the high crime rates in the now predominantly black neighborhoods. Children of first-generation Jewish or Italian immigrants, who often received a college education, tended to establish themselves as white-collar workers and refused to take over their parents' businesses (Aldrich and Reiss, Jr. 1976; I. Kim 1981; Waldinger 1986).

In addition to these demographic changes, civil disorders in black areas during the 1960s—especially those following Dr. Martin Luther King's assassination in April 1968—caused many white businesses to move out (Aldrich and Reiss, Jr. 1970). The arson and looting that accompanied civil disorders not only caused direct financial and physical damage to small businesses but also had indirect effects. White business owners found it increasingly difficult to obtain insurance in riot-torn areas, which in turn prevented them from obtaining financial credit. In this way, civil disorders, in combination with rising insurance problems and decreasing profits, fueled white business owners' desire to move to other areas. Thus, even before Korean immigrants arrived in the early 1970s, the turmoil of the 1960s had set in motion the interethnic succession of businesses in black areas.

Recent Korean and Arab immigrants established their businesses in these areas primarily because of the low barriers to entry compared to those in white areas (Kim and Hurh 1985; Min 1988; Light and Bonacich 1988; Yoon 1991a). The rental cost of stores in black areas is less than that in white areas, and a limited knowledge of English is often sufficient for owners. Besides the minimal requirements of capital and managerial skill, the absence of competition from local black businesses lowers the barriers to entry. Korean business owners often mention that when they first moved into black areas, they did not experience the same level of hostility and resistance from local residents that Jewish and Italian business owners had. For these reasons, Korean immigrant businesses in Chicago and Los Angeles are concentrated in predominantly low-income black and Latino neighborhoods.

The peripheral sector of open markets. According to Piore (1979), product markets tend to be separated into two noncompeting sectors: a primary sector, in which large-scale firms cater to the predictable and largely stable segment of demand, and a peripheral sector, in which smaller-scale firms cater to the unpredictable and/or fluctuating portion of demand. In the peripheral sector, immigrant and ethnic small businesses have a competitive edge over large businesses, which do not wish to contend with unstable demands for production, low economies of scale, and small, overly differentiated markets (Waldinger 1986).

The garment industry is a good example of how the division of labor between large manufacturers and small subcontractors provides business opportunities to small-scale immigrant businesses. This industry, which is prone to seasonal fluctuations or unpredictably rapid changes in fashion, is divided into two components: the manufacturer, who is responsible for designing and merchandising, and the subordinate contractor, who is charged with production (Waldinger 1986, 52).[16] The contracting arrangement allows the manufacturer to limit investment in fixed capital, thereby reducing risks—an important consideration in an industry so prone to instability. The same arrangement relieves subcontractors of the heavy requirements of capital and technology, allowing them to start their own businesses with limited capital and skills. The segmentation of the garment industry, a joint function of the division of labor and the instability of demand, thus provides opportunities for small-scale immigrant businesses, whose labor ultimately serves the interests of large businesses.

Still another environment favorable to small businesses is one in which a market is too small or too differentiated to support the large centralized structures needed for mass production or distribution (Waldinger 1986, 24). Waldinger explains the prevalence of immigrant retail grocery stores in New York in terms of the heterogeneous racial and ethnic mixture of the population. In his view, small retail stores are more efficient than large, centralized chain stores in meeting New York's highly differentiated market demands. I suspect that its geographical compactness and urban lifestyle also provide a favorable environment for small retail stores by creating a constant flow of pedestrians on the streets. Stores open long hours are better suited for such a busy lifestyle. Immigrant businesses, most of them family-run, have a competitive advantage over large firms in extending business hours, thanks to a free and loyal family labor force.

The import–export trade. Previous research on Asian immigrant entrepreneurship has tended to focus on the American setting, with little attention to its global dimension. This lack of attention can be attributed partly to the relative newness of economic development in several Asian countries and of massive Asian immigration to the United States, which gained momentum only in the early 1970s. Another important reason is thought to be the inadequacy of our present social science concepts for explaining transnational processes and activities that cross boundaries of individual nation-states.

Our present concept of immigration, for example, is unidirectional and ideologically biased toward assimilation in the host society. In other words, we assume that people migrate from less developed countries to more developed countries and that once they arrive in the country of destination, they are interested only in their social and economic well-being there. Such a dichotomized concept cannot adequately explain the multiple and simultaneous relationships—familial, economic, social, and political—that contemporary immigrants develop and maintain between their countries of origin and settlement. As we can see from the experiences of those who have come to the United States from St. Vincent, Grenada, Haiti, and the Philippines, immigrants are not rooted in one location. Rather, they are able to cross geographic and cultural boundaries by building transnational social networks, economic alliances, and political ideologies. Through these activities, they not only maintain their ties with their home countries but also actively participate in and even influence the political and economic development of these countries (Basch, Schiller, and Blanc 1994). Thus, our theoretical perspective on immigration and immigrant entrepreneurship should be more global and transnational, and we should pay greater attention to the role that home countries play in the business development and overall economic mobility of Asian immigrants in the United States.

Since the mid-1960s, some Asian immigrant groups have been engaging in the import–export trade, which includes importing, distributing, and retailing cheap consumer items manufactured mainly in their home countries (Sung 1976; Koos 1982; Wong 1987). The growth of this import–export trade was greatly facilitated by the rapid growth of export-oriented industries in several Asian countries, which in turn was promoted by the increased reliance of the United States on imported goods. For instance, wigs became the major export item of South Korea in the late 1960s and early 1970s thanks to a cheap labor force and government-aid loans to the wig industry (I. Kim 1981; Yoon 1995). When the demand for wigs declined in the early 1970s, Korean wig manufacturers switched to other labor-intensive industries, such as garment, footwear, and general merchandise manufacturing, with little disruption to their existing production mode. South Korean manufacturers also established branch offices in the United States and actively recruited Korean immigrants as importers, wholesalers, and retailers of Korean-made products, creating a strong vertical integration of businesses. This integration has provided Korean immigrants with initial business opportunities in the U.S. economy, particularly in low-income minority neighborhoods.

The import–export trade is not something uniquely associated with post-1965 immigrants. In fact, international trade by Asian immigrant entrepreneurs has a long history, although it has not received adequate attention from researchers. For instance, as early as 1852, Chinese merchants in San Francisco were importing rice, tea, silk, sugar, opium (opium smoking was legal in California until 1881), wheat, flour, ginseng, mercury, dried seafood, and other products from China (Ma 1984, 101). These merchants, in turn, exported gold and silver, wheat, flour, ginseng, mercury, and dried seafood back to their home country. After they began to fish in California waters, they also started to export dried fish, abalone, and shrimp to China (Chan 1986, 85). Like their Chinese counterparts, many Japanese immigrants engaged in international trade by importing "cooking ingredients for fellow immigrants, and curios and goods such as lacquerware, china, parasols, fans, scrolls, tea, and silk goods for Euro-American customers" (Chan 1991, 40–41). In the 1880s, silk became the most valuable item in the commerce between Japan and the United States.

While this nineteenth-century import–export trade emerged to meet the demands of Asian and Euro-American customers for Asian cultural goods, the international trade of the late twentieth century developed as part of a global economic restructuring in which several East Asian countries supply labor-intensive manufactured goods to more developed countries such as the United States. For this reason, the market for goods imported by recent Asian immigrants often extends to members of the general population (Chin, Yoon, and Smith 1996).

International trade is one of the fastest growing business opportunities in the Asian American community, and its growth is likely to continue in the Pacific Rim era, in which commodities, capital, information, and people are exchanged across the Pacific Ocean at increasing rates. Furthermore, the cultural, social, and economic ties between Asian countries and their emigrants to the United States are becoming stronger with the advancement of communication and transportation technology. For these reasons, the capability of immigrant entrepreneurs to link overseas markets and capital with coethnic entrepreneurs in the United States will become increasingly important for the development of Asian immigrant entrepreneurship.

In summary, opportunity structures theory claims that immigrant and ethnic businesses are prevalent in industries in which the barriers to entry are low with respect to capital, technology, and competition from local or large businesses. Immigrant businesses also find economic niches in the import–export trade. However, this theory is still unable to explain why business opportunities are unequally utilized by members of different racial and ethnic groups. Alone, it cannot explain why outsiders such as Koreans and Arabs took advantage of such opportunities in racially transitional areas while black residents did not. In order to explain these intergroup differences, we need to pay attention to how members of different groups perceive and interpret business opportunities and how they mobilize resources to take advantage of them.

An Interactive Model of Immigrant and Ethnic Entrepreneurship

From our literature review, three factors emerge as key variables in explaining the entrepreneurial propensity and success of some immigrant and ethnic groups in the United States: (1) employment opportunity structures in the general labor market; (2) business opportunity structures; and (3) the relative capacity of individual members and the group as a whole to organize and mobilize resources for business opportunities (Aldrich, Jones, and McEvoy 1984; Kim, Hurh, and Fernandez 1989;

Waldinger, Aldrich, and Ward 1990; Light and Rosenstein 1995). I propose that intergroup variation in business participation is an outcome of the interaction among these three factors. This interactive model represents an advancement over previous theories, which fail to provide us with an overall and integrated view of the relationships among various aspects of immigrant and ethnic entrepreneurship.

In this model, each factor is a necessary condition of business participation but is not sufficient in its own right. For example, business opportunities have little relevance to an individual who does not possess the resources necessary to take advantage of them. By the same token, resources increase that person's likelihood of being self-employed only when self-employment is a desired goal. The desirability of self-employment is, in turn, largely determined by the person's employment opportunities in the general labor market. For this reason, immigrants—who are often more disadvantaged in the labor market than native-born Americans—have stronger incentives for becoming independent business owners.

The types of resources available and the ways in which immigrants and members of ethnic groups mobilize them for business opportunities depend in part on individuals' background characteristics and in part on their cultural heritage. For theoretical purposes, I divide these resources into three types: ethnic resources, class resources, and family resources.[17]

Ethnic resources are defined as "resources and forms of aid preferentially available from members of one's own ethnic group or derived from the ethnic group's heritage" (Min and Jaret 1984, 432). These resources are, roughly speaking, equally available to all members of an ethnic group who share a common origin and culture and actively participate in activities in which these commonalities are important ingredients. Therefore, the important criteria for drawing on such resources are membership in one's own ethnic group and active participation in its shared activities. Ethnic resources may be material (for example, financial aid), informational (business advice), or experiential (job training). Ethnic customers, employees, suppliers, media and publications, and social organizations can all be considered ethnic resources.

In contrast, class resources are "private property in the means of production and distribution, wealth, and investments in human capital" (Light 1985, 173). These resources can be "either cultural, such as values, attitudes, and knowledge and skills transmitted intergenerationally, or material, such as property used for production and distribution, human capital, and financial capital" (Light 1984). Class resources, which may include education, wealth, and occupational skills and experiences, are available only to those members of an ethnic group whose social and economic position has enabled them to invest in human capital or to be endowed with these resources from their parents.

It is difficult to classify resources from one's own family members. Some researchers include them under ethnic resources because they think the assistance of family members is derived from culture and is not class-specific. However, it is important to distinguish between resources that are available from one's own family members and those that derive from membership in a larger nonkin group of coethnics (Min and Jaret 1984). Family resources are private goods that are exchanged and kept within a closed circle of family and kin, whereas ethnic resources are like public goods to which all coethnics have free access. It is also important to distinguish between resources that come from one's own family members and those that derive from membership in a socioeconomic class. While class resources can be obtained through an investment in human capital, family resources are available by virtue of family relations. The size of one's family and the participation of its members in unpaid labor can affect an individual's chance of business ownership and successful management independently of his or her human capital. Thus, financial aid, business advice, or labor from immediate family members can be considered a separate type of resource.

Portes and Zhou (1992) use the concept of social capital, which is similar to what I define as ethnic resources. It includes captive ethnic markets for culturally defined products and services, access to informal sources of capital based on "enforceable trust," informal international commerce between countries of origin and destination, access to a cheap and reliable immigrant labor force, and opportunities for employment and future business ownership. Portes and Zhou view ethnic solidarity ("bounded solidarity," to use their term) and trust among coethnics, which are basic sources of social capital, as situationally induced coping mechanisms against disadvantageous minority status in the host country. Thus, the solidarity and trust that foster ethnic businesses do not originate in the values acquired in the country of origin; rather, they derive from the fact that immigrants are treated as culturally and phenotypically different from natives in the host country.

The concept of social capital was first elaborated by James Coleman (1988) to explain social action in the context of social structure. According to Coleman, individuals' actions are shaped and constrained by norms, interpersonal trust, networks, and social organization. Unlike physical or human capital, social capital is thought to inhere in the structure of the relationships among actors, not in the actors themselves or in the physical implements of production.

From the social capital perspective, then, intergroup differences in business ownership are explained primarily by group-level characteristics such as ethnic solidarity and trust. The human capital of individual members of an ethnic group is not regarded crucial in this regard. This approach has explanatory power when the members of a group do not possess a high level of human capital but still show a high rate of business ownership, as in the experience of recent Cuban and Chinese immigrants. For example, the Cuban bourgeoisie in Miami, who escaped from Cuba with little money but with class, social, and human capital intact, could build a prosperous ethnic economy by tapping the abundant cheap labor of post-Mariel coethnics and the paternalistic ideology of ethnic solidarity, which are ethnic rather than class resources (Portes and Bach 1985; Light and Rosenstein 1995). Similarly, postwar Chinese immigrants, who possessed little capital and few business skills, could establish numerous restaurants and garment businesses—the two bases of the enclave economy in New York's Chinatown—thanks to the availability of reliable, low-wage Chinese labor and the efficient mobilization of ethnicity that curbs conflicts between employers and workers (Waldinger 1986; Zhou 1992).

The social capital approach, however, offers only a partial explanation of the social origins of Korean immigrant entrepreneurship. Their high rate of business ownership is largely the result of their high levels of formal education and their professional and white-collar occupational backgrounds.[18] Individual differences in levels of education and English-language proficiency are found to influence significantly their probability of business ownership and success. For example, an analysis of self-employment among Korean Americans using data from the 5 percent Public Use Microdata Sample (PUMS) of the 1980 U.S. census reveals that four-year college graduates have a higher probability of business ownership than non–college graduates, a pattern more evident among foreign-born individuals than among the native-born. In addition to materialistic class resources, middle-class values and attitudes, which advocate upward social and economic mobility, have been a driving force in the massive entry of Korean immigrants into the self-employment sector. Family structure and relations (as measured by household type, family size, and hours of unpaid family labor) also significantly affect the probability of business ownership and success. For example, married persons are 76 percent more likely than the unmarried to become self-employed, and the larger the family size, the greater the income from business. These findings show that intragroup differences in business ownership are as substantial as intergroup differences, and personal- and family-level characteristics are as important as group-level characteristics in determining the probability of business ownership and success (Yoon 1991b; 1996).

The distinction among class, family, and ethnic resources is therefore useful for two reasons. First, it helps us analyze how immigrant businesses are organized and how their organizational patterns differ from one ethnic group to another. If groups differ in the types and magnitudes of their resources, this fact may provide us with a key to understanding why certain groups are successful in entrepreneurial careers while others are not. Second, this categorization helps us observe the changing significance of class, family, and ethnicity at different stages of immigrant business development. As my earlier study of Korean immigrant businesses in Chicago suggests (Yoon 1991a), ethnic and family resources are important in the initial stages because they are the only resources available (or easily available) to prospective business owners. However, they may become less important or even irrelevant at later stages, when more resources are available from outside narrow ethnic and family boundaries.

In the following chapters, I examine how employment opportunity structures, business opportunity structures, and resource mobilization have affected interdependently the formation and growth of Korean immigrant entrepreneurship. I also examine how Korean immigrants perceive small business in American society and how they personally interpret their businesses and their lives in this country. In order to understand the social origins of their entrepreneurship, however, we first need to know under what circumstances, from what backgrounds, and with what motivations they came to the United States. These questions are the main topics of inquiry in chapter 2.

TWO

Immigrant life consists of constant doubt and justification of one's reasons for being in a foreign land. Whether voluntary or involuntary, immigration does not automatically separate people from their home country, at least not mentally. The struggles and humiliation they face in their adopted country make them wonder why they immigrated in the first place. Thoughts of returning to their homeland for good do not diminish with time and become more appealing when immigrants are made to feel small. However, for many people, return migration is not a realistic option despite the difficult, marginal, and dissatisfying aspects of immigrant life. It would not only be a humiliating proof of their failure but would also deprive them of any investments, whether small or large, that they had made in their new country through hard work and frugality.

Faced with this dilemma, Korean immigrants to the United States selectively contrast positive aspects of American life with negative aspects of South Korean life so as to justify their decision to live in the United States. America is viewed as an open and fair place, whereas South Korea is viewed as a closed and unfair place for those who do not have social connections. Military threats from North Korea, authoritarian political establishments, favoritism, overcrowding, and the extremely competitive college entrance examination in South Korea make America a safer and better place for them and their children to live. Nonetheless, the language barrier, prejudice, discrimination, and the glass ceiling Korean immigrants face in their everyday lives undermine their belief in the American system and rekindle their desire to return to a place where they are members of the dominant group. It is this constant mental negotiation between opportunities and constraints that makes Korean immigrant life a bittersweet experience.

In this chapter, I explain first the social, economic, and political con-

48

ditions that initiated and continue to sustain Korean immigration to the United States. Second, I explain the motivations and entry mechanisms that brought these immigrants into the country. Finally, I document and explain the changes in the class backgrounds of Korean immigrants during the last three decades. This analysis is especially important for understanding changing patterns of social and economic adaptation among the different waves of immigrants. Although the primary focus of this chapter is on the period since 1965, a brief summary of Korean immigration to the United States from 1903 to the end of World War II is presented to illustrate the historical context for current trends.

A Historical Overview of Korean Immigration to the United States

Korean immigration to the United States can be divided into three phases: the early period, from 1903 to 1944; the intermediate period, from 1945 to 1964; and the recent period, from 1965 to the present. Each wave of Korean immigrants was caused by different factors in Korea and the United States, and the motivations and characteristics of the immigrants in each period were substantially different.

The Early Period of Korean Immigration, 1903–44

Three sets of factors played important roles in initiating and sustaining the early phase of Korean immigration to the United States: push factors that drove Koreans out of their homeland; pull factors that attracted Koreans to Hawaii and the West Coast; and agents who linked the two.

The push factors in Korea consisted of a series of political and economic upheavals and disasters at the end of the declining Chosŏn (or Yi) dynasty. After a reign of five centuries (1392–1910), the Chosŏn government lost its control over the ownership of land and taxation as the *yangban* ruling class appropriated more land from which to extract taxes and rent directly from farmers. Consequently, the financial basis of the government became increasingly precarious, and farmers found themselves squeezed more and more by the oppressive taxation of yangban landlords and corrupt officials (Pomerantz 1984, 280).

The internal disintegration of the Chosŏn dynasty's feudal order paved the way for the penetration of such imperialist powers as Japan, the United States, and Russia. After the Meiji Restoration of 1868, Japan had emerged as an industrial country and had become interested in Korea as a source of foodstuffs and other raw materials and as a market for its own manufactured goods. In 1876, it succeeded in forcing the Chosŏn rulers to sign the unequal Kanghwa Treaty, which opened Inch'ŏn, Wŏnsan, and Pusan to the Japanese for trade and residence and allowed the Japanese to exercise extraterritorial rights. Within two decades, Japan had achieved unequivocal control over Korea after defeating China in the Sino-Japanese War (1894–95) and Russia in the Russo-Japanese War (1904–5).

In the 1880s, pressed by poverty and food shortages during frequent famines, many Korean farmers had begun to accept cash advances for the future sale of their crops from Japanese merchants. This resulted in a cycle of debt and dependency on these merchants that further eroded the self-sufficiency of farmers. The entry of Japanese manufactured goods, such as textiles and metal products, into the Korean market also undermined Korea's primitive handicraft industries. As a result, many farmers and artisans went bankrupt. A nationwide famine in 1901 made matters worse.

All of these factors combined to produce intolerable conditions for many farmers. In 1894, such conditions led to a massive peasant uprising called the Tonghak Rebellion in the southwestern province of Chŏlla, where agriculture was most highly developed and hence the oppression was most pervasive. Similar conditions forced many farmers in the northwestern province of Hamgyŏng to migrate northward to Siberia and establish farms on land under Russian control. Impoverished farmers, uprooted from their villages by famines and wars, fled unemployed and dispossessed into cities such as Seoul and Inch'ŏn, where they engaged in miscellaneous low-skilled forms of labor. Rootless refugees in their own country, they were cut off from traditional social norms and obligations and consequently became receptive to new ideas, such as Christianity, and new opportunities far from their homeland (Patterson 1988, 104).

These laborers were pulled into the United States by the demand for cheap labor in Hawaii's sugar plantation camps (Pomerantz 1984, 285). Since the establishment of these large-scale, labor-intensive plantations in the 1830s, immigrant laborers had been recruited from various countries to work in their fields. Chinese laborers began to arrive in sizable numbers in 1852, and before the end of the nineteenth century, some 50,000 of them had immigrated to Hawaii (Chan 1991, 26–27). However, anti-Chinese agitation and legislation, such as the Chinese Exclusion Act of 1882, began to restrict the numbers allowed to enter Hawaii, and in 1886 the importation of Chinese laborers came to an end. Hawaii's sugar planters then recruited Japanese laborers, who began to arrive in 1885 and comprised nearly 80 percent of the workforce on the plantations at the turn of the twentieth century (Pomerantz 1984, 294). As the Japanese gained a labor monopoly on the plantations in the 1890s, they launched numerous strikes against the planters, demanding higher wages and better conditions. Growing numbers of Japanese laborers also migrated to the U.S. mainland in search of higher-paying jobs in railroad construction camps and California's burgeoning agricultural economy. Under such circumstances, Koreans were recruited to the plantations— to meet the labor shortage on the one hand and to offset Japanese dominance on the other.

Individuals such as Dr. Horace N. Allen, David W. Dashler, and several American missionaries (including the Reverend George H. Jones) were crucial in linking the demand for cheap labor in Hawaii and the supply of such labor in Korea. Allen had arrived in Korea in 1884 as a Presbyterian medical missionary and soon earned the trust of King Kojong (1864–1907) after he saved one of the king's brothers-in-law, who was injured during an attempted coup. After he gained entry into Korean politics, Allen vigorously sought concessions and franchises for American businesses from the Koreans. He believed that the United States would become involved in Korean politics as its economic interests in Korea increased. Such involvement, Allen hoped, would in turn counter Japanese influence and help the Koreans regain independence (Patterson 1988, 20).

Allen became involved in Korean immigration to Hawaii after he met a representative of the Hawaiian Sugar Planters' Association, who was eager to recruit Koreans as laborers. He then persuaded his friend the king to allow Koreans to emigrate. His arguments appealed to Kojong, who thought that emigration would relieve the sufferings of famine victims, increase U.S. economic interests in Korea, and consequently strengthen the relationship between Korea and the United States.

Following Allen's recommendations, the Department of Emigration was established in 1902, and David W. Dashler, an American businessman, was put in charge of recruiting Korean laborers. Dashler's initial recruiting efforts, however, met with little success, primarily because of Koreans' fear of going abroad. Although many Koreans had migrated to Siberia and Manchuria beginning in the 1880s, overseas emigration was a totally new experience. The intervention of the Reverend George H.

Jones of the Methodist Episcopal Church of Inch'ŏn was crucial in over-coming the initial resistance. Jones, a personal friend of Allen, believed that emigration to Hawaii would be beneficial for Koreans—and that his mission work among them would be more successful there. He per-suaded his congregations to emigrate, and half of them joined the first shipload of Koreans to Hawaii on December 22, 1902 (Patterson 1988, 49).

This shipload, carrying 101 emigrants, sailed from Inch'ŏn and ar-rived in Honolulu on January 13, 1903. Fifteen additional shiploads in 1903 brought 1,133 more Koreans. By 1905, when Korean immigration came to a halt because of Japanese opposition, 7,226 immigrants had arrived in Hawaii (Houchins and Houchins 1974, 553). Of these, 6,048 were male adults in their twenties, 637 were women, and 541 were chil-dren. Thus, the majority of the early Korean immigrants to Hawaii were young, single males who came to Hawaii to make a quick fortune and return home rich and respected.

These immigrants came from diverse geographic and occupational backgrounds. The majority of them had been manual laborers in port cities and towns. The remainder included former soldiers in the Korean army, household servants, policemen, woodcutters, miners, students, churchmen, and Buddhist monks. Farmers were underrepresented among the early immigrants, accounting for only one-seventh of the to-tal (Houchins and Houchins 1974, 555; Ryu 1988, 29). But this small proportion conceals the fact that the majority of the immigrants had in fact originally been farmers before they had drifted into the port cities and towns (Patterson 1988, 104).

A distinctive characteristic of the early Korean immigrants was their Christianity. It was estimated that nearly 40 percent of them had become Christians in Korea, and gradually most of them became churchgoers (Choy 1979, 77). The overrepresentation of Christians in this group re-sulted partly from the fact that American missionaries had encouraged their Korean congregations to emigrate to Hawaii. It also resulted from the fact that the majority of the early Korean immigrants were recruited in port cities and towns in the Seoul–Inch'ŏn area and in northern Ko-rea, where Christianity was more prevalent than elsewhere. Because of the strong religious connection and the absence of traditional associa-tions based on kinship and region of origin among the early immigrants, Christian churches became the center of the social, cultural, and political activities of the Korean community in the United States (Ryu 1988).

Another important characteristic of the early Korean immigration to Hawaii was an unbalanced sex ratio: there were ten men for every woman. A sojourning orientation among these immigrants was responsible for this skewed ratio. To redress the problem, Korean women were brought into Hawaii through the exchange of pictures between prospective brides and grooms. Between 1910 and 1924, when this practice was banned, almost 1,000 Korean brides arrived in Hawaii and another 115 in California in this fashion (H. Kim 1980, 602).

Picture brides made significant contributions to the Korean immigrant community. First of all, their arrival led to the establishment of families in the community and to the creation of a new generation of American-born Koreans. Second, these brides were generally more educated and enlightened than their husbands, whom they encouraged to change occupations from plantation work to small businesses or other urban trades. As a result, Koreans left the plantations more quickly than any other ethnic group in Hawaii. Between 1903 and 1915, 1,087 of them moved to the U.S. mainland in search of higher wages in railroad construction camps and orchards (Patterson 1976, 83). The picture marriage also had a tragic consequence on Korean families, however. Because of the large age discrepancy between husbands and wives—on average, 14 years—Koreans recorded the highest rate of divorce among all racial and ethnic groups in Hawaii.

During the decade after 1910, some 541 Korean students came to the United States to study at American schools and universities (Houchins and Houchins 1974, 558). Although at the time of entry they were classified as students, they were essentially political refugees who tried to escape Japanese rule over Korea (1910–45). They soon became the intellectual and political leaders of the Korean immigrant community, and they organized and sponsored the Korean independence movement overseas. Between 1924, when the Immigration Act effectively curtailed Asian immigration, and the end of World War II, there was virtually no immigration from Korea (E. Yu 1983, 23). By 1945, when Korea regained its independence from Japan, Koreans in the United States represented a small and largely isolated minority, with about 6,500 members in Hawaii and about 3,000 on the mainland (L. Shin 1971, 32).

The Intermediate Period of Korean Immigration, 1945–64

Shortly after regaining its independence from Japan, Korea was divided along the 38th parallel into a communist North Korea and a democratic South Korea. The United States ruled South Korea through a military government between 1945 and 1948 and became more deeply involved in the area during the Korean War (1950–53). After this war, the United States stationed more than 40,000 troops in South Korea until 1990, when a small reduction in this number occurred. The presence of U.S. troops resulted in a sizable number of intermarriages between Korean women and American military servicemen, and between 1950 and 1964, 6,000 of these women immigrated to the United States. During the same period, 5,000 children, either war orphans or children of mixed parentage, were adopted by American families. These women and children accounted for two-thirds of the Korean immigrants admitted to the United States between 1950 and 1964. Unlike the early Korean immigrants, who formed their own communities, they were already attached to American families and were scattered throughout the United States. They are still cut off from the Korean immigrant community and live isolated and marginal lives in the United States (B. Kim 1978; E. Yu 1983, 23–24).

Post–World War II military, political, and cultural relations between the United States and South Korea were also responsible for the migration of about 6,000 Korean students to the United States between 1945 and 1965 (W. Kim 1971, 26). They entered the United States in expectation of finding social prestige back in South Korea after obtaining diplomas from American colleges and universities. Many of them, however, settled in the United States after completing their studies and laid a foundation for succeeding waves of Korean immigrants.

Korean Immigration since 1965

Korean immigration to the United States entered a new phase when the United States changed its immigration policy in 1965. Since 1970, when this new wave of immigration gained momentum, large numbers of Koreans have crossed the Pacific Ocean to start a new life in the United States. As table 2.1 shows, 18,346 Koreans were admitted as permanent residents in 1971 alone. Since the second half of the 1970s, about 30,000 Koreans have immigrated annually, and during the peak years of 1985 to 1987, more than 35,000 arrived annually, making South Korea the third largest country of origin for U.S. immigrants after Mexico and the Philippines. In sum, more than 660,000 Koreans entered the United States as permanent residents between 1965 and 1990. As a result of this massive immigration, the Korean population in the United States has increased dramatically—from 69,150 in 1970 to 357,393 in 1980 and 798,849 in 1990 (Barringer, Gardner, and Levin 1993, 39).

The zeal of Koreans for immigration to the United States began to dwindle after 1988, as a deepening economic recession made the United States a less attractive destination than before. Since then, the total population of Korean immigrants—particularly the number of new arrivals—has been declining. In contrast, the number of Koreans who have returned permanently to Korea has been growing since 1988, when South Korea successfully hosted the Olympic Games in Seoul. This event raised South Korea's international status and aroused Koreans' pride and nationalism. In addition, the success of Korean conglomerates such as Hyundai and Samsung in the world market has lured a growing number of American-educated and -trained Korean professionals and technicians back to South Korea.

The Immigration and Nationality Act of 1965 also dramatically changed the demographic and socioeconomic profiles of Korean immigrants (see table 2.2). As noted in the preceding section, more than half of the immigrants between 1950 and 1964 were young women between the ages of 20 and 29 who had married American servicemen serving in south Korea and children less than five years of age adopted by American parents. Those who arrived after 1970 were quite different. First of all, they were permanent immigrants, not sojourners, so they immigrated as nuclear families. Their stable family structure and strong family ties later became important assets for their economic adaptation to the United States. They also came from urban backgrounds in South Korea. More than half of them came from Seoul, and the remainder came from Pusan, Taegu, and other large cities.

Data from the 1980 U.S. census also show that about 30 percent of the Korean immigrants aged 25 and older who were admitted between 1970 and 1980 had received four years of college education. The corresponding figures were 22 percent for new immigrants of all nationalities who had arrived during the same period and 16 percent for the U.S. native-born population (U.S. Bureau of the Census 1984, 12). In addition, the majority of the post-1965 Korean immigrants were professional, technical, managerial, or clerical workers—in other words, white-collar workers—before immigration. Laborers and farmers, in contrast, have been uniformly underrepresented in this group, although they made up more than half of the Korean labor force as recently as

Table 2.1. Number of Koreans Admitted to the United States as Permanent Residents, 1950–90

Year of Entry	Status at Entry		Total
	New Arrivals	Adjustments[a]	
1950–54	538	N/A	538
1955–59	4,990	N/A	4,990
1960–65	11,686	1,583	13,269
1966	2,492	598	3,090
1967	3,956	1,424	5,380
1968	3,811	1,098	4,909
1969	6,045	1,820	7,865
1970	9,314	2,079	11,393
1971	14,297	4,049	18,346
1972	18,876	5,513	24,389
1973	22,930	4,961	27,891
1974	28,028	4,658	32,686
1975	28,362	2,364	30,726
1976	30,803	1,881	32,684
1977	28,437	2,480	30,917
1978	25,830	3,458	29,288
1979	26,646	2,602	29,248
1980	29,387	2,933	32,320
1981	28,819	3,844	32,663
1982	27,861	3,863	31,724
1983	29,019	4,320	33,339
1984	28,828	4,214	33,042
1985	30,532	4,721	35,253
1986	30,745	5,031	35,776
1987	32,135	3,714	35,849
1988	31,071	3,632	34,703
1989	28,248	5,974	34,222
1990	25,966	6,335	32,301
Total			
Number	589,652	89,149	678,801
Percentage	87	13	100

Sources: U.S. Immigration and Naturalization Service, *Annual Reports*, 1966–77; *Statistical Yearbook*, 1978–90.

a. Adjustments refers to persons who had previously entered the United States with nonimmigrant status (student, visitor, or businessperson) and who changed their status to that of permanent resident.

1980 (KEPB 1980). Thus, recent Korean immigration to the United States has been primarily a movement of middle-class Koreans.

Nevertheless, the proportion of professional and technical workers, especially medical practitioners, among Korean immigrants has been declining during the last two decades, whereas that of Koreans from lower socioeconomic backgrounds has been increasing. More individuals have reported working in Korea as operatives, laborers, or farmers—occupations that generally constitute the lower class and the working class in South Korea. Why have Koreans of middle-class background been overrepresented in the post-1965 Korean immigration? Why have Koreans of lower- and working-class background responded to the immigration opportunity only in more recent years? Why did this immigration occur in the first place, and why on a large scale after 1965? These four questions are the central issues to be explored in the remainder of this chapter.

Light and Bonacich (1988) explain the immigration as a response to economic and political dislocations in South Korea resulting from its involvement in the world capitalist system. They argue that American and Japanese capitalists penetrated the Korean economy to take advantage of its cheap labor force, which created the dislocations. The classes that were most likely to be dislocated and that had the greatest incentive to emigrate, they say, were agricultural workers, who migrated to cities in search of employment; educated white-collar workers, who could not find jobs commensurate with their training; and indigenous capitalists, who had to compete with foreign investors. Light and Bonacich summarize their position as follows:

> One cannot but be struck by the coincidence of the rise in manufactured exports from South Korea to the U.S. and the rise in emigration. . . . In our view, both processes were rooted in the emergence of a proletariat (that is, free wage labor) in South Korea and reflect U.S. capitalist efforts to make use of this labor force. This emergence was partly a product of internal development in South Korea, but *U.S. capitalist involvement* there (backed by political and military involvement) contributed substantially to the process of *proletarianization* and thus to the loosening of Koreans for work in U.S. invested plants and firms specializing in manufactured imports, and for emigration. Finally, the U.S. presence contributed to the harsh conditions of political and economic life in the republic, which made it both a fertile ground for

Table 2.2. Age and Sex of Korean Immigrants, 1956–90 (Percentages)

	Year of Entry																		
Age/Sex	1956	1957	1958	1959	1960	1961	1962	1963	1964	1965	1966	1967	1968	1969	1970	1971	1972	1973	1974
Under 5																			
Males	9.4	13.2	21.6	15.9	9.7	13.4	7.3	3.4	5.5	5.9	3.8	3.2	3.9	3.9	4.2	4.4	5.2	6.6	6.5
Females	14.0	13.6	25.2	27.6	22.0	31.6	19.4	9.2	11.5	11.5	9.6	6.6	8.1	7.5	7.0	7.4	8.9	10.0	9.2
5–9																			
Males	4.2	2.9	6.7	6.1	4.8	5.1	4.2	3.2	3.3	3.7	2.7	3.6	3.2	3.8	3.7	4.3	4.2	4.5	5.2
Females	3.7	3.6	6.6	7.1	5.0	6.6	4.9	3.7	5.5	4.3	4.8	4.4	4.5	4.1	4.8	4.9	4.8	4.7	5.0
10–19																			
Males	8.0	4.0	1.7	2.8	2.5	2.7	2.7	2.7	3.3	2.6	3.2	3.3	3.6	2.7	4.1	4.1	4.9	5.9	6.9
Females	5.9	2.1	2.8	2.6	3.2	4.0	4.1	4.5	6.6	6.5	5.7	6.4	5.8	5.8	5.9	6.0	6.4	7.7	8.2
20–29																			
Males	3.3	4.2	2.8	2.9	4.0	3.5	4.9	7.1	3.4	2.4	4.2	4.9	5.8	5.9	7.4	6.8	7.5	7.1	6.6
Females	36.1	42.1	23.6	26.4	37.2	22.4	38.7	46.4	45.3	45.7	39.6	33.5	35.5	35.2	33.1	29.2	25.1	22.3	21.3
30–39																			
Males	4.4	4.6	2.9	2.3	2.5	2.6	3.7	6.1	2.8	3.3	8.3	13.0	10.1	10.8	10.0	12.7	12.2	9.7	9.4
Females	7.5	5.2	4.1	4.6	7.5	6.1	7.7	10.9	9.9	11.9	14.0	14.8	12.9	12.5	12.3	12.7	11.7	10.4	10.1
40–49																			
Males	1.2	0.6	0.5	0.6	0.2	0.5	.05	.08	0.4	0.4	1.1	2.0	1.7	1.9	2.0	1.9	2.8	3.0	3.6
Females	1.4	1.5	0.7	0.5	0.7	0.7	0.7	0.6	1.1	0.6	0.8	1.6	1.6	1.7	2.1	2.1	2.5	2.8	3.2
50–59																			
Males	0.3	0.4	0.4	0.3	0.3	0.2	0.1	0.2	0.3	0.2	0.2	0.3	0.4	0.5	0.7	0.6	0.9	1.0	1.0
Females	0.3	0.8	0.1	0.0	0.2	0.2	0.6	0.4	0.4	0.3	0.7	0.8	1.1	1.0	1.0	0.9	1.3	1.9	1.4
60 and over																			
Males	0.0	0.6	0.0	0.1	0.2	0.5	0.2	0.2	0.3	0.2	0.2	0.5	0.3	0.2	0.3	0.4	0.5	0.7	0.7
Females	0.2	0.4	0.1	0.1	0.1	0.2	0.3	0.5	0.5	0.6	0.8	0.8	0.8	0.7	0.7	0.7	1.1	1.7	1.4
Total percentages																			
Males	30.9	30.6	36.8	31.0	24.2	28.3	23.5	23.6	19.2	18.7	24.0	31.0	29.0	31.0	33.0	36.0	38.0	39.0	40.0
Females	69.1	69.4	63.2	69.0	75.8	71.7	76.5	76.4	80.8	81.3	76.0	69.0	71.0	69.0	67.0	64.0	62.0	61.0	60.0
Total number	573	477	1,604	1,719	1,507	1,534	1,538	2,580	2,362	2,165	2,492	3,956	3,811	6,045	9,314	14,297	18,876	22,930	28,028

Table 2.2.

Age/Sex	1975	1976	1977	1978	1979	1980[a]	1981[a]	1982[b]	1983[b]	1984[b]	1985[b]	1986	1987	1988	1989	1990
Under 5																
Males	7.3	8.0	6.7	5.4	4.6	11.6	10.6	—	—	—	—	8.4	8.0	7.3	6.2	5.1
Females	10.1	11.1	10.5	8.8	7.0			—	—	—	—	11.1	10.6	8.8	6.4	5.2
5–9																
Males	5.6	5.0	5.0	5.1	4.9	9.0	7.3	—	—	—	—	3.1	3.1	3.2	3.0	2.7
Females	5.8	5.0	5.1	5.2	4.8			—	—	—	—	3.2	3.0	3.2	2.7	2.6
10–19																
Males	8.0	6.6	6.9	6.4	7.4	15.4	14.3	14.3	16.3	17.8	18.1	6.7	7.1	8.0	7.8	8.7
Females	8.8	8.3	8.3	8.1	7.8			18.3	20.2	21.8	20.7	6.5	6.6	7.5	7.0	7.8
20–29																
Males	7.4	7.3	7.7	6.9	7.6	29.3	30.8	11.1	9.7	9.4	9.3	8.7	8.9	7.2	8.0	6.9
Females	18.2	22.1	21.1	20.8	21.8			19.2	17.4	17.3	17.0	15.5	15.9	14.5	15.2	13.5
30–39																
Males	8.2	7.0	6.9	7.6	6.7	15.0	14.4	5.4	5.9	5.9	6.0	6.4	6.3	6.9	7.6	8.0
Females	9.4	8.4	8.3	8.6	8.3			6.6	6.9	7.2	7.6	7.3	7.5	8.3	9.2	10.0
40–59																
Males	3.4	3.0	3.3	3.8	3.6	7.8	7.7	3.4	3.9	4.0	3.8	3.7	3.8	4.7	5.3	6.5
Females	3.0	2.9	3.1	3.7	3.8			3.9	4.1	4.2	4.1	3.9	4.2	5.2	5.5	6.7
50–59																
Males	1.1	1.1	1.4	1.7	1.9	5.3	6.7	2.2	2.0	2.0	2.0	2.3	2.3	2.8	3.7	3.9
Females	1.3	1.7	1.9	2.6	3.4			4.6	3.5	3.8	4.0	4.7	4.4	4.6	4.5	4.7
60 and over																
Males	0.8	0.9	1.3	1.7	2.2	6.7	8.3	2.9	2.4	2.5	2.7	3.2	3.2	3.0	3.2	3.0
Females	1.5	1.7	2.5	3.5	4.1			5.4	3.8	4.0	4.6	5.2	4.9	4.8	4.8	4.7
Total percentages																
Males	42.0	39.0	39.0	39.0	39.0	u	u	40.0	42.0	42.0	42.0	43.0	43.0	43.0	45.0	44.8
Females	58.0	61.0	61.0	61.0	61.0	u	u	60.0	58.0	58.0	48.0	57.0	57.0	57.0	55.0	55.2
Total number	28,362	30,803	30,917	29,288	29,248	32,320	32,663	31,724	33,339	33,042	35,253	35,776	35,849	34,703	34,222	32,301

Source: Same as for table 2.1.

u = data unavailable.

a. In 1980 and 1981, males and females were not counted separately.

b. Between 1982 and 1985, males and females under 20 years old were counted in a single category. Percentages for this group are shown in the rows for ages 10–19.

profitable investment and trade and provided an impetus for emigration [emphasis added]. (117)

This explanation, however, does not square with the actual class composition of Korean immigrants, nor does it adequately explain why Koreans
of lower- and working-class backgrounds have begun to immigrate to
the United States in increasing numbers only in recent years.

In this chapter I provide an alternative explanation of Korean immigration patterns. First, such immigration has been primarily a movement
of middle-class Koreans seeking better opportunities in the United
States. Second, political, military, and cultural relations between the
United States and South Korea since World War II have been as important as economic relations for initiating Korean immigration. Third,
the immigration of middle-class Koreans was set in motion by the rapid
expansion of a new urban middle class whose members were experiencing a widening gap between their expectations of upward mobility and
the limited opportunities available to them in South Korea. Finally, there
has been a gradual increase of Korean immigrants from lower- and
working-class backgrounds because of a change in U.S. immigration policy in 1976 and also because of the increasing importance of social networks as an entry mechanism.

Social and Economic Changes in South Korea

During the late 1960s and the 1970s, South Korea underwent a dramatic structural transformation from an agricultural society to a capitalist,
industrialized one. After President Park Chung Hee came to power
through a coup d'état in 1961, his military government initiated a program of economic development modeled after the economies of Western
countries. Following the advice of U.S. economic advisors and Korean
economists educated in American universities, South Korean economic
planners directed the economy toward export-oriented industrialization
(Mason et al. 1980; Koo 1987). In the absence of natural resources, capital, and technology, such development using Korea's inexpensive and
disciplined labor force was thought to be the right choice.

The basic pattern has been "to import raw materials, intermediate
goods, and heavy capital goods and to produce finished products for
overseas markets" (I. Kim 1981, 82). The United States and Japan were
the primary suppliers of capital and technology as well as the largest

overseas markets. Thus, from the beginning, South Korea stressed a dependent form of development, relying heavily on foreign capital, technology, and markets. So, too, did Taiwan. But its development distinguished South Korea from many Latin American countries, where economic stagnation, structural unemployment, and growing inequality were regarded as inevitable consequences of dependent development.

What made South Korea and Taiwan different from most Third World countries was their politico-strategic position in East Asia as bulwarks against communist expansion (Koo 1987; Ong and Liu 1994, ch. 2). As a result, the United States has supported the undemocratic but anticommunist South Korean governments since the end of World War II by providing them with military and economic assistance. Of the $222.4 billion spent by the United States worldwide in resisting communist expansion, 5.7 percent, or $12.6 billion, was spent on South Korea, second only to South Vietnam (Light and Bonacich 1988, 42). In addition, by 1975, U.S. commercial banks had extended $2.3 billion in loans to South Korea, which constituted 83.5 percent of all commercial loans to South Korea (I. Kim 1981, 83). Thus, by the time South Korea became part of the world economy and opened its doors to foreign capitalists, "adequate economic foundations in both infrastructure and human capital had been laid, and the state was in firm control of the economy" (Koo 1987, 169).

The special treatment that South Korea received from the United States was not restricted to military and economic aid. South Korea has also been one of the countries benefiting from duty-free manufactured exports to the United States, and in 1977 alone it exported $515 million worth of manufactured commodities under the U.S. government's Generalized System of Preference, which constituted 16.5 percent of total Korean exports to the United States (Light and Bonacich 1988, 59).

Aside from South Korea's political and economic relations with the United States, the international division of labor and the growing willingness of the United States to rely on imported goods turned out by the 1970s to be important factors in the rapid growth of the South Korean economy. Under the international division of labor, core countries have been increasingly specializing in labor requiring professional, technical, and managerial skills, while semiperipheral countries have been taking over labor-intensive production in traditional industries (Portes and Walton 1981). The decision to concentrate on export-oriented development was a timely one for South Korea because in more recent years the growing competition from labor-rich developing countries has made it increasingly difficult for Third World countries to follow this pattern.

The successful combination of a strong and efficient government, a cheap and industrious labor force, and an ability to draw on foreign capital, technology, and markets has led to remarkable economic growth in South Korea during the last three decades. Exports rose dramatically from $41 million in 1961 (in 1976 constant U.S. dollars) to $10 billion in 1977 and $24.4 billion in 1983. The gross national product (GNP) also increased from $2.3 billion in 1962 to $35 billion in 1977 and $62 billion in 1981 (KEPB 1983, 3). Throughout the 1960s and 1970s, the Korean economy maintained about a 10 percent annual increase in GNP, and the rate in the manufacturing sector was even greater because of the export-oriented development. In 1966, manufacturing accounted for 13.4 percent of the GNP; by 1983, it had increased to 33.4 percent.

Export-oriented development has dramatically changed the industrial structure of South Korea in a short period of time. Agriculture declined rapidly during the 1960s and 1970s, but manufacturing and the service industries posted large gains during the same period (see table 2.3). In 1960, two out of three workers were farmers, but by 1970 this proportion had declined to one-half and by 1985 to only one-quarter. According to the latest South Korean census, in 1990, only 18 percent of the labor force remained in agriculture, fishing, and forestry.

In contrast, less than 8 percent of the labor force worked in the mining and manufacturing industries in 1960, but by 1970 that figure had risen to 14 percent and by 1980 to 23 percent. These industries continued to expand during the 1980s, and by 1990 they accounted for about 27 percent of the Korean labor force. As in many such countries, the service industry had developed well before South Korea started to industrialize in 1962. In 1960, this and other tertiary industries employed one-quarter of the labor force, and they continued to grow during the next three decades. Today, more than half of Korean workers are employed in the service sector and in commerce.

During the course of industrial restructuring, large numbers of rural out-migrants were drawn into the booming manufacturing industries or marginal service sectors in large cities. Between 1960 and 1975, an estimated 6.9 million farmers left their land to seek their fortunes in the city (Han 1977, 60). The general pattern of rural-to-urban migration was one in which single migrants under the age of 30 became production workers in the manufacturing industries, while members of migrant

Table 2.3. Distribution of the South Korean Labor Force, 1960–90
           (Percentages)

Industry	1960	1965	1970	1975	1980	1985	1990
Agriculture, fishing, and forestry	65.9	58.6	50.5	45.9	34.0	24.9	18.3
Mining and manufacturing	7.5	10.4	14.3	19.1	22.6	24.5	27.3
Service and commerce	26.6	31.0	35.2	35.0	43.4	50.6	54.4
Total number (thousands)	7,028	8,206	9,745	11,830	13,706	14,935	18,036

Sources: Korean Economic Planning Board, *1960 Population and Housing Census Report; Annual Report on the Economically Active Population,* 1965, 1970, 1975, 1980, 1985, 1990.

households engaged in either small businesses or informal economic activities (such as peddling, daily construction work, or small-scale transportation work) in urban areas (J. Kim 1986).

Such migration occurred primarily because of the widening economic disparities between rural and urban households. In 1970, the average income of rural households was 25 percent less than that of urban households, excluding those of high-income wage and salary workers (CISJD 1986, 64–65). The Park Chung Hee government had prevented the price of rice from rising in order to keep urban workers' wages down, a condition essential to maintaining the competitiveness of Korean manufactured products in the international market. As the price of locally produced rice and other grains did not rise with that of industrial products such as fertilizers and pesticides, the economic condition of farmers deteriorated. Thus, Korean economic development was achieved at the expense of agricultural workers.

This situation is often explained as a result of farmers' passivity and failure to mobilize politically. Peasant struggles in South Korea led neither to a successful revolution nor to a radical shift in the Korean political power structure (Koo 1987). College students, on the other hand, have been an active political force throughout modern Korean history. The student revolution in April 1960 toppled the corrupt Syngman Rhee government and gave birth to the first democratically elected government, that of Chang Myon (1960–61). This was primarily an urban, middle-class movement. Park Chung Hee, who seized power in 1961, was quite aware of the political clout of the urban middle class, and therefore he continued to emphasize rapid economic growth in the urban manufacturing sector at the expense of the agricultural sector (Koo 1987). Thus, uneven economic development in South Korea was partly the result of the political economy of the Park regime, which wanted to enhance its political legitimacy through rapid economic growth.

Massive out-migration from rural areas led to rapid urbanization and the concentration of the population in several large cities, especially Seoul. Seoul contains 25 percent of the nation's population in only 0.6 percent of its area. The concentration of economic resources in Seoul was the major reason for the massive migration to the capital. In 1976, Seoul accounted for 28 percent of the GNP, with 42 percent of all manufacturing companies, 45 percent of all banking institutions, and 66 percent of all savings (T. Kim 1983, 164). The political, cultural, and educational dominance of Seoul over the rest of the country also drew many Koreans, who dreamed of enjoying a sophisticated urban culture. In 1975, 57.9 percent of all privately owned cars, 44 percent of all telephones, 49 percent of all hospital beds, and 60 percent of all college students in Korea were concentrated in Seoul. For young people, migration to the capital for education was an opportunity for upward social and economic mobility.

Education has often been identified as one of the most important factors in the rapid economic growth of South Korea. Korean workers represented cheap yet educated labor, whereas in many other Third World countries cheap laborers were mainly uneducated. A substantial investment in education was made before South Korea's economic development started in 1962. By 1965, Korea's human resources development was equivalent to that found in countries with three times its GNP (McGinn et al. 1980, 62).

U.S. assistance was critical for the rapid expansion of educational opportunities at the primary level, both at the end of World War II and after the Korean War. During the three years when the American military governed South Korea (1945–48), the United States tried to inculcate the American concept of democracy in the Korean population through school reforms. It mandated equal opportunity in education, coeducation in schools, and a shift of control from national and provincial governments to townships and counties (McGinn et al. 1980, 12).

But these efforts met with little success because the Korean governments used education to foster anticommunist and progovernment ideas to justify their authoritarian rule. Thereafter, the United States channeled its investments mainly toward physical facilities, especially the construction of primary schools. Between 1952 and 1966, it spent about $100 million for education in South Korea. A smaller sum of money ($19 million) went to improving higher education. Much of this went to Seoul National University, to help upgrade its faculty. The United States also contributed to a program to send Korean students to the United States for study. By 1956–57, the third largest foreign student enrollment in the United States was from Korea, behind only Canada and Taiwan (McGinn et al. 1980, 92). In the context of its total foreign aid to South Korea, however, the U.S. government's contribution to the expansion of higher-level educational opportunities was minimal.

The U.S. private sector—most notably, Protestant churches—was a more significant source for the expansion of higher education in South Korea. As early as 1882, even before Korea developed diplomatic and trade relations with the United States, American missionaries came to Korea to convert its people to Christianity. From the beginning, they built schools, hospitals, and other social service institutions as part of their mission. Several prominent private secondary and higher-level schools were founded by American missionaries: Yonsei Medical Center (by Dr. Horace Allen in 1885), Yonsei University (by Dr. H. G. Underwood in 1915), Ewha Women's University (by missionary Mary F. Scranton in 1886), Catholic Medical School (by Roman Catholics in 1855), and Soongjun University (by W. M. Baird in 1897). Theological seminaries, such as the Methodist Theological Seminary established by G. H. Jones in 1905, were also founded throughout Korea by American missionaries who represented the Presbyterian and Methodist denominations. Many Korean elites were educated in these private Christian schools. Christianity became a symbol of modern ideas and thus spread rapidly among the educated urban class. Thanks to such assistance from both the public and private sectors of the United States, Korea was able to expand its secondary and higher education even when its economy alone could not have allowed it.

Despite the significant role of foreign aid, the major source for the expansion of higher education in Korea since the 1960s has been the Korean people themselves. The Park Chung Hee government tried unsuccessfully to curtail enrollment in higher education, partly because of the high unemployment rate among college graduates and partly because of its fear of another student revolution (McGinn et al. 1980, 95). Despite government restrictions and increasing tuition, Koreans maintained a strong desire for such education. In 1987, almost 90 percent of all parents expected to provide college or higher-level education for their sons, and 70 percent expected to provide the same level of education for their daughters. Even parents with only primary schooling themselves had high expectations for their children's education: 60 percent desired higher education for their sons, and 40 percent desired it for their daughters (KEPB 1987, 155).

This strong desire and fierce competition for educational opportunity can be traced to the fact that education has been the most viable avenue of upward social and economic mobility in Korean society. Korea is unusually homogeneous in race, language, religion, and culture. Beginning in the early twentieth century, a series of social and political upheavals—including Japanese colonialism (1910–45), rule by the U.S. military government (1945–48), land reform (1948–50), the Korean War (1950–53), and the massive migration of refugees from North Korea during the war—destroyed the old class structure and made South Korea a more fluid and egalitarian society (Koo 1987, 170). In the absence of a traditional class structure, education became the most reliable means to advance individual social and economic status.

The immediate social and economic rewards of higher education reinforce the strong desire for it. Income differences by educational level are quite large in South Korea. In 1976, graduates of two-year junior colleges and high schools earned 63 percent and 44 percent, respectively, of the average income of graduates from four-year colleges (Korean Ministry of Labor 1985, 24). Since then, this income discrepancy has steadily narrowed. Thus, in 1990, male graduates of junior colleges and high schools earned 70 percent and 65 percent, respectively, of the income of male graduates of colleges and universities (KEPB 1992, 92). Among females, the percentages were 69 percent and 55 percent. Despite this moderate wage increase among non–college graduates (particularly high school graduates), the income difference by educational attainment is still wide.

Beyond the immediate economic rewards of a college education, the contemptuous attitude of college graduates toward non–college graduates in a face-saving culture motivates people to seek higher education with little specific reference to economic returns. Particularly for women, a college education is a means to enhance one's position in the marriage market. Graduates from prestigious women's universities in Seoul have a better chance than their less fortunate peers of marrying men of high social and economic status. For this reason, women's education and labor force participation are inversely related to each other in South Korea: college-educated women are not strongly inclined to work because their high-status husbands earn enough money to support their families, whereas less well educated women are more likely to work to supplement their low-status husbands' meager earnings (K. Kim 1990).

Foreign aid to education and the strong desire for higher education in South Korea led to the expansion of such education beyond the demands of the labor force. As table 2.4 shows, on average about 30 percent of all male college graduates (including those from two-year junior colleges) during the last three decades could not find employment after graduation. Unemployment has been more serious for women. More than half of all female graduates did not or could not participate in the labor force after graduation. The imbalance between the demand for and the supply of college graduates in South Korea led some Koreans to migrate overseas for employment.

Some sought to emigrate permanently to the United States, whereas others went to West Germany and the Middle East as contract mining workers, construction workers, and nurses. After their contracts expired, most of the former miners and construction workers did not return to South Korea, where they would have become unemployed again. Instead, they entered the United States as spouses of Korean nurses, whom they had married overseas and whose training qualified them as immigrants with special skills.

Class Formation in South Korea

As the scale of the Korean economy expanded, especially in manufacturing, large numbers of people became wage or salary workers in private corporations and government institutions. The movement of labor between industries was accompanied by changes in occupational distribution (see table 2.5). In 1960, two-thirds of the labor force consisted of self-employed farmers and rural laborers. Their absolute numbers and relative proportion of the total labor force dropped rapidly between 1960 and 1990, when less than one-fifth of Korean workers remained on farms. Large numbers of rural out-migrants went to work in manufacturing industries. In 1960, production workers and manual laborers accounted for only 13 percent of the labor force, but that figure had risen to 22 percent by 1970, 28 percent by 1980, and 35 percent by 1990.

Rapid proletarianization was accompanied by an increase of white-

Table 2.4. Employment Status of College and University Graduates in South Korea, 1965–90

Year	Males					Females			
	Graduates	Advanced[a]	Enlisted[b]	Employed	Employment Rate (%)[c]	Graduates	Advanced[a]	Employed	Employment Rate (%)[d]
1965	35,153	1,772	6,286	13,249	48.9	9,593	660	3,277	36.7
1966	23,438	1,910	4,275	10,810	62.7	7,290	991	3,378	53.6
1967	22,914	1,979	4,748	11,306	69.8	10,502	1,171	4,682	50.2
1968	26,829	2,040	2,978	15,738	72.2	12,016	731	5,133	45.5
1969	23,365	1,354	3,300	14,408	77.0	10,798	570	5,967	58.3
1970	24,877	1,753	3,669	15,906	81.8	10,894	641	6,399	62.4
1971	27,593	2,280	4,693	16,246	78.8	11,030	549	6,595	62.9
1972	30,038	2,486	4,388	16,801	72.5	12,049	582	7,097	61.9
1973	30,805	2,913	5,586	16,131	72.3	12,171	637	6,068	52.6
1974	32,290	2,390	5,497	16,870	69.1	14,482	894	5,871	43.2
1975	36,203	2,676	6,145	18,878	68.9	17,551	788	7,820	46.7
1976	38,746	2,381	7,618	21,424	74.5	19,940	802	9,629	50.3
1977	42,699	3,861	8,330	23,926	78.4	21,214	970	10,244	50.6
1978	51,794	4,526	11,404	27,666	77.1	23,183	1,012	11,966	54.0
1979	60,452	6,231	13,132	32,814	79.9	26,586	1,437	14,725	58.6
1980	72,246	8,484	16,363	32,966	69.5	31,916	2,221	15,696	52.9

1981	78,795	11,992	21,191	30,256	66.3	34,036	2,411	15,005	47.4
1982	82,510	10,283	21,106	34,930	68.3	42,472	2,801	18,846	47.5
1983	103,083	10,880	29,683	43,501	69.6	51,250	3,521	22,873	47.9
1984	104,283	11,498	25,683	47,693	71.1	57,827	4,168	24,896	46.4
1985	118,260	14,577	28,590	50,779	67.6	78,628	5,251	29,519	40.2
1986	130,416	13,016	31,505	53,076	61.8	88,889	5,029	32,216	38.4
1987	139,080	12,110	33,354	61,980	66.2	100,971	5,619	37,509	39.3
1988	149,851	12,526	29,477	71,363	66.2	104,895	5,730	44,218	44.6
1989	150,073	12,319	27,793	73,208	66.6	107,348	6,281	49,575	49.1
1990	147,646	12,582	22,670	76,966	68.5	110,366	6,931	54,786	53.0
Total	1,783,439	170,819	379,464	848,891	70.2	1,027,897	62,398	453,990	49.7

Source: Korean Ministry of Education, *Statistical Yearbook of Education,* 1965–90.

Note: Totals include graduates of four-year colleges and universities, two-year junior technical and vocational colleges, and teacher's colleges.

a. Advanced to higher level of education.

b. Enlisted in the army.

c. Employment rate = employed / (graduates minus advanced and enlisted).

d. Employment rate = employed / (graduates minus advanced).

Table 2.5. Occupational Distribution of Employed Workers in South Korea, 1960–90 (Percentages)

Occupation	1960[a]	1966[a]	1970	1975	1980	1985	1990
Professional and technical	2.4	2.8	3.2	3.3	4.6	5.8	7.2
Administrative and managerial	1.3	0.9	0.9	0.8	1.0	1.5	1.5
Clerical	2.6	4.3	5.8	6.7	9.5	11.5	13.0
Sales	8.3	10.7	10.1	10.4	12.1	15.4	14.5
Service	6.0	5.3	6.7	6.4	7.0	10.9	11.1
Production, transportation, and other manual labor	13.2	19.2	21.7	22.8	28.2	30.3	34.6
Agriculture, fisheries, and forestry	65.4	56.8	50.7	48.8	37.6	24.6	18.1
Others	0.8	0.0	0.9	0.8	0.0	0.0	0.0

Sources: Korean Economic Planning Board, *1960 Population and Housing Census Report; Annual Report on the Economically Active Population,* 1962, 1965, 1970, 1975, 1980, 1985, 1990.

a. Workers in transportation and communication were included in the category of production, transportation, and other manual labor during these years.

collar workers in professional, technical, managerial, sales, and clerical occupations. In 1960, professional and technical workers (such as medical doctors, lawyers, and professors) accounted for 2.4 percent of the labor force, but by 1980 that figure had grown to 4.6 percent, an increase of almost 100 percent. The number of professional and technical workers continued to expand during the 1980s, and by 1990 their share of the labor force was 7.2 percent. The growth of this group of highly skilled workers was a result of the expansion of higher education and professional institutions such as hospitals, universities, and research institutions.

The fastest growth among white-collar occupations occurred in clerical positions. In 1960, they accounted for only 2.6 percent of the labor force, but by 1980 about one-tenth of all workers were clerical workers—almost a fourfold increase. This growth was caused partly by the expansion of government institutions and large-scale private corporations and partly by the increasing participation of women in the labor market. In 1960, only 6 percent of clerical workers were women, but by 1980 one-third were (Koo 1990, 673).

The feminization of clerical work was facilitated by automation and the increasing division of labor into a series of standardized and repetitive tasks. As Braverman (1974) and Piore (1979) point out, when work is structured in this way, the worker is not required to know more than the few tasks he or she actually performs. As a result, the feminization of clerical work was accompanied by the downgrading of job qualifications and economic rewards for such labor. In 1976, clerical workers earned 55 percent more than the average income of all workers, but by 1990 their income advantage had been reduced to only 3 percent (KEPB 1992, 92).

When professional, technical, administrative, managerial, clerical, and sales workers are combined into a broad category of white-collar workers, their proportion in the labor force is seen to have grown from nearly 15 percent in 1960 to 20 percent in 1970, 27 percent in 1980, and 36 percent in 1990. Thus, the expansion of the white-collar workforce occurred side by side with the expansion of the manual production workforce during the course of Korean industrialization.

Changes in occupational distribution in turn brought about changes in class composition. Hong and Surh (1985) have developed a model that bases Korean class membership on four factors: (1) occupation; (2) class of worker (whether the worker is employed by others or self-employed); (3) employment sector (whether the worker is employed in the traditional agricultural sector or the industrial–corporate sector); and (4) level of social control at work. Using these four factors, they distinguished seven classes: (1) the upper-middle class[1] (capitalists, high-ranking business administrators, high-ranking government officials or army officers, doctors, lawyers, and professors); (2) the new middle class (intermediate-ranking administrative, managerial, sales, and clerical workers); (3) the old middle class (self-employed business owners, technicians, and professionals); (4) the working class (manual production workers); (5) the urban lower class (peddlers and unemployed or underemployed urban laborers); (6) self-employed farmers; and (7) the rural lower class (poor farmers with less than 0.5 hectares of land and unemployed or underemployed rural laborers). Table 2.6 illustrates the relationship among these classes.

Hong and Surh identified several major changes in South Korea's class composition. First, the number of self-employed farmers and people in the rural lower class declined rapidly during the 1960s and 1970s. Second, the working class grew rapidly during the same period. In 1960, before South Korea started to industrialize, less than 10 percent of the economically active male population (ages 20–64) belonged to the working class, but by 1980 working-class males accounted for almost

Table 2.6. Korean Class Model

Level of Social Control	Industrial Sector		
	Corporate	Self-Employed	Agricultural
High	Upper-middle class	Upper class	
Middle	New middle class	Old middle class	Self-employed
Low	Working class	Urban low class	Rural low class

Source: Hong and Surh 1985, 18. Reprinted by permission of Hanul Publishing Co.

Table 2.7. Class Composition in South Korea, 1960–80 (Percentages)

Class	1960	1970	1975	1980
Upper-middle class	0.9	1.3	1.2	1.8
New middle class	6.6	14.2	15.7	17.7
Old middle class	13.0	14.8	14.5	20.8
Self-employed professionals	0.3	0.5	0.6	0.6
Self-employed business owners	6.7	9.6	9.7	12.0
Self-employed service workers	0.4	0.5	0.6	0.8
Self-employed technicians	5.7	4.2	3.6	7.4
Working class	8.9	16.9	19.9	22.6
Urban lower class	6.6	8.0	7.5	5.9
Self-employed farmers	40.0	28.0	28.2	23.2
Rural lower class	24.0	16.7	12.9	8.1
Total number	5,210,137	59,332	61,715	154,630

Source: Hong and Surh 1985, 21. Reprinted by permission of Hanul Publishing Co.

Note: Percentages are based on the economically active male population (ages 20–64).

one-quarter of the labor force. Third, the new middle class, which consisted mainly of college-educated, white-collar workers, also grew rapidly. Finally, contrary to the predictions of an inevitable decline (Mills 1951), the old middle class in South Korea continued to grow (see table 2.7).

In summary, class formation in South Korea in the course of industrialization has been more complex than most theorists have thought. Proletarianization accelerated as South Korea became industrialized, but it did not lead to the predicted demise of self-employed business owners. Instead, it entailed an increase in both manual production workers and urban, professional, white-collar workers. When the three middle classes are combined, they account for 20 percent of the population in 1960, 30 percent in 1970, and 40 percent in 1980.

In their explanation of Korean emigration, Light and Bonacich (1988) emphasized the proletarianization of workers while downplaying the growth of the middle classes. This position has led them to portray Korean industrialization as a series of social and economic dislocations and Korean emigration as a movement of cheap labor. However, if we look at the growth of the middle classes as well, we can see that Korean industrialization has brought economic advancement to them, although at the expense of farmers and the working class. These new middle and upper-middle classes, whose members have been the main beneficiaries of South Korea's economic growth, ironically became the major sources of Korean emigrants to the United States.

Emigration as a Solution to Structural and Cultural Imbalances

It may seem paradoxical that the new middle class has supplied the largest number of South Korean emigrants while the working class and farmers, who have suffered the most in the course of industrialization, have not responded as actively to immigration opportunities. Three key factors help explain these different class responses: motivations for emigration, resources, and national policies on emigration and immigration.

Motivations for Emigration to the United States

The new middle-class Koreans were motivated to emigrate mainly by a sense of limited opportunity for social and economic mobility in South Korea, not only for themselves but also for their children. As they obtained college educations and became professional and white-collar workers, their aspirations for such mobility grew. As noted earlier, however, one of the most serious structural imbalances in South Korea has been the extent to which the supply of college graduates exceeds the demand for such a highly educated labor force. Between 1965 and 1990, the average unemployment rate for male college graduates was 30 percent (Korean Ministry of Education 1965–90). If there were no three-year compulsory military service for males, the unemployment problem would be even more serious. This trend has not only encouraged the emigration of middle-class Koreans but has also affected the economic well-being of those who remain behind, subjecting them to fierce competition, delayed promotion, and underemployment and making them constantly compare their long-term rate of return on their education in South Korea to that in other countries with more opportunities.

Favoritism in Korean society. The existence of favoritism in Korean society makes social mobility even more unlikely for those who have no connections with persons in important positions. Kinship, region of origin, and school ties still influence access to employment and prestige.

Regionalism has often been the single most important source of political mobilization. For example, in the 1992 presidential election, Kim Dae Jung, an opposition leader from Chŏlla, received 98 percent of the electoral votes in his home province, whereas Kim Young Sam, the candidate from the ruling party, received 90 percent of the votes in his native province of Kyŏngsang.

Such polarization of electoral votes is a symptom of deep-seated regionalism among Koreans. People from Chŏlla, a traditionally agricultural area, tend to believe that they have been victims of discrimination in their attempts to secure important positions in government, business, and the army. Their suspicion has some justification because since General Park Chung Hee took power on May 16, 1961, every subsequent president—Chun Doo Hwan (1980–87), Rho Tae Woo (1987–92), and Kim Young Sam, elected in 1992 as the first civilian president since 1960—has come from Kyŏngsang, an industrialized area and the archrival of Chŏlla.

The continuing dominance of Korean politics by people from Kyŏngsang has widened the economic inequality as well as the social distance between people from Kyŏngsang and those from Chŏlla. With the backing of native-born presidents, Kyŏngsang has experienced dramatic industrial development and a rapid rise in its standard of living, whereas Chŏlla has been excluded for decades from the course of South Korea's industrialization and modernization.

As a result of such imbalanced economic growth, people from Chŏlla have migrated to Seoul in large numbers and now account for about 30 percent of the population there. Because of their agricultural backgrounds and their recent arrival, however, they constitute the majority of the working and urban lower classes of Seoul. Discrepancies in economic standing, centuries-old prejudice and discrimination against people from Chŏlla, and the appeal to regionalism by the ruling political parties in every presidential and parliamentary election have combined to widen the social distance between residents and migrants from Chŏlla and those from the other parts of the nation. People from Chŏlla have become the object of suspicion and contempt (a common stereotype portrays them as treacherous and opportunistic), and they are often excluded from friendship, marriage, and employment. It is possible that they have been overrepresented in the flows of Korean emigrants, but no studies have examined this issue.

Regional favoritism and prejudice have had an even worse effect on North Korean refugees than on people from other parts of South Korea. Between 1945 and 1951, 1.2 million North Koreans made their way south to escape political persecution, economic hardships, and downward social mobility under communist rule (E. Yu 1983, 30). According to Illsoo Kim (1981, 35), these refugees and their descendants numbered some 5.1 million and constituted 14 percent of the South Korean population in 1977. Disproportionately large numbers of them had been landlords, intellectuals, and government employees, who had more to lose than did peasants and working-class people in the communist Democratic People's Republic of Korea. Christians in search of religious freedom that was denied them in the north also joined the southbound exodus in large numbers and thus constituted a large proportion of North Korean refugees. This partly explains why they have subsequently been overrepresented among the Korean immigrant population in the United States.

Despite their privileged class backgrounds, North Korean refugees found it very difficult to establish a solid economic foothold in South Korea because they had left all their wealth and social networks in the north. Although there has been no discrimination against people of North Korean origin at the government level, the fact that they had to start from scratch without social support networks put them at a disadvantage in competing with South Koreans for wage employment in the private and public sectors. As a result, these refugees have engaged in commerce at a higher rate than the national average—the same pattern of economic adaptation repeated by Korean immigrants in the United States.

When the South Korean government began to encourage massive emigration in 1962, North Korean refugees were among the first to respond, leaving in the early waves of post-1960 immigration to South America and the United States. One study estimated that they constituted 50.6 percent of the 423 Korean emigrant families who entered Latin American countries from 1962 to 1968 (I. Kim 1981, 35). Their immediate grasp of emigration opportunities was a result of their sense of rootlessness in South Korea and their fear of another war on the Korean peninsula.

School ties have also contributed to the formation of exclusive elite classes in Korean society. Graduates of prestigious high schools (such as Kyonggi High School) and universities in Seoul (Seoul National University, Korea University, and Yonsei University) have virtually monopolized the important positions in government, business, and the universities. Graduates of less prestigious schools believe they have little chance of being promoted to important positions, no matter how hard they try. In a national survey (ISS 1987, 107), Koreans were asked whether they believed it was difficult to succeed if they did not have connections or a good family background; about 70 percent of the respondents answered in the affirmative. This result indicates how deeply favoritism is rooted in Korean society and how frustrated people feel about it. For those who have received a college education and been influenced by Western concepts of democracy and justice, favoritism based on family ties, school ties, and region of origin has become increasingly intolerable, providing push factors toward emigration.

Education for children. The highly competitive and expensive Korean education system has been another important reason for middle-class families to emigrate, primarily for the sake of their children. Until 1969, only a primary education was compulsory in Korea, and it was free of charge. That year middle schools (equivalent to the seventh, eighth, and ninth grades in the American school system) were also made compulsory, but parents had to pay fees and other expenses. Since then, parents have borne two-thirds of the costs of education (McGinn et al. 1980, 27), and in recent years tuition fees for high schools and colleges have risen much higher than wages of household heads.

Besides the high cost, the severe competition for a college education has led middle-class parents to emigrate to the United States. The strong demand for higher education and the government's decision to restrict enrollment at the college and university level have resulted in fierce competition for a limited number of slots in these institutions. Every year more than 70 percent of college applicants fail the entrance examination and have to spend one or two more years preparing to retake it. These students are called *Chae-soo-saeng* (second-time applicants) or *Sam-soo-saeng* (third-time applicants), terms that used to imply that the applicants were failures. But in recent years, as the number of such failures has reached an alarming level, they have lost their negative connotation. The annual number of reapplicants is around 300,000, placing tremendous financial and psychological stress on students, their families, and society at large. Increasing numbers of middle-class Korean families have come to the United States to seek a second chance for their children or to bypass the stressful rite of passage altogether. For this reason, aspirations for children's education have provided one of the most important reasons for Korean immigration to the United States.

Cutthroat competition to pass the college entrance examination has also led to serious social problems in South Korea. High school students not only attend school for long hours during the regular day but also receive additional private tutoring in the evening. Tutoring has become prevalent among middle- and upper-class families as well as among lower-class families, extracting more than 10 percent of their incomes. Some wealthy families spend more than 1 million won ($1,250) per month for private tutoring, an amount exceeding the average monthly income of many wage workers.

Fearing a widening inequality and division among socioeconomic classes, the Korean government banned private tutoring during the 1980s, but concerned parents continued to hire college students, high school teachers, and even college professors as tutors for their children. Professors, particularly in the performing arts and music, have been reported to offer expensive and exclusive private lessons for high school students, who then receive favorable evaluations from their teachers at the time of the entrance examination. As a result of this unethical arrangement, better qualified but less fortunate students are denied an opportunity for fair competition.

The strong desire for a college education has given birth to a number of syndicates of high school teachers and college administrators who help students who have failed the entrance examination to be admitted to the universities in return for hundreds of thousands of dollars. To accomplish their goal, the syndicates either change the applicants' examination scores or hire college students to take the examination on behalf of the applicants. College administrators desperately need the money to maintain and expand their institutions, given the meager government support for education and the heavy dependence of colleges on students' tuition. In March 1993, sixty-one defendants—students, parents, high school teachers, and college administrators (including the president and vice president of Kwang Woon University, a Seoul-based private university)—were indicted for participating in such a scheme. Since then, numerous private universities have been investigated by the police on suspicions of wrongdoing. After the public began to demand a more thorough investigation of corruption in the Korean higher educational system, the Korean Ministry of Education revealed that more than 2,000 students had been illegally admitted to colleges and universities during the period between 1986 and 1993. As suspected, those students were from the upper and upper-middle classes, the children of politicians, government officials, army officers, entrepreneurs, and college professors.

As the competition for a college education has increased, so has the cost of education in general because preparation for the college entrance examination starts at the middle-school level. Since the mid-1970s, therefore, education has been steadily transformed from a means of upward social mobility to one of status maintenance. Middle-class families with high aspirations for their children's education but without the means to pay for the expensive preparation for the examination or for college tuition have had a greater motivation than either lower-class or upper-class families for emigrating to the United States in pursuit of educational opportunity. California has been the preferred U.S. destination for most because its state universities provide quality education at a low cost.

Although large numbers of middle-class Korean families have come to the United States for their children's education, some Koreans have come alone to attend institutions of higher learning. Between 1953 (the end of the Korean War) and 1980, a total of 15,147 Korean students entered the United States to study at American universities or colleges; fewer than 10 percent of them returned to South Korea after finishing their studies. In 1985, about 13,000 such students were enrolled in American universities and colleges (I. Kim 1987, 329). From the beginning, Korean students who have gone abroad have shown a strong preference for American schools: of the total number of Korean students in overseas study programs between 1953 and 1980, 83 percent were enrolled in U.S. institutions (KOIS 1983, 703). This preference has resulted partly from the similarity between the Korean and American education systems and curricula and partly from the prestige an American education confers in Korean government, businesses, and universities. For example, in 1988, 46 percent of the faculty of the Seoul National University received their degrees abroad, and 72 percent of these individuals were educated in U.S. institutions (Population and Development Studies Center 1988, 2–8).

Because of the high social prestige attached to an American education, many Korean students coming to the United States aspired to return home to careers as politicians, professors, and top-ranking government officials. After graduation, however, many of them could not find jobs there commensurate with their training; they were overeducated and overspecialized. As a result, many of them decided to settle in the United States and changed their nonimmigrant status to that of permanent resident aliens. Their eligibility for this status derived largely from the special training or professional skills they had acquired in the United States. Thus, between 1966 and 1980, more than 9,400 Korean students became U.S. permanent residents. Because the majority of these students came from middle-class and upper-middle-class backgrounds in South Korea, they have augmented the representation of these groups in the Korean immigrant population.

Cultural imbalance. The United States has had troops stationed in South Korea since the end of the Korean War in 1953. Currently numbering about 40,000, the troops have transmitted American mass culture to South Korea. During the war, poverty-stricken Koreans were deeply impressed by America's affluence and mass consumption. Illsoo Kim (1981, 33) describes the cultural impact of this encounter on the urban middle classes as follows:

> For Korean urbanites, wearing American-made shoes, hats, gloves, sunglasses, and wristwatches, most of which flow illegally from the PX's of United States military compounds, has been a powerful means of enhancing status. American popular songs and movies have fascinated Korean urban youth, and many Korean urban intellectuals today tend to ignore Korean television and radio programs in favor of the American ones that are beamed by the United States Army station, American Forces Korea Network (AFKN).

American mass culture has had cumulative effects on Korean culture. As Koreans began to yearn more and more for American films, music, and other products, the Korean entertainment industry lost ground and became progressively outmoded. Korean cultural entrepreneurs, such as television program producers and movie distributors, grew increasingly dependent on imported American products. This dependency, in turn, further eroded the base of the Korean cultural industry, rendering its products less and less competitive.

Developing countries such as South Korea have become culturally dependent on richer countries such as the United States because it is relatively less expensive for them to consume ready-made cultural products than to produce these products themselves. The requirements of capital and technology, along with constantly changing styles, discourage local entrepreneurs from investing in cultural novelties. The initial disadvantages faced by developing countries pave the way for the dominance of imported cultural products and perpetuate a vicious circle of cultural dependency.

The diffusion of American lifestyles and mass consumption among middle-class Koreans radically raised expectations about what constitutes a satisfactory standard of living, but the South Korean economy made the fulfillment of such expectations difficult. The widening gap between expectations and limited opportunities for social and economic mobility led the new middle-class Koreans to become skeptical about their long-term prospects in Korea. Consequently, emigration to the United States became an attractive alternative.

Resource Mobilization: Human Capital and Social Networks

The overrepresentation of middle-class Koreans among immigrants to the United States can also be attributed to their relative advantage in mobilizing resources compared to their lower- and working-class counterparts. As discussed in chapter 1, resources consist not only of wealth but also of human capital (for example, investment in education), information, and social networks. Until recently, middle-class Koreans had the advantages of a higher level of education, stronger English-speaking skills, and early exposure to American mass culture, which gave them confidence in their ability to overcome risks and uncertainties. In contrast, lower- and working-class Koreans, for whom economic survival is a daily struggle, had neither the wealth nor the time to plan for such a long-term commitment as international migration.

After 1975, however, immigration to the United States started becoming easier for these groups of Koreans. Although they remained disadvantaged in terms of human capital, their growing social networks substantially reduced the uncertainty and satisfied the requirements of international migration. As immigration became routine and institutionalized, a growing number of privately operated emigration companies and travel agents delivered all necessary services to would-be immigrants, and lower- and working-class Koreans began taking advantage of these services.

In addition, Korean immigrant communities have been established throughout the United States during the last two decades. Recent immigrants who do not have specific job skills or cannot speak English fluently can nevertheless find employment in Korean-owned small businesses in Korean ethnic enclaves. These protected settings provide immigrants with employment, housing, and recreation, thus lowering the qualifications for immigration.

South Korean Emigration Policy and U.S. Immigration Policy

No matter how willing Koreans were to emigrate, had the South Korean government been unwilling to let its people move abroad or the U.S. government been unwilling to admit them into the country, Korean immigration would not have occurred. The size and composition of this immigrant flow have also been greatly affected by the policies of the two nations.

The South Korean government established an emigration policy in 1962 as part of its national development plan. Between 1960 and 1975, the South Korean population grew from 24.0 million to 34.6 million, a 44 percent increase. This rapid growth was the result of three factors: (1) a sharp reduction in the mortality rate, caused by the introduction of Western medical technology at the end of the nineteenth century and especially at the end of the Korean War; (2) the postwar baby boom; and (3) an influx of North Koreans during and after the war. The Korean government regarded this population growth, which exceeded the rate of GNP growth, as a threat to balanced economic development. It therefore encouraged emigration as a means of relieving population pressure.

Another goal of the 1962 emigration policy was to secure foreign exchange through remittances sent home by Koreans working or living abroad. For example, about 17,000 Korean nurses and miners migrated to West Germany as contract workers between 1963 and 1974 (I. Kim 1981, 53). During this period, they sent about $720 million to their families in South Korea.

Under the 1962 policy, emigration was divided into three categories. The first, called group emigration, involved individuals whose entry into specific nations was arranged through negotiations between the South Korean government and the receiving nations. The second category was termed contract emigration, in which each individual entered a contract with a prospective employer in the receiving nation. Most of these contracts were arranged by emigration companies in South Korea, and many people in this group became "occupational" or "skilled" immigrants to the United States. The third category, called special emigration, consisted of those emigrants who had been invited by individuals or by public or private organizations in the receiving country. It included those who had "relative preference"—family members of earlier emigrants, Korean war brides, and orphans (S. Hong 1979; I. Kim 1981, 53).

The policy also prohibited some categories of persons from emigrating. Social outcasts—such as ex-convicts, alcoholics, psychotics, and those who could not perform useful physical labor—were excluded. Military deserters were excluded for reasons of national security and political dissidents for fear that they might engage in antigovernment activities abroad.

After this emigration policy was established, some wealthy Korean businessmen, high-ranking government officials, and professionals managed to emigrate to the United States on tourist visas. Many of them brought large amounts of money with them and invested in U.S. business enterprises for the purpose of acquiring permanent resident status, as permitted under U.S. immigration law. In 1976, the minimum capital investment required for classification as a businessman and investor was $40,000; currently, the minimum amount is $500,000 in less developed regions of the United States and $1 million in other regions. Between 1966 and 1975, 2,617 Koreans gained their permanent resident status in this manner (see table 2.8).

Fearing a continued cash outflow and a national "brain drain," the Korean government amended its emigration policy in 1975 to prevent three classes of Koreans from leaving: (1) persons owning properties valued at more than $100,000; (2) military officers and retired generals; and (3) high-ranking government officials, incumbent or retired, including national assembly members, judges, presidents of national corporations, and others of similar status (I. Kim 1981, 65). Thus, the revised policy has generally excluded upper-class Koreans from emigration. There is no evidence, however, that the policy was designed to encourage middle- or lower-class Koreans to emigrate, so the overrepresentation of the middle class in the Korean emigration stream was not simply a byproduct of this policy.

Table 2.8. Adjustments to Permanent Resident Status among Korean
Immigrants, 1966–90

Year	Status upon Entry				
	Temporary Visitors for Pleasure	Students	Businessmen and Investors[a]	Others[b]	Total
1966	105	360	13	120	598
1967	283	861	29	151	1,424
1968	289	595	31	183	1,098
1969	470	850	93	407	1,820
1970	614	907	141	417	2,079
1971	879	975	250	1,945	4,049
1972	1,071	1,011	448	2,983	5,513
1973	1,151	811	708	2,291	4,961
1974	924	775	624	2,335	4,658
1975	436	397	280	1,251	2,364
1976	407	339	247	888	1,881
1977	515	393	262	1,310	2,480
1978	883	516	452	1,607	2,415
1979	780	328	434	1,060	2,602
1980	u	u	u	u	2,933
1981	u	u	u	u	3,844
1982	1,628	378	497	1,360	3,863
1983	1,475	419	781	1,645	4,320
1984	1,655	522	843	1,194	4,214
1985	1,796	720	764	1,441	4,721
1986	2,049	1,007[c]	817[c]	1,158	5,031
1987	1,539	903[c]	461[c]	811	3,714
1988	1,345	976[c]	432	879	3,632
1989	1,836	1,161[c]	360	2,617	5,974
1990	1,612	1,114	466	3,112	6,335

Source: Same as for table 2.1.

u = data unavailable

a. Numbers include temporary visitors for business, treaty traders (a nonimmigrant class of aliens who come to the United States temporarily under the provisions of a treaty of commerce and navigation with foreign states), and investors.

b. Numbers include government officials, exchange visitors, temporary workers and trainees, and dependent spouses and children.

c. Numbers include spouses and children.

In fact, U.S. immigration policy has had a far greater influence on the class background of Korean immigrants than has Korean emigration policy. In 1965, the United States abolished the quota system under which visas for permanent residence had been distributed according to the ethnic composition of the U.S. population. This system, which began in 1921, used an individual's country of birth to determine whether he or she could enter as a legal alien and used the number of previous immigrants from a country and their descendants to set the quota of how many new immigrants from that nation could enter annually. These quotas were based on figures from the 1910 census until 1924, when officials decided to use figures from the 1890 census to further reduce the quotas. In 1929, numbers from the 1920 census became the basis for the system until it was repealed in 1965 (Schaefer 1988, 127). Few Asians had been admitted to the United States prior to 1965, first because of laws specifically excluding them and, after such laws were repealed, because of quotas based on the tiny proportion of Asians in the U.S. population.

The national origins quotas were criticized as a discriminatory system favoring northern and western European immigrants and resulting from an intricate set of racist assumptions. Northern and western Europeans were seen as innately more adaptable to the American social system, and other groups were viewed as naturally lacking in favorable social and moral qualities (Marger 1991, 30). Under the 1929 immigration system, almost 70 percent of the quota from the Eastern Hemisphere went to only three countries: Great Britain, Ireland, and Germany.[2] But the liberal social and political atmosphere of the 1960s, when the Civil Rights movement was in full swing, created pressure for immigration reform. The discriminatory immigration policy was also seen as damaging to U.S. foreign relations at a time when the country was engaged in the Cold War.

Not just political considerations but also domestic labor issues led to the dramatic shift in U.S. immigration policy in 1965. Economists were forecasting a substantial increase in demand for workers in the professional, technical, and managerial sectors (Light and Bonacich 1988, 133). The shortage of professional workers was most critical in the medical industry and in engineering, especially in space science. The medical system was expanding rapidly, but U.S. medical schools were not supplying enough doctors and other professionals. Hospitals—especially those run by federal and state governments—wanted to import foreign physicians to fill the vacant positions (I. Kim 1981, 147; Shin and Chang 1988, 623).

Under the new immigration law, national origins quotas were abolished; instead, immigrant visas were to be issued on a first-come, first-served basis. In addition, annual limits of 170,000 immigrants from the Eastern Hemisphere and 120,000 from the Western Hemisphere were established. In 1971, a single worldwide ceiling of 290,000 persons re-

placed these hemispheric distinctions, and in 1980 the number was reduced to 270,000. Each country in the Eastern Hemisphere was then
given an annual limit of 20,000 immigrants. Within this numerical limitation, a potential immigrant was given a visa for permanent residence
on the basis of either his or her family relationship with a U.S. citizen or
legal permanent resident or his or her possession of a job skill needed in
the United States. Immediate relatives of U.S. citizens (parents, spouses,
and minor children) were excluded from the annual limits.

The Immigration and Nationality Act of 1965 brought about two
fundamental changes in the characteristics of immigrants to the United
States. The more substantial change was a pronounced shift in their geographic origins. During the century and a half between 1820 and 1965,
about 81 percent of the 43 million immigrants to the United States had
been from Europe. After the 1965 act went into operation on July 1,
1968, however, immigration from Europe dropped sharply while that
from Asia and Latin America increased substantially. During the periods
1960–64 and 1970–74 alone, the European share of total immigration
dropped from 45 to 25 percent, while the Asian share increased from 8
to 30 percent and the Latin American share increased from 34 to 40
percent (Warren 1980, 2).

The second important change brought about by the 1965 act was a
greater emphasis on family relationships as a basis for selecting immigrants. Under the Immigration and Nationality Act of 1952 (also called
the McCarran–Walter Act), 50 percent of immigration visas had been
reserved for skilled immigrants and for the spouses and children of such
immigrants; the remaining 50 percent were for family members of U.S.
citizens and permanent residents. Under the new law, however, members
of the professions, scientists, and artists of exceptional ability were third
among preference groups while highly skilled workers and low-skilled
workers in occupations for which labor was in short supply in the United
States were sixth. Together, these groups were given only 20 percent of
the annual quota of visas, whereas immigrants admitted under the
family-preference categories received 74 percent of them.

Economic recessions during the 1970s led to political pressures on
Congress to amend the act of 1965 to curtail even further the flow of
immigrants admitted under occupational preferences and to increase the
proportion of those admitted under family-reunification preferences.
Congress responded in 1976 by passing the Eilberg Act and the Health
Professions Educational Assistance Act (Yochum and Agarwal 1988).

The Eilberg Act required alien professionals to receive job offers from U.S. employers as a precondition for admittance as legal immigrants. The Health Professions Educational Assistance Act in effect removed physicians and surgeons from eligible categories of labor certification. Since the late 1970s, the U.S. Department of Labor has also discouraged other types of occupational immigration by not issuing labor permits to many qualified prospective immigrants. As a result, the proportion of occupational immigrants has been drastically reduced since the late 1970s.

The 1990 Immigration Act represents another change in U.S. policy. Basically, this act aims at attracting highly skilled workers into the United States in the belief that they will increase national productivity rates. To achieve this goal, it allocates 140,000 employment-based visas annually, which is 2.6 times more than the previous level of 54,000. This change will benefit immigrants from such countries as the United Kingdom and Canada, which have used employment preferences more extensively than family preferences as entry mechanisms. Another important change is the establishment of a flexible annual cap of 480,000 family-related immigrants. This cap includes immediate relatives of U.S. citizens, who had previously been excluded from the numerical limitation. This change will result in a decline in the number of immigrants admitted under family preferences and will adversely affect countries such as Mexico and the Philippines, which have relied on these preferences (U.S. INS 1990; Vialet and Eig 1991). The Immigration Act of 1990 is not, however, expected to have as great an impact on Korean immigration as it will have on that from the Philippines, mainland China, and India. This is because the zeal for immigration to the United States has been dwindling among Koreans in recent years while it remains high among the other Asian groups.

These changes in U.S. immigration policy have greatly altered the entry mechanisms and class backgrounds of Korean immigrants (see table 2.9). Because of the small number of naturalized Koreans in the United States before 1965, new immigrants could not use relative preferences as much as other, more established ethnic groups. Thus, between 1965 and 1974, occupational preferences were the most widely used entry mechanism among Korean immigrants, accounting for approximately 30 percent of those admitted to the United States each year. As a growing number of Koreans became U.S. citizens after five years of permanent residence and thereby became eligible to sponsor the immigration of their brothers and sisters from South Korea, the proportion of relative-preference immigrants increased. From 1975 to 1981, those who entered under the fifth preference category (brothers and sisters of U.S. citizens) accounted for more than 30 percent of the total.

As an increasing number of Koreans applied for immigrant visas under this category, a huge backlog of applications built up. Prospective Korean immigrants had to wait five to six years for admission to the United States. Today the waiting period is ten years. Koreans, therefore, began taking advantage of the second preference category—spouses and unmarried sons and daughters of permanent resident aliens—which had not been used extensively earlier. Thus, since 1981, such individuals have accounted for more than 20 percent of all Korean immigrants.

Some cunning strategies are employed by those who are eager to come to the United States by any means. For example, Koreans who have acquired U.S. citizenship first sponsor the immigration of their parents—in many cases their mothers, who are not only exempt from the annual numerical limitation under the current U.S. immigration law but are also eligible for their green cards within six months. Upon arrival in the United States, these parents immediately file for family reunification visas on behalf of their unmarried sons and daughters, who can obtain their immigrant visas within a year under the second preference category.

In many cases, older parents do not intend to stay permanently in the United States, but they nonetheless become U.S. permanent residents for the sake of their children. Some of them discard their resident status by simply returning permanently to South Korea after their children accomplish their goal. Others travel to the United States for only a short period of time each year (usually one month) to maintain their permanent resident status while they continue to live and work in South Korea.

Another reason for the increase in immigrants admitted under this preference category is the growing number of women who come to the United States as spouses of male Korean permanent residents, who often look for marriage partners in Korea rather than in America. Many of these men prefer native Korean women, whom they believe to be docile and willing to submit to their husbands, over Korean women in the United States, who have become "too Americanized." But while male immigrants have this option, their female counterparts have great difficulty finding husbands of Korean descent, not only in South Korea but

Table 2.9. Entry Mechanisms for Korean Immigrants, 1966–90 (Percentages)

Year of Entry	Admitted under Numerical Limitations					Exempt from Numerical Limitations				Total Number
	1st Pref.ᵃ	2nd Pref.ᵇ	4th Pref.ᶜ	5th Pref.ᵈ	Occupa-tional Pref.ᵉ	Parents of U.S. Citizens	Spouses of U.S. Citizens	Children of U.S. Citizens	Other Special Immigrantsᶠ	
1966	0.5	2.2	0.0	0.2	17.6	1.7	52.0	23.8	0.8	2,492
1967	0.2	5.7	0.3	4.3	32.7	1.6	37.3	16.4	1.2	3,956
1968	0.1	7.6	0.6	4.6	27.8	2.2	37.1	18.1	1.7	3,811
1969	0.1	8.6	0.1	8.8	30.1	1.9	33.8	15.7	0.6	6,045
1970	0.2	8.8	0.4	14.2	30.8	1.9	29.4	13.0	1.0	9,314
1971	0.1	7.7	0.2	13.5	41.9	1.5	23.2	11.0	0.8	14,297
1972	0.1	7.9	0.2	15.2	45.1	1.8	18.3	11.4	0.8	18,876
1973	0.1	14.0	0.2	22.0	32.2	2.6	16.3	11.6	1.1	22,930
1974	0.0	15.0	0.3	21.6	33.5	2.3	14.8	10.2	2.6	28,028
1975	0.1	16.7	0.3	30.0	22.2	3.1	10.7	11.7	4.8	28,362
1976	0.1	14.2	0.3	35.4	13.0	4.0	15.9	14.3	0.8	30,803
1977	0.1	13.1	0.3	42.3	8.5	5.5	14.5	14.1	0.6	30,917
1978	0.1	15.7	0.5	35.0	8.9	7.4	15.1	12.2	1.1	29,288
1979	0.1	19.8	0.7	35.0	5.2	9.7	16.6	10.2	1.4	29,248
1980	0.1	18.9	0.5	39.1	2.9	10.2	13.7	10.2	0.7	32,320

1981	0.1	27.7	1.6	23.3	8.3	13.0	13.3	9.7	0.9	32,663
1982	0.2	31.3	1.7	19.8	3.4	13.5	13.2	12.2	1.6	31,724
1983	0.2	27.3	1.3	22.3	8.3	9.7	11.9	14.9	1.3	33,339
1984	0.2	24.5	1.8	21.7	8.8	9.9	12.0	17.7	0.9	33,042
1985	0.3	25.5	2.3	19.4	7.7	11.1	12.2	18.3	1.0	35,253
1986	0.2	23.4	2.6	19.2	8.4	12.7	12.7	19.2	0.8	35,776
1987	0.2	25.1	2.1	24.5	3.4	11.9	12.7	18.5	0.7	35,849
1988	0.2	20.1	2.2	27.0	8.7	11.3	12.9	16.2	1.0	34,703
1989	0.2	22.6	2.3	21.9	9.0	10.1	13.5	12.5	1.0	34,222
1990	0.4	17.4	2.3	27.7	9.9	9.7	12.6	10.2	10.0	32,301

Source: Same as for table 2.1.

a. The first preference category applies to unmarried sons and daughters of U.S. citizens and their children.

b. The second preference category applies to spouses and unmarried sons and daughters of resident aliens and their children.

c. The fourth preference category applies to married sons and daughters of U.S. citizens and their spouses and children.

d. The fifth preference category applies to brothers and sisters of U.S. citizens and their spouses and children.

e. The occupational preference category applies to immigrants in professions and with special skills and their spouses and children. It includes the third preference, sixth preference, and nonpreference categories.

f. Other special immigrations include ministers of religion and employees of the U.S. government abroad and their spouses and children. In 1990, this category included 2,244 Korean aliens legalized under the Immigration Reform and Control Act (IRCA) of 1986.

also in the United States because of their nontraditional attitudes toward the appropriate gender roles of Korean men and women. This incompatibility may increase the rates of interracial marriage and nonmarriage among Korean women who are raised and educated in America.

Under the current immigration law, spouses of U.S. permanent residents whose marriages took place abroad are required to wait in their home countries for more than two years before being admitted to the United States. Such a long waiting period is not only painful for newlywed couples but also harmful to their marriages. To avoid this two-year separation, wives of Korean male permanent residents come to the United States as temporary visitors or students, hiding their marital status from the customs officers at airports. Upon his wife's arrival, a husband applies for a family reunion visa for her. It usually takes a person two and a half years to be called for an interview after filing a visa application; meanwhile, the wife can stay with her husband in the United States, although she is technically a "visa abuser." When the time comes for her visa interview at the American Embassy in Seoul, she returns to Korea and then reenters the United States, this time as a legal immigrant. Despite the fear of being caught and deported to South Korea by the U.S. Immigration and Naturalization Service, this practice is becoming increasingly popular among Korean immigrants. It seems to explain in part why the number and the proportion of status adjusters among Korean immigrants have been increasing in recent years while those of the regular immigrants have declined.

The Changing Class Backgrounds of Korean Immigrants

The increasing role of family networks as an entry mechanism has resulted in the declining occupational selectivity of Korean immigrants since 1976. A close examination of the trends in occupational backgrounds among immigrants of the last three decades reveals three patterns. First, the proportion of professional workers has steadily declined (see figure 2.1). Second, the proportion of white-collar workers in managerial, sales, and clerical occupations has steadily increased. Finally, the proportion of manual laborers, farmers, and service workers, who generally constitute the lower classes in South Korea, has increased, although its growth has been erratic over this period (see figure 2.2). This may be a reflection of the frequent changes in the demand for precision production workers, craft and repair workers, operators, and service workers in

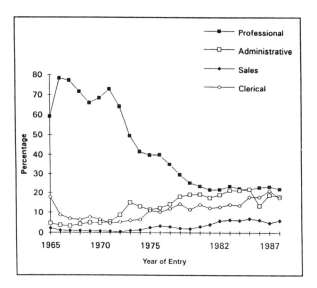

Figure 2.1. Occupational Backgrounds of Korean White-Collar Immigrants, 1965–90

Source: Same as for table 2.1.

Notes: Data for 1980 and 1981 are unavailable. Professional refers to professional specialty and technical workers. Administrative refers to executive, administrative, and managerial workers.

the U.S. labor market. As figure 2.3 shows, since the early 1980s, blue-collar workers have caught up with white-collar workers within the immigrant population.[3]

Although the increasing role of family networks and the changes in U.S. immigration policy in 1976 are the main reasons for such changes in the class backgrounds of Korean immigrants, the economic situation in South Korea is another contributing factor. As already discussed, income inequality there has been growing in recent years. The Gini Index, a measure of this inequality, increased noticeably between 1970 and 1975—from 0.332 to 0.391—and decreased only slightly in 1980, to 0.387.[4] The income share of the bottom 40 percent of the population declined from 19.6 percent in 1970 to 16.9 percent in 1975 and 16.1 percent in 1980, whereas the share of the upper 20 percent increased from 41.6 percent to 45.4 percent over these years. Absolute poverty in Korea has been significantly reduced, but relative poverty—measured by the percentage of the population below one-third of the national median income—has increased from 5 percent in 1970 to 14 percent in 1978 (Koo 1984, 1030).

In addition, as already mentioned, the desire for emigration to the

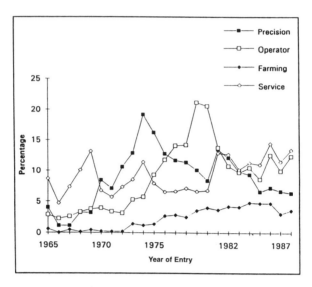

Figure 2.2. Occupational Backgrounds of Korean Nonwhite-Collar Immigrants, 1965–90

Source: Same as for table 2.1.

Notes: Data for 1980 and 1981 are unavailable. Precision refers to production, craft, and repair workers. Operator refers to operators, fabricators, and laborers. Farming refers to farmers, forestry workers, and fishers.

United States has been diminishing among the middle and upper-middle classes in recent years because their economic conditions at home have improved and they have become aware of the limited opportunities in the United States. They have realized that a large number of immigrants who had been white-collar workers in Korea now engage in small businesses in minority areas or in ethnic markets simply because they do not have other choices. Thus, middle-class Koreans have become increasingly reluctant to exchange their secure positions in South Korea for lower social and economic positions in the United States.[5]

While economic conditions have been improving for the middle and upper-middle classes, a sense of relative deprivation has spread among lower-class Koreans. According to a recent national opinion survey (ISS 1987, 107), they are now more strongly motivated to emigrate than their socioeconomic superiors: higher proportions of the working class (29 percent) and the urban marginal class (45 percent) favor emigration than do those of the upper-middle class (22 percent), the new middle class (24 percent), and the old middle class (22 percent). It is expected that the

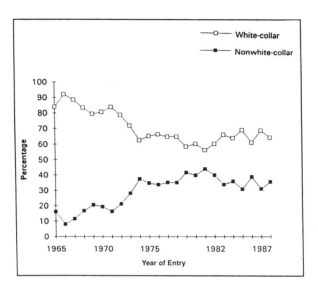

Figure 2.3. Class Backgrounds of Korean Immigrants, 1965–90
Source: Same as for table 2.1.
Note: Data for 1980 and 1981 are unavailable.

number of immigrants from lower- and working-class backgrounds will therefore continue to increase as long as their relative economic conditions do not substantially improve.

Such changes in class background are expected to affect significantly the rate and pattern of social and economic mobility among different cohorts of Korean immigrants in the United States. Statistics from the 1990 U.S. census confirm that those who arrived before 1975 had higher levels of education and higher social and economic status (SES) than the later arrivals. They had achieved more adequate labor utilization (as measured by a higher labor-force participation rate, a lower unemployment rate, and a higher percentage of full-time workers), filled more prestigious occupations, earned greater personal and family income, and developed better command of English than their later counterparts.

The higher SES of these cohorts may simply be due to their longer residence in the United States, however. As earlier arrivals, they may have had more opportunities than the post-1975 cohorts to learn English and acquire job skills and interpersonal networks, which in turn have increased their chances of earning higher wages and filling more prestigious occupations. For this reason, the cross-sectional comparison of co-

Table 2.10. Social and Economic Status of Korean Immigrants (Percentages)

		Year of Entry			
Characteristics	All Periods	1985–90	1975–84	1965–74	Before 1965
Educational level					
Some high school or less	17.3	17.1	17.7	16.9	17.0
High school graduates	26.1	28.9	28.1	19.2	18.4
Some college	21.0	17.2	22.5	22.2	22.4
Four-year college graduates	22.8	22.5	21.6	26.1	20.7
Graduate school graduates	12.8	14.4	10.0	14.7	21.5
Mean years of schooling (no.)	11.2	11.2	11.1	11.5	11.7
Employment status					
Labor force participants	72.3	60.6	75.8	77.6	77.6
Unemployed	4.2	6.4	3.9	3.2	2.4
Year-round full-time[a]	41.4	26.2	44.5	50.7	51.2
Occupational distribution					
Professional workers	13.6	12.6	10.8	18.3	23.8
Managerial workers	12.4	10.5	12.1	14.3	15.7
Service workers	15.5	18.5	15.4	13.8	11.1
Operators and laborers	13.7	15.3	13.6	13.0	9.7
Occupational prestige scores[b] (no.)	42.0	40.0	41.0	44.9	47.3
Economic well-being					
Mean personal income ($)	19,226	10,313	18,894	27,907	30,909
Mean family income ($)	46,812	30,679	46,084	63,425	64,852
Percent below poverty level	13.0	25.0	10.3	5.7	7.5
English-speaking ability					
Speak only English	6.9	3.0	4.1	11.0	36.5
Speak English very well	25.8	14.8	24.5	38.4	40.5
Speak English well	34.7	27.0	39.4	37.4	18.3
Do not speak English well	28.1	44.8	28.5	12.8	3.8
Do not speak English at all	4.5	10.3	3.5	0.6	1.0
Total number	18,598	4,911	8,614	4,208	865

Source: U.S. Bureau of the Census, 5 percent PUMS of the 1990 census.

Note: Only adult immigrants between the ages of 25 and 65 were included in the analysis.

a. Year-round full-time is defined as working 50 to 52 weeks per year and working 35 or more hours per week.

b. Occupational prestige scores were based on the 1989 NORC occupational prestige score scheme (see Appendix F of the *General Social Surveys, 1972–1991: Cumulative Codebook*, NORC 1991).

horts is problematic. To compare more accurately different rates of socioeconomic mobility, we therefore need to control for the different lengths of residence in the United States. To that end, I have looked at the 1970–74 cohort in 1980 and the 1980–84 cohort in 1990, groups that had each spent between seven and eleven years in the United States but were separated by the 1976 changes in immigration policy (see table

2.11). Because I have used non-Hispanic whites as the comparison group for each cohort, changes in dollar values between 1980 and 1990 do not pose a problem for the comparison of personal and family incomes.

Compared to the 1980–84 cohort in 1990, the 1970–74 cohort in 1980 filled more prestigious occupations, earned greater personal and family income, had a lower chance of being below the poverty level, had a higher chance of owning homes, and achieved better command of English given the same length of residence in the United States. Members of this group earned 95 percent of the personal income and 101 percent of the family income of whites, whereas their counterparts in 1990 earned only 72 percent and 89 percent, respectively. The proportion of people in poverty increased from 7.3 percent among the 1970–74 cohort to 12.1 percent among the 1980–84 cohort. Partly because of their weaker earning power, only 47 percent of the latter owned homes, as compared with 61 percent of the former. All these statistics tend to suggest that rates and patterns of socioeconomic mobility are different among different cohorts of Korean immigrants and so-called model minority images of Korean Americans are increasingly outdated for more recent cohorts.

In other words, the entry of growing numbers of immigrants from lower- and working-class backgrounds into the existing Korean American community during the late 1970s and 1980s does seem to have lowered the overall economic status of Korean Americans in comparison to whites. According to published data from the 1980 and 1990 U.S. censuses, the median family income of Koreans was 97.4 percent of that of whites in 1980 but declined to 91.3 percent in 1990 (see table 2.12). During the same period, the proportion of Korean Americans living below the official poverty line increased from 13.1 percent to 14.7 percent. (A family of four is below the poverty line if it earns less than $12,647 per year.) As a result, Korean Americans were twice as likely as whites to live below the poverty line in 1990 (see table 2.13).

The declining economic status of Korean American families becomes even more significant if we compare it with the improving economic status of Asian Americans as a group. Asian American families earned 108.7 percent of the median income of white families in 1980 and 111 percent in 1990. During the same period, the poverty rate of Asian Americans declined from 14.3 percent to 11.6 percent.

In addition to changes in the class backgrounds of Korean immigrants, the increasing proportion of the elderly is another factor in the

Table 2.11. Social and Economic Status of Different Cohorts of Korean
Immigrants, 1980 and 1990 (Percentages)

	1980		1990	
Status	1970–74 Cohort	Whites	1980–84 Cohort	Whites
Employment status				
Labor force	74.2	72.6	74.6	78.0
Unemployed participants	4.7	4.3	4.1	4.1
Year-round full-time	42.9	48.5	42.3	52.9
Occupational distribution				
Professional workers	14.8	14.1	10.2	15.3
Managerial workers	9.8	12.0	11.9	13.7
Service workers	16.9	10.4	16.1	10.7
Operators and laborers	19.4	16.3	13.2	14.1
Occupational prestige scores (no.)	47.6	43.6	40.0	44.4
Economic well-being				
Mean personal income ($)	13,670	14,458	16,941	23,377
Mean family income ($)	26,532	26,262	41,174	45,810
Poverty status	7.3	6.4	12.1	7.3
Public assistance	1.7	2.5	1.7	2.7
Home ownership	61.0	76.4	47.1	76.2
English-speaking ability				
English only	4.7	94.1	3.3	95.0
Very well	23.9	4.1	20.2	3.5
Well	47.5	1.3	39.4	1.0
Not well	21.7	0.5	32.2	0.5
Not at all	2.2	0.1	4.9	0.1
Total number	2,848	890,014	4,911	989,295

Source: U.S. Bureau of the Census, 5 percent and 1 percent PUMS of the 1980 and 1990 censuses.

Note: Only adult immigrants aged 25 to 65 were included in the analysis. Non-Hispanic whites were used as the comparison group.

declining economic status of Korean Americans between 1980 and 1990.
In 1970, only 1 percent of the Korean immigrants were more than 60
years old, but this figure increased to 6.7 percent in 1980 and 7.7 percent
in 1990. These elderly immigrants are less likely to participate in the
labor force and more likely to be poor and dependent on welfare than
younger immigrants, and their increasing representation in the Korean
American community seems have to increased its overall poverty and
welfare dependence rates. All of these changes suggest that the community is becoming increasingly diverse and heterogeneous in terms of age,
occupations, socioeconomic status, and class positions.

Table 2.12. Median Family Income by Race, 1980 and 1990

Race	1990 Income ($)	% of White Family Income	1980 Income ($)	% of White Family Income
Total population	35,225	94.8	19,917	94.8
White	37,152	100.0	21,014	100.0
Black	22,429	60.4	12,627	60.1
Hispanic	25,064	67.5	14,712	70.0
Asian	41,251	111.0	22,849	108.7
Korean	33,909	91.3	20,459	97.4

Sources: U.S. Bureau of the Census, *1990 Census of Population, Social and Economic Characteristics, United States,* 1993a, 48–117; *1980 Census of Population, General Social and Economic Characteristics, U.S. Summary,* 1983, 63–162.

Table 2.13. Poverty Rate by Race, 1980 and 1990

Race	1990 Rate (%)	% of White Poverty Rate	1980 Rate (%)	% of White Poverty Rate
Total population	10.0	140	9.6	140
White	7.0	100	7.0	100
Black	26.3	380	26.5	380
Hispanic	22.3	320	28.3	400
Asian	11.6	170	14.3	200
Korean	14.7	210	13.1	190

Source: Same at for table 3.12.

Summary

Contemporary Korean immigration to the United States has evolved in the context of the U.S. government's political and military involvement in South Korea. Since the Korean War ended in 1953, a large number of Korean women have entered the United States as spouses of American servicemen who had been stationed there. American political and military dominance over South Korea has extended into cultural dominance. Over the past four decades, a sizable number of Korean students have entered the United States to receive higher education in American colleges and universities in the expectation of returning to South Korea with greater social prestige. Many of them, however, settled in the United States after they finished their studies and laid the foundation for chain migration among succeeding generations of Koreans.

Massive immigration began to occur after the United States changed its policies to admit immigrants from all countries of the world on an equal basis. Social changes in South Korea were equally important to this process. In 1962, the Korean government established its first policy to encourage emigration as a means of controlling population size, alleviating unemployment, and securing foreign exchange.

Along with these changes in policies, a series of social changes during the 1960s and 1970s—in particular, industrialization, urbanization, and the expansion of higher education in South Korea—produced a new urban middle class that had growing expectations of upward mobility. Nevertheless, it was difficult for the members of this class to realize these expectations in South Korea, and therefore many of them adopted emigration to the United States as a solution to structural and cultural imbalances. This movement of middle-class people seeking better economic and educational opportunities in the United States became the dominant strand of Korean immigration.

After a change in U.S. immigration law in 1976 placed greater emphasis on family reunification than on individual job skills as qualifications for entry, the proportion of Korean immigrants from lower- and working-class backgrounds began to increase. Social networks also contributed to this trend by reducing the risks and uncertainties of international migration.

Changes in the class backgrounds of Korean immigrants have also had important implications for patterns of adjustment in American society. Because of their occupational backgrounds, the pre-1976 immigrants established themselves as professionals or successful entrepreneurs and moved to white suburbs with little resistance from residents. Their children attended private schools or the better public schools in the suburbs and had close interactions with their non-Korean peers. This social and cultural assimilation into mainstream society was a dominant pattern among the Korean immigrants who came to the United States in the late 1960s and early 1970s.

In contrast, the more recent immigrants, especially those from lower-class backgrounds, have tended to settle in ethnic communities for employment, residence, and recreation. They work as employees in Korean-owned businesses, live in apartments in close proximity to Korean stores, and watch Korean television programs and movies.[6] Their children speak Korean most of the time and interact mostly with Korean peers. Retarded economic mobility, confinement in ethnic communities, and resistance to social and cultural assimilation are thus common among these immigrants. It is difficult for them to follow the paths of their predecessors because they have fewer resources and because opportunities for economic advancement, such as business ownership, have already been claimed by the earlier arrivals. As the number of Koreans who immigrate through family connections and depend on assistance from family members for employment and residence increases, the concentration of immigrants in ethnic communities and their consequent segregation from the larger society are likely to increase as well. And as the number of Korean immigrants from less privileged socioeconomic backgrounds grows, the immigrant community will become more heterogeneous and class will become more important as a basis for interpersonal relations.

Ironically, then, many Korean immigrants who came to the United States to seek greater economic mobility instead found only limited opportunities. It is this realization that has driven these immigrants to start businesses of their own. In the next chapter, I explain how patterns of immigration have affected the growth and current state of Korean immigrant entrepreneurship in urban America.

THREE

CLASS, FAMILY, AND ETHNICITY IN

KOREAN IMMIGRANT ENTREPRENEURSHIP

Immigrant entrepreneurship among contemporary Koreans departs from traditional patterns in several important respects. First, while previous immigrants (such as the Italians, Chinese, and Filipinos before World War II) were mostly uneducated and from rural and lower-class origins, recent Korean immigrants are mostly well-educated, urban, and of middle-class backgrounds. Because of their greater human capital, these immigrants are more likely than their predecessors to take an individualistic approach to establishing and maintaining businesses (Light 1984). Second, traditional social relations based on extended kinship and regions of origin have little influence on Korean immigrant businesses, which are instead shaped largely by modern ethnic institutions, such as Korean immigrant newspapers, churches, and business associations (I. Kim 1981). Third, economic development in their home country and international trade between this country and the United States provided the initial business opportunities for Korean immigrants (I. Kim 1981; Min 1988; Chin, Yoon, and Smith 1996). They imported Korean-made products and distributed them to Korean retailers in minority areas of large cities. This international trade linkage among Korean manufacturers, importers, and retailers provided the immigrants with a competitive edge over the members of other ethnic groups. Fourth, while previous immigrants had started businesses in their protected ethnic markets and then expanded into open markets, Korean immigrants started businesses in both ethnic markets and areas dominated by other minorities from the outset. In fact, the other minority markets have proved to be far more important than the Korean ethnic markets in terms of the number of businesses involved and the size of gross sales.

For these reasons, the contemporary Korean experience provides us with an opportunity to examine new aspects of immigrant entrepreneurship that have been overlooked by previous studies. In this chapter, I first explain the data and methodology of my research. Second, I survey the growth of the Korean community and immigrant entrepreneurship in Chicago. The primary goal of this historical overview is to examine how structural forces of the 1950s and 1960s—such as the interracial succession of residence in American central cities, the global economic restructuring, and the economic growth of South Korea—enabled Korean immigrants to establish their businesses in low-income minority neighborhoods. Third, I examine how individual Korean immigrants have responded to such structural forces and mobilized class, family, and ethnic resources in their pursuit of self-employment in business. Throughout the chapter, I try to compare the experiences of Koreans with those of other immigrant and ethnic groups in U.S. history. This will help us understand how Koreans are similar to and different from these groups in their patterns of adaptation to the United States.

Data and Methodology

The primary data for this study came from field observations and interviews with Korean business owners in Chicago and Los Angeles. The Chicago survey, which was conducted between September 1987 and May 1988, involved interviews with the owners of 103 businesses in black neighborhoods on the West and South Sides and 96 businesses in Koreatown on the Northwest Side. The Los Angeles survey, which was conducted between December 1993 and March 1994, consisted of interviews with the owners of 93 stores in South Central Los Angeles, a predominantly black and Latino neighborhood, and 105 stores in Koreatown, only three miles west of downtown.

The two surveys featured almost identical questions and wordings to ensure that the findings would be commensurate. However, the Los Angeles survey also incorporated several new sets of questions in order to investigate important topics that had not been adequately examined in the Chicago survey. For instance, a series of questions was asked about sources of capital for the respondents' first and current businesses in the United States and about sources of future business loans. These questions were designed to examine the changing importance of class, family, and ethnic resources in immigrant business formation and development. A special module on Koreans' perceptions of and feelings of social distance from members of different races was another addition. This section was designed to uncover the attitudes of Korean store owners toward blacks and Latinos as employees, customers, and neighbors. Such information can help us understand why Korean businesses experience greater rejection from the black community than from the Latino community.

The interviews included both closed- and open-ended questions focused on four major topics: (1) personal characteristics of Korean business owners and their family members; (2) characteristics of Korean businesses, such as size, racial composition and socioeconomic status of the customer base, resource utilization patterns, and business-related problems; (3) Koreans' attitudes toward and relations with members of other racial and ethnic groups, including whites, Asians, blacks, and Latinos; and (4) policy recommendations for improving Korean businesses and race relations among minority groups.

The two surveys also employed the same sampling method insofar as information about Korean businesses was available. In the Chicago survey, interviewees from Koreatown were randomly drawn from a complete list of businesses in the Korean Business Directories of 1987 and 1988. However, random sampling was not possible with interviewees from black areas because Korean businesses catering to non-Korean customers are rarely advertised in such directories.

As an alternative, the cluster sampling method was used to select a sample of respondents in Korean business concentration areas (KBCAs for short).[1] Thirteen KBCAs were located with the help of the *Korea Times of Chicago* (1986), and six of them were chosen as sites for sampling. These six were located in predominantly black areas and were more established than the others in terms of size and history. Figure 3.1 shows the locations of the KBCAs and Koreatown as well as the percentage of households below the poverty level in most of the black areas. The KBCAs are clearly concentrated in predominantly low-income black neighborhoods.[2]

For the Los Angeles survey, I was able to compile a list of businesses in both Koreatown and South Central Los Angeles from the Korean business directories and the membership directories of major Korean business associations, such as the Korean Grocers' Association, the Korean Dry Cleaner–Laundry Association, and the Korean Wig and Hairgood Retailers Association. Membership directories were essential for locating Korean businesses in South Central because, as in Chicago, businesses that are not dependent upon Korean patronage are rarely

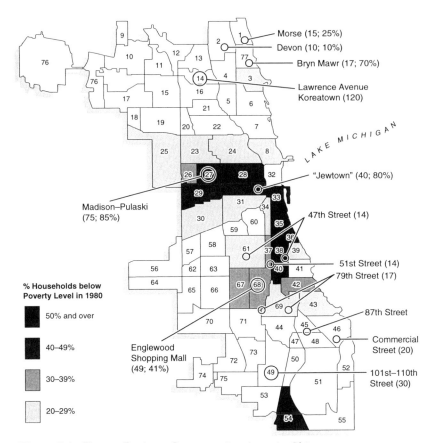

Figure 3.1. Korean Business Concentration Areas in Chicago

Source: The *Korea Times of Chicago*, 1986. The Chicago community poverty areas map was adopted from William J. Wilson, *The Truly Disadvantaged*, 1987, 52.

Note: In parentheses are the number (and sometimes the percentage) of Korean stores in each KBCA.

listed in the general Korean business directories. If I had relied solely on the latter, I would have excluded those businesses that are located outside Koreatown.

By combining the information in both types of directories, I compiled a list of 5,375 Korean businesses whose zip codes are between 90001 and 90072, which puts them within the boundaries of the city of Los Angeles. The zip codes were also used to delineate the boundaries of Koreatown and South Central (see fig. 3.2). Koreatown includes the area covered by zip codes 90004, 90005, 90006, 90010, 90015, and

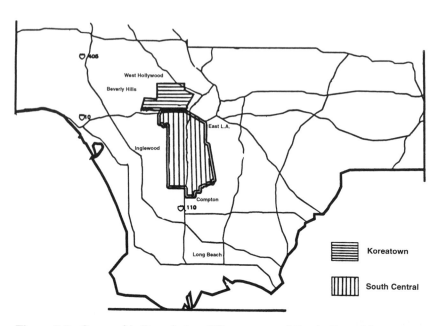

Figure 3.2. Geographic Boundaries of Koreatown and South Central Los Angeles

90020.[3] The Korean business and membership directories yielded the names of 3,745 Korean businesses located within these zip codes. A random sample of 280 businesses was made, and 97 of these were dropped because of an incorrect address and phone number, discontinued ownership, or the temporary absence of the owner. Out of 183 eligible candidates, 105 business owners participated in the survey, yielding a response rate of 59 percent.

South Central includes the area covered by zip codes 90001, 90002, 90003, 90007, 90008, 90011, 90016, 90018, 90037, 90043, 90044, 90047, 90059, 90061, 90062, 90089, 90301, 90302, 90303, 90304, and 90305. Out of 978 Korean businesses in this area, a random sample of 180 was made, and 26 of these were dropped for the same reasons as indicated for those in Koreatown. Out of 154 eligible candidates, 93 participated in the survey, yielding a response rate of 60 percent.

Findings from the two sample surveys were supplemented by readings of the Chicago and Los Angeles editions of the *Korea Times*, the oldest and most widely circulated Korean-language newspaper in the United States. Since its first publication in 1970, the newspaper has been keeping a record of every aspect of Korean immigrants' lives. Furthermore, it has been providing on a regular basis in-depth analyses of the state and problems of Korean small businesses. In the aftermath of the civil unrest in Los Angeles in April 1992, the newspaper launched a series of news reports and analyses over a period of several months that examined the historical development and future directions of Korean businesses. By any measure, the *Korea Times* is the richest data base for studying the Korean community and its immigrant businesses in the United States. By reading this newspaper from 1970 up to 1994, I was able to document the first types of Korean businesses in Chicago and Los Angeles and the directions in which these businesses have developed.

In addition to my readings of the newspaper, I used other qualitative research methods, such as participant observation and in-depth interviews with some Korean immigrant business owners, in order to obtain detailed information on Korean business owners and their businesses. My interviews with several of these owners are included in this chapter to offer an inside perspective on how they themselves interpret their experiences. As historian Ronald Takaki (1989, 8) puts it, the voices of these ordinary people who have been ignored "contain particular expressions and phrases with their own meanings and nuances, the cuttings from the cloth of languages."

The Growth of Korean Immigrant Entrepreneurship in Chicago

Korean businesses in Chicago can be broadly classified into four types, depending on whether the customers are Koreans or members of other ethnic groups and whether the products and services originate in South Korea or in the United States. Table 3.1 displays the four types and their characteristics.

The businesses in the first cell developed from the demand of Korean immigrants for their own cultural products, such as Korean food and movies. These businesses, which I call Korean-oriented businesses, concentrate in the Korean community to offer fast and convenient service to their customers. The businesses in the third cell developed from the international trade between the United States and South Korea. These businesses, which I call minority-oriented businesses, sell Korean-made consumer goods in minority areas of large cities, primarily to low-income blacks and Latinos. These two types of Korean businesses

Table 3.1. Typology of Korean Businesses

Origin of Supply	Ethnicity of Customers	
	Korean	Other
	I	III
South Korea	**Korean-oriented businesses** Korean food and gift stores; travel agencies; newspaper and bookstores; Korean video rental stores	**Minority-oriented businesses** wig stores; clothing stores; footwear stores; miscellaneous general merchandise stores
	II	IV
United States	**Ethnic professional businesses** accounting, legal, and health services; real estate and insurance brokers; auto repairs and dealers	**Majority-oriented businesses** fruit and vegetable stores; dry cleaning and laundry; snack shops; gas stations; garment subcontractors

Source: Adopted from I. Kim, *New Urban Immigrants*, 1981, 105, and modified to fit Korean businesses in Chicago.

were the first to be established in Chicago, and they continue to be the backbone of the Korean business community. The same pattern is generally true in other large cities where Koreans are concentrated, such as Los Angeles and New York City (I. Kim 1981; Kim and Hurh 1985; Min 1988; Light and Bonacich 1988; Chang 1990).

The businesses in the second cell developed from the demand of Korean immigrants for professional and technical services. These businesses, which I call ethnic professional businesses, are usually run by Korean immigrants who came to study at American universities and earned professional licenses in their specialty. The businesses in the fourth cell do not have any economic connection with either Korean customers or South Korea. Instead, they cater to the general population, providing products and services at low cost. I call these majority-oriented businesses.

In this chapter, I focus on the businesses in the first and third cells, Korean-oriented and minority-oriented businesses, because they were the entry points of Korean immigrants into small business in Chicago.

Korean-Oriented Businesses in Koreatown

The Korean community in Chicago began to form in the early 1970s. The first Korean immigrants consisted mainly of students and former miners and nurses who had been contract workers in West Germany before entering the United States. Most of the former miners had graduated from college in South Korea and had had no prior skills or experience in mining. Along with more than 2,000 other Koreans, they had gone to West Germany during the 1960s and 1970s to escape the high unemployment rates among college graduates. After their contracts expired, a majority of them did not return to South Korea, where they could expect only unemployment. Instead, they entered the United States as the spouses of Korean nurses, whom they had married in Germany and whose professional skills were in demand in the American medical industry in the late 1960s. About 200 of these former miners settled in Chicago.

These early immigrants played a very important role in the formation of Chicago's Korean community by laying a basis for chain migration. When the United States changed its immigration policy in 1965, they sponsored the immigration of their family members from South Korea. In December 1973, they also founded the Dong Woo Club, a social club designed to ease the transition to the United States that went on to produce many successful Korean entrepreneurs and influential community leaders (*KTC* 8 November 1983). In recognition of its contribution to the Korean community of Chicago, Governor James Thompson designated every December 25 as the Day of the Dong Woo Club (*KTC* 21 March 1991).

The precise number of Koreans who settled in Chicago in the early 1970s is hard to determine, but it is estimated to be somewhere between 7,000 and 10,000. The center of the Korean community was located on Clark Street, between Belmont Avenue and Addison Avenue. The area, now known as Lake View, had become an Asian shopping area, with a scattering of restaurants and stores offering Asian goods, as the Japanese and Filipinos began to move in during the 1960s. In 1960, Asians made up 3 percent of the total population in this area; by 1980, they accounted for 5 percent (Fadragas 1984, 14). Koreans were drawn into the area because of the Oriental foods available at Japanese grocery stores. Korean businesses began to multiply on Clark Street to meet the demands of immigrants for their ethnic foods and to help arrange travel to their home country. In 1971, there was a total of thirteen Korean businesses in the community: five restaurants, six grocery stores, one travel agency, and one bookstore. In 1972, this number increased to twenty-four, even though most of the Korean businesses catered exclusively to Korean customers.

In the late 1970s, the center of the Korean community moved from

Clark Street to Lawrence Avenue. The number of Korean immigrants in Chicago increased rapidly after 1970, and the recent arrivals looked for apartments with low rental rates. Albany Park, located on the Northwest Side of Chicago, had many inexpensive multiunit apartments and was located in close proximity to the original Korean community on Clark Street. Such conditions attracted immigrants to the area.

Albany Park is about eight miles from downtown Chicago. The heart of Koreatown is centered at the intersection of Lawrence and Kimball Avenues. Unlike many communities on the Northwest Side, which grew from initially independent villages, Albany Park was settled in the course of the peripheral expansion of Chicago itself, particularly through the growth of established residential areas nearby, such as Irving Park, Ravenswood, and Mayfair. It was annexed to Chicago in 1889, and the installation of an electric streetcar line on Lawrence Avenue in 1896 stimulated development of the area. The extension of the Ravenswood branch of the elevated line to Kimball and Lawrence Avenues in 1907 started a building boom (Royer 1984, 35). The Ravenswood line, which connects the Kimball CTA station to the Loop, remains the main source of transportation for Korean immigrants who do not have their own cars. As in other major U.S. cities, the availability of such a mass transit line to downtown has been a major factor in the current location of Koreatown. The other factors include the availability of less expensive housing, the proximity to downtown, and an avoidance of black residential areas.

Albany Park had once served as a first stop for many European immigrants and as a stepping-stone community for successive population groups moving away from the older and more densely populated parts of the city to the outlying areas and the suburbs. It is still a racially diverse residential area. As table 3.2 shows, almost three-quarters of the residents in 1980 were of mixed European origins; 20 percent were Hispanic, mostly Mexicans and Puerto Ricans; 5 percent were Asian, mainly Korean, Indian, and Filipino. The proportion of blacks increased during the 1970s, but it was still negligible at 0.6 percent. At Von Steuben, one of two high schools in the area, more than 30 languages are reported to be spoken by the families of students (Royer 37).

The early settlers in Albany Park were Germans and Swedes. Many of them eventually moved farther north, although some remained in the northern and eastern areas of Albany Park, especially in Ravenswood Manor. After 1912, there was a large influx of Russian Jews, and the com-

Table 3.2. Population Characteristics of Korean Business Concentration Areas in Chicago 1970–80

Characteristic	Albany Park 1970	1980	West Garfield Park 1970	1980	Englewood 1970	1980	Near West Side 1970	1980
Total population	47,092	46,075	48,464	33,865	89,713	59,075	78,703	57,296
% White	97.6	74.0	2.8	0.7	3.0	0.6	25.2	16.3
% Black	0.1	0.6	96.9	98.9	96.4	98.9	72.2	74.7
% Other nonwhite races	2.3	25.4	0.3	0.4	0.6	0.5	2.6	9.0
% of Hispanic origin	6.1	19.7	0.7	0.8	1.9	0.8	8.9	10.0
% Foreign-born	22.2	36.3	0.5	0.8	0.6	0.7	6.7	9.0
Median school years	11.3	12.2	10.3	10.9	10.5	11.2	9.4	10.8
% Female-headed households	12.1	19.7	29.1	57.8	29.7	57.2	36.7	65.6
Median family income ($)	11,021	19,793	7,532	10,922	7,509	10,597	6,012	7,532
% Below poverty level	6.2	10.5	24.5	37.2	24.3	35.8	34.7	48.9
% White-collar workers	23.2	49.9	8.8	34.9	10.9	39.7	16.2	46.9
% Civilian unemployed	2.5	6.9	8.0	20.7	7.7	18.2	8.0	15.8

Source: Chicago Fact Book Consortium, *Local Community Fact Book: Chicago Metropolitan Area Based on the 1970 and 1980 Censuses,* 1984.

munity included a large Jewish population through the 1950s. In the late 1960s and early 1970s, however, the Jewish community continued to move north, especially to the northern suburbs, and Dempster Street in Skokie became the new center of Jewish businesses. The vacancy rate of apartments and stores in Albany Park subsequently increased, and large apartments became available for low rental rates, drawing Koreans into the area (*KTC* 4 December 1980). Most of the Korean businesses in the area were also purchased from Jewish business owners.

By the early 1960s, Albany Park had begun to deteriorate. Very little residential development has taken place since 1930, and nearly all of the housing stock was built before 1939. Parts of the shopping strip along Lawrence Avenue, especially the large buildings, were showing the signs of deferred maintenance. Absentee ownership had become common. Retail locations closed up, while clusters of blocks along Kedzie, Lawrence, Montrose, Elston, and Pulaski Avenues were becoming slums (Royer 1984, 37). Before the Koreans arrived, 30 percent of the stores on Lawrence Avenue were vacant (*KTC* 14 November 1983).

The entrance of Koreans revived the area as a business district. According to the Lawrence Avenue Development Corporation (LADCOR), Koreans and other ethnic business owners invested $38 million in the area between 1979 and 1989, and the number of retail stores increased from 100 in 1976 to 290 in 1989. During this period, Korean investment in real estate on Lawrence Avenue tripled (*KTC* 21 November 1989). The first Korean store there was a photo studio that opened in 1977; there were 81 Korean businesses in the area by 1981 and 118 by 1983 (*KTC* 14 February 1983). The boundaries of the Korean business district in Albany Park have continued to expand, and the current Koreatown covers a wide area bounded by Foster, Western, Montrose, and Pulaski Avenues. According to the 1991 Korean Business Directory, there are now 428 Korean businesses (excluding insurance and real estate agencies) in Koreatown.

Minority-Oriented Businesses in Black Neighborhoods

Korean immigrants entered black areas in the early 1970s to meet the exploding demand for wigs among blacks. The use of wigs had become popular in the United States in the early 1960s, and nationwide retail sales jumped from $10 million in 1960 to $500 million in 1969. It was estimated that 38 percent of American women aged 17 and over pos-

CLASS, FAMILY, AND ETHNICITY

sessed at least one wig (Chin, Yoon, and Smith 1996). As so many Americans were suddenly adopting the fashion, American wig makers could not meet the demand through domestic production, and they began to import Korean hair, which had once been shunned because of its dark color and stiff texture, as a substitute for scarce European hair. Improved dyeing techniques made it look like the European variety. Korean hair exporters subsequently emerged to meet this demand.

These hair exporters soon became aware of the economic opportunities in manufacturing the wigs themselves, and they began to export them almost exclusively to the United States. In 1967, the Japanese invention of a synthetic thread called Kanekalon, which could be used as a substitute for human hair, revolutionized the wig business. Korean manufacturers acquired the exclusive rights to the new product and became the major suppliers of wigs to the United States. The number of such manufacturers increased from 43 in 1967 to 169 in 1972 and dropped to 96 in 1977, when the demand for wigs declined. But during the late 1960s and early 1970s, wigs were a major export item of South Korea. In 1966, they were the third largest such item, accounting for roughly 4.8 percent of total exports, and this figure increased to 6.5 percent in 1971 (see table 3.3).

The price of Korean-made synthetic wigs was low enough for low-income blacks to afford: about $30 in 1970. Natural hair wigs, which were ten times more expensive, were sold exclusively at department stores and were virtually inaccessible for low-income black customers.

Korean manufacturers thus sent their sales representatives to black neighborhoods to open retail stores. Wig importers actively recruited Korean immigrants as retailers and peddlers in black areas to expand their businesses. They even supplied the wigs on credit so that Korean retailers could start their own businesses with very little initial capital. Large numbers of Korean students became involved in the wig business to supplement their tuition during vacations, but many decided to pursue the business after finding that they made unexpectedly large profits.

In parallel with the number of retailers, the number of wig importers increased rapidly during the so-called golden era of wigs of the late 1960s and early 1970s. As of March 1973, there were almost seventy Korean wig importers throughout the United States, including twenty-eight in Los Angeles (Chin, Yoon, and Smith 1996). Many successful Korean businessmen in Chicago made their fortunes in the wig business in the early 1970s:

Table 3.3. Korean Exports of Selected Commodities, 1966–81
(In Millions of U.S. Dollars)

Commodity	1966	1971	1975	1980	1983
Clothing	33.4	304.3	1,148.2	2,946.9	3,701.4
	(13.3)	(28.5)	(22.6)	(16.8)	(15.1)
Footwear	5.5	37.4	191.2	874.5	1,234.8
	(2.2)	(3.5)	(3.8)	(5.0)	(5.1)
Travel goods, handbags, and similar articles	0.4	5.4	79.5	262.8	285.4
	(0.2)	(0.5)	(1.6)	(1.5)	(1.2)
Wigs, false beards, and similar articles	12.0	69.9	75.3	55.6	51.6
	(4.8)	(6.5)	(1.5)	(0.3)	(0.2)
Miscellaneous manufactured articles	59.2	445.4	1,882.6	5,298.4	6,797.4
	(23.6)	(41.7)	(37.1)	(30.3)	(27.8)
Total exports	250	1,068	5,081	17,505	24,445
Percentage of exports sent to the U.S.	38.3	49.8	30.2	26.3	33.7

Source: Bank of Korea, *Economic Statistics Yearbook*, 1966, 1971, 1975, 1980, 1983.

Note: The numbers in parentheses are the percentage shares of each commodity in total exports.

Mr. Ku, now an owner of a general merchandise store at the 63rd Street Shopping Mall, came to the United States in 1971 at age 28 as a sales representative for Korean wig-manufacturers back home. He had roots in a potentially lucrative business and all the stock he needed. At the time, Afro wigs were a hot item in the black community, and the cheapest were those made in Korea. It did not matter that Ku's English was spotty. His wigs cost less. His business boomed. "Some Koreans came over here and made five to six million dollars selling wigs to black people," says Ku. "They cleaned up. It was big business. We rented a store for $300, maybe $500 a month top. We got Korean wigs, so we didn't need credit. For 1975 and 1976, the streets were jammed with Korean wig stores everywhere." (Joravsky 1987)

But the Korean wig business started to fall off in the mid-1970s. An economic recession beginning in 1971 and a sudden change in the American fashion world were responsible for lessening the demand for wigs. Severe intraethnic competition among Korean wig retailers was another reason for this decline. As the number of Koreans in the business increased, retailers lowered the price of each wig to $20 or less. Contrary to the expectations of the retailers, the lower price undermined the value of wigs rather than increasing the demand for them. The price-cutting war reduced profit margins and drove many small wig retailers out of business. In response to the shrinking demand, Korean wig manufacturers reduced production after the mid-1970s.

Korean retailers in black areas responded to these changes by adding other merchandise items, such as handbags and jewelry, to their inventories or by changing over to other lines of goods, such as clothing or footwear. Like the wigs, all of this merchandise was manufactured in South Korea and imported by Korean immigrants. Korean manufacturers themselves responded by switching to other labor-intensive industries, such as garment manufacturing, with little disruption to their existing production mode. In 1975, South Korea exported $1.1 billion worth of men's and women's wear, which accounted for 23 percent of all exports. In the same year, $191 million worth of Korean-made footwear was sold (see table 3.3). Most of this merchandise was imported by big American chains such as Nike, Sears Roebuck, and J. C. Penney. Yet large numbers of Korean importers emerged as agents in the international trade between the United States and South Korea and distributed this merchandise to Korean retailers in minority areas.

By 1991, there were 115 Korean importers and wholesalers in the Chicago area (*Central Daily News of Chicago* 1991). Most of them concentrated on the importation of general merchandise, clothing, electronics, and food. Geographically, they were centered on the North Side of Chicago along Clark Street, Lawrence Avenue, and Lincoln Avenue, which increased their accessibility to Korean retailers in both the Korean community and the black areas of Chicago's West and South Sides. As of 1991, it was estimated that there were 850 Korean businesses in Chicago's minority areas. Some Korean community leaders claimed that this number would be more than 1,000 if numerous small stores in indoor and outdoor flea markets and swap meets were also counted.[4]

In these ways, Korean-oriented businesses and minority-oriented businesses provided the entry points for many Korean immigrants into the American economy. These immigrants accumulated capital and experience in such businesses and then advanced into more capital-intensive enterprises, such as gas stations and garment manufacturing. Immigrant professionals, such as CPAs, lawyers, and real estate brokers, began to enter the Korean ethnic economy on a large scale in the early 1980s, after the foundation of this economy had already been established.

We have also seen how Korean-oriented businesses and minority-oriented businesses developed almost simultaneously in the early 1970s. While the former found an economic niche in the demand of Koreans for cultural products, the latter found their niche in the export–import trade between South Korea and the United States. Because they accepted these different economic niches, the two types of businesses developed independently of each other.

History Hangs on Hair: The Political Economy of the Korean Wig Industry

The rise and fall of the Korean wig industry unexpectedly changed the course of modern South Korean politics. The story of Yung Ho Chang, founder of the wig and garment manufacturing firm YH Trade, illustrates how closely Korean immigration and immigrant entrepreneurship were related to the South Korean political economy in the turbulent period of the 1970s.

Chang arrived in New York City in January 1962 as a vice-director of the Korean Trade Promotion Corporation (KOTRA), a government agency established in 1962 to encourage overseas marketing. He and his wife ran a general merchandise store in Queens while he worked for KOTRA, and they also busied themselves by selling general merchandise at the New York World Trade Exhibition held in Flushing in 1964–65. This experience motivated Chang to change his status from that of a salary worker to that of an entrepreneur. He returned to South Korea and started YH Trade, named after his English initials. He bought a bean sprout dugout in Wangshipri, Seoul, with $2,000 he and his wife had saved in New York and formed a wig manufacturing firm with ten female workers in May 1965. He himself had once worked for an American wig manufacturer to learn how to make wigs out of human hair, and his firm grew by taking advantage of cheap Korean hair and labor. The invention of the synthetic thread Kanekalon in 1967 helped his firm become a leading manufacturer and exporter of wigs to the United States. Because his products sold so well in the U.S. market, he once said bluntly, "Wigs are money." At this time, of course, the industry was enjoying its golden era and serving as a lifeline for many Korean immigrants.

Chang's success was remarkable. The gross sales of YH Trade were only $13,000 in 1965, but by 1970 they exceeded $10 million, and between 1965 and 1978 the company exported $100 million worth of wigs to the United States. YH Trade expanded into a big firm employing

4,000 workers and moved to a five-story building. For his contribution to Korean exports, he was awarded a medal of honor by President Park Chung Hee, and he returned the favor by building a commemorative tower in the vicinity of Kimpo International Airport. Because exporting goods was regarded as the only way that South Korea could survive, he was considered a patriot. During his heyday, he was elected president of the New York Korean Association (1969–70), and he gave generous donations to many big and small events in the Korean community there.

The recession in the wig industry in the early 1970s, however, struck a harsh blow to the growth of YH Trade. It began to record deficits, and a growing number of workers were fired. To recover from this recession, Chang switched to garment manufacturing, specializing in men's and children's wear, ski wear, and raincoats. But his transformation could not save him. He fell into insurmountable debt after he acquired an electronics firm for $1.7 million, almost three times its actual value. On his last trip to Seoul in May 1978, he discovered that his debts to banks totaled $6.2 million, almost twice what he had expected. Faced with this crisis, he decided to close YH Trade and obtained a permit of business discontinuance from the Department of Labor.

But his action was met by angry protests from the YH workers, who claimed that they had not been paid for many months' work and that Chang intentionally closed YH Trade after smuggling money to the United States. They launched a sit-in demonstration at the headquarters of the New Democratic Party (NDP), the leading opposition party against the dictatorial Park government, demanding that the government recall Chang from the United States and save YH Trade from bankruptcy. To emphasize their desperate situation, some of the 172 demonstrators, all of whom were female, threatened to commit suicide if the police tried to arrest them. Against their fierce resistance, the police invaded the building at 2:00 A.M. on August 11, 1979, and arrested all of them. During the arrest, the demonstrators, newspaper reporters, national assemblymen, and staff of the NDP were severely beaten and assaulted by the police, and walls, windows, and office equipment were broken and damaged. One demonstrator committed suicide by cutting an artery in her left arm.

Kim Young Sam, then head of the NDP, was pulled from the building and sent home by the police. He was humiliated and upset by the brutal handling of the case, and he called the police action a coup against the people and their democracy. In an interview with the *New York Times*, he said that U.S. troops were stationed in South Korea to preserve democracy and for that reason the U.S. government should put greater pressure on the Park regime to end its dictatorship. His remark irritated Park, who had had difficult relations with Jimmy Carter over human rights issues and the withdrawal of U.S. troops from South Korea. Park called Kim a worshiper of the powerful and ordered the National Assembly to deprive him of his membership in that body. Then a less militant, pro-Park individual replaced Kim as the interim president of the NDP. Park's actions provoked a violent protest of students and citizens in Pusan and Masan, Kim's strongholds, on October 16, 1979. Emergency martial law was then enforced in this area.

President Park's oppressive stance toward the YH workers resulted from the political economy of his military regime, which lacked political legitimacy and tried to overcome this problem through operation politics and the promise of rapid economic growth. Park used this promise, along with the fear of an invasion by North Korea, as justifications for his dictatorship. At the same time, to play operation politics, he required enormous amounts of secret funds, and a few giant conglomerates were the main providers of such funds. In return, these firms received special favors from the government in the form of huge bank loans, low interest rates, contracts for big projects, and oligarchic control over the market. The Park regime also suppressed labor strikes and union movements so that workers would remain cheap and docile to management. Throughout the two decades of his reign, his government had always sided with the capital and oppressed the labor, and the swift and brutal suppression of the YH workers in 1979 was part of this anti-labor position.

President Park took such drastic action against Kim Young Sam over the objections of some of his close aides. He seemed to think that this was the best strategy to counter the challenge of opposition groups to the constitutional amendment of October 1972, which had allowed him to run for the presidency for three consecutive terms. His noncompromising strategy conflicted with that of Kim Jae Kyu, then director of the Korean Central Intelligence Agency (KCIA), who surveyed the Pusan–Masan incident himself and sensed that Park had already lost the support of the people. He persuaded Park not to expel Kim Young Sam from the National Assembly and not to take military action against the demonstrators in Pusan and Masan. But he was repeatedly rebuked by Park and Cha Ji Chol, then head of Park's security guard. He felt particularly embarrassed and resentful about Cha's arrogant attitude toward him and abuse of power. He finally came to believe that Park was the stumbling block to South Korea's democracy and had to be eliminated. When he heard a rumor that he would soon be replaced by Cha as the KCIA director, he assassinated Park and Cha at a dinner party he held at an inner house of the KCIA on December 12, 1979. His revolt was more incidental than planned, and his attempt to seize power through emergency national martial law failed. He was later arrested by Chun Doo Hwan, then commander of the army's Defense Security Command, and sentenced to death for high treason in a hurriedly processed military trial.

The vacuum in power caused by Park's sudden death provided a good opportunity for Chun and his followers, who had been secretly building up a power base inside the Korean army, to steal power with little resistance. After they proclaimed national martial law and stopped the formal system of law and order, they sent their opponents to prison, defamed established politicians by labeling them as either communists or bribe takers, seized their wealth, and banned them from any political activities. Kim Young Sam was put under indefinite house arrest, and Kim Dae Jung, another opposition leader, was arrested and tortured by Chun's new military circle, which framed him as an instigator of a student demonstration in Kwangju. His arrest provoked a violent uprising of students and citizens on May 18, 1980, which resulted in an estimated 2,000 deaths (although the official toll was only 240). The Kwangju Uprising is remembered as the most tragic massacre of civilians by the Korean army.

After having suppressed the uprising, Chun ran for the presidency while keeping other candidates from competing. He became the eleventh president by winning 99.9 percent of the electoral votes in a government-setup election held in a stadium in August 1980. He was succeeded by Rho Tae Woo, who had helped in Chun's military coup, in the 1987 presidential election, in which Kim Young Sam and Kim Dae Jung competed against each other and dashed people's hopes for democracy. But in the subsequent National Assembly election in April 1988, Rho's ruling party failed to obtain the majority of seats. The political situation became very unstable as three opposition parties overpowered the ruling party, which needed to form a coalition with at least one of the opposition parties to secure the majority of votes. Rho chose Kim Young Sam and Kim Jong Phil, whom he thought to be less militant than Kim Dae Jung, and together they formed the Democratic Liberty Party (DLP) in 1992. That year, Kim Young Sam won the presidential election as the candidate of the DLP. He was the first civilian president since

1960, and after his election he initiated many reforms in politics, banking, education, and other areas. Under his leadership, former presidents Chun and Rho, who had supported Kim in the belief that he would not prosecute them for their past wrongdoings, were charged with bribe taking, a military coup, and the Kwangju massacre. In August 1996, Chun was sentenced to death and Rho to a twenty-two-year prison term. Four months later, however, the sentence was reduced to life imprisonment for Chun and a 17-year prison term for Roh.

All of these events of the past three decades can be summarily called democratization, a process of overthrowing military dictatorship and restoring civilian rule. Some scholars claim that this process is inevitable as South Koreans seek greater political freedom after they have achieved economic prosperity. From this perspective, the expansion of the new middle class is regarded as crucial. Of course democratization is a complex structural process, and a single event cannot cause it to take place. But it may be fair to say that the YH incident was one of the key events that triggered the long sequence of political processes that has finally led to democratization. In this sense, the rise and fall of the Korean wig industry had the unintended consequence of speeding up the pace of political change in South Korea.

Ethnic Succession of Businesses in Minority Areas

Until the early 1970s, the portions of Chicago's West and South Sides in which Korean businesses eventually became concentrated had been dominated by Jewish and Italian business owners. The ethnic succession of businesses is well illustrated by the examples of three such areas: the Madison–Pulaski shopping district, the Englewood Shopping Mall, and the neighborhood known by some as "Jewtown."

The Madison–Pulaski shopping district, located at the intersection of Madison Street and Pulaski Road in West Garfield Park, is the biggest Korean business concentration area in any of Chicago's black areas. In 1986, there were 75 Korean stores in this area, accounting for 85 percent of the 98 stores there. This shopping district, which used to be called "the downtown of blacks," had been dominated by Italian and Jewish business owners until Korean immigrants entered the area beginning in the early 1970s. The exploding demand for wigs among blacks enabled Korean businesses to enter the area and flourish. One former wig store owner in the area recalls:

I made money as if I grabbed leaves scattered on the ground. Because business was so good, I did not have time to count my takings at the site. I dumped money into a laundry bag and spent the night by counting all the money I had earned during the day. (Personal interview)

When the demand for wigs declined in the mid-1970s, Korean business owners switched to selling clothing or general merchandise. By 1986, thirty-one stores sold clothing, thirty sold general merchandise, and eight sold footwear, representing the majority of Korean businesses in the area.

The Englewood Shopping Mall, located at 63rd and Halsted Streets in Englewood, was constructed as part of the Chicago South Areas Redevelopment Project in 1966. Shortly after the construction of the mall, the businesses there came to be monopolized by Jewish owners. In 1968, a Korean wig dealer who imported his products and owned several wig retail stores in black areas opened a store in the mall. He made huge profits during the late 1960s and early 1970s, and his success attracted a growing number of Korean business owners to the mall in the mid-1970s and early 1980s. By 1986, there were twenty clothing stores, seventeen general merchandise stores, ten footwear stores, and two snack shops in the mall owned by Koreans, accounting for 40 percent of the one hundred twenty businesses there.

"Jewtown," located at Halsted and Maxwell Streets on the Near West Side, is the Korean business concentration area nearest to downtown Chicago. This was the center of the Jewish business community at the turn of the century. Even though it had become a residential neighborhood for blacks, Latinos, and Italians by the 1940s, Jewish business owners continued to dominate the area into the late 1960s. In 1971, a Korean immigrant opened the first Korean wig and clothing store in the area. During the mid-1970s, Koreans began to take over Jewish stores, and by 1986, they owned thirty-seven, or 80 percent, of the forty-six businesses in the area.

All three of these black neighborhoods had been residential areas for various ethnic groups over time. Germans, Irish, and Scandinavians had occupied them between the early 1850s and late 1890s, when they were replaced by Italians and Russian Jews. As little as a decade later, the three areas became the center of Jewish and Italian businesses, and the Englewood shopping district became the second busiest commercial area in Chicago (Leslie 1984, 174).

Blacks began to move into these areas in the 1950s and by 1980 constituted more than 90 percent of the population. The arrival of black residents coincided with a series of events that eventually led to a decline in the prosperity of these neighborhoods. Changes in the racial composition of the population led to the exodus of white residents in the 1960s, which in turn naturally gave rise to the interethnic succession of businesses beginning in the early 1970s. But such business succession was slower than residential succession because Jewish and Italian business owners remained in these racially transitional areas even after their own ethnic groups moved to the North and Northwest Sides of Chicago.

Most of these business owners were first-generation immigrants, and they were not succeeded by their children or by subsequent groups of coethnic immigrants. As members of such ethnic groups seek out salaried employment, they set up a vacancy chain. Glazer and Moynihan (1970) describe the problem of business succession among Jewish Americans in a somber tone:

> Jewish businessmen in large part are not as acculturated as Jewish professionals. Many have not gone to college, they are often self-made, even today they are often immigrants, and they may lack social polish or be aggressive and crude. For these reasons "succession," the problem of what their sons will do, is intense for them. When the father is an immigrant and not a college man, and not the sort of person one sees in the pages of *Fortune*, and the son has gotten a good education, there is a great strain involved in his taking up the family business. Too, being a Jewish business, it is likely to be of low status—a small clothing firm, an umbrella factory, a movie-house, a costume jewelry manufactory serving Negro or Puerto Rican trade. Though such a business supplied enough to send the children to college and support the family, it might not seem quite the right thing to a son with an expensive education. Thus very often the son of such a businessmen goes into the professions, and the family business is regretfully sold or abandoned to partners. (150)

In addition to interethnic residential succession, the civil disorders of the 1960s were responsible for the exodus of white businesses from black areas (Aldrich and Reiss, Jr. 1970). Between 1965 and 1968, blacks attacked and burned the stores of white merchants in 128 U.S. cities (Light, Har-Chvi, and Kan 1994, 79). Faced with a rising crime rate and decreasing profitability, and surrounded by blacks hostile to their businesses, these owners had a strong incentive to move to other locations.[5] The combination of changing ethnic composition and civil disorders had thus created new business opportunities in these black areas before the arrival of Korean immigrant entrepreneurs.

As recent immigrants, Koreans did not meet with severe discrimination and resistance from local black residents, at least not initially. In fact, one of the important reasons why they chose to locate their businesses in these areas was the lower level of discrimination and hostility compared to that in white areas. Blacks were perceived by Koreans as easy to please, whereas whites were seen as condescending. Some of the respondents in this study attributed the attitudes of blacks toward Koreans to their shared minority status in a white-dominated society. The mild reception of Koreans by blacks might also be a result of their uncertainty about how to react to these new immigrants. Thus, although this interethnic relationship has deteriorated in recent years, when Koreans first entered black areas, they were not subject to the same level of antipathy and rejection as Jewish and Italian business owners had been.

While the most competitive, lower-status businesses in these neighborhoods were abandoned, those that brought higher profits and were more difficult to enter often retained their previous owners. By the 1970s, the Jews and Italians who remained in business in these areas had become building owners, wholesalers, or importers. Many Korean retailers in these areas now depend on Jewish wholesalers, especially in the shoe repair, dry cleaning, and laundry businesses. In 1985, for example, there were 170 Korean shoe repair stores in Chicago, accounting for a third of all such businesses in the city. However, there was only one Korean supplier in the business at that time, so the Korean owners had to depend on Jewish suppliers (*KTC* 22 July 1987).

Likewise, almost all of the Korean dry cleaners and laundry owners in Chicago are dependent on Jewish suppliers. In 1991, there were 2,000 such businesses in Chicago, accounting for 66 percent of those in the city (*KTC* 14 July 1990), but there was only one Korean supplier. Korean laundry owners and dry cleaners prefer Jewish suppliers to the Korean supplier because of the larger stock and more professional service they offer.

In summary, the timing of Korean immigration to the United States proved to be critical for the growth of Korean businesses. Before the massive immigration started in 1970, South Korea had expanded its trade with the United States, and a large number of Korean immigrants had emerged as agents between the two countries. Selected Korean export items, such as wigs, provided initial business opportunities to many immigrants. Furthermore, the interethnic succession of residence, which had occurred in large U.S. cities before the large-scale Korean immigration, resulted in vacated business opportunities in minority areas, enabling the immigrants to enter these areas without great resistance from existing local businesses.

While these structural factors created the initial business opportunities, a sense of blocked mobility in professional and white-collar wage employment has been largely responsible for driving many Korean immigrants toward self-employment in small businesses. In the following sections, I examine how Korean immigrants have responded to such labor market disadvantages and how they have mobilized resources on the basis of class, family, and ethnicity to realize their goal of being on their own.

Background Characteristics of Korean Business Owners

Korean business owners, like Korean immigrants in general, have distinctive demographic and socioeconomic characteristics (see table 3.4). The overwhelming majority of my respondents (95 percent in the Chicago survey and 87 percent in the L.A. survey) were currently married. The average number of children among the married respondents was two, and 43 percent of the children in the L.A. survey were 16 years of age and over. In addition to their own children, 15 percent of the respondents in Chicago and 27.5 percent of those in Los Angeles lived in the same household as their parents, brothers, sisters, or other relatives. As a result, according to the L.A. survey, the average number of persons in a Korean entrepreneur's household was 3.94, which was 50 percent higher than the average size of the U.S. household (2.63) and 24 percent higher than the average size of the Korean American household (3.19) (U.S. Bureau of the Census 1993a, 53). The stable family structure and large household size of Korean business owners can be important assets for low-cost business management.

These business owners also received very high levels of education. Between 60 and 70 percent of the respondents received four or more years of college education, whereas only 27 percent of U.S. civilian employees between the ages of 25 and 64 did so (U.S. Bureau of the Census 1988, 391). Their level of education is even higher than that of Korean immigrants as a group, 46 percent of whom were graduates of four-year colleges in 1990 (see table 2.10).

In one sense, Korean business owners are overeducated for their role; managing a small business hardly requires a college education or formal training. The mismatch between education and employment must be understood as a result of their difficulty in finding appropriate occupations in the United States. Many respondents said that if white-collar jobs had been available, they would have chosen them, but the language barrier precluded such a possibility. Many of them found that they had to start off as factory workers, dishwashers, or pumpers at gas stations. Given such bleak employment prospects, small business owner-ship was viewed as the best choice.

The predominantly urban background of Korean business owners is revealed by the finding that more than 80 percent of the respondents came from Seoul, the capital city of South Korea. The remaining re-spondents came from other big cities of South Korea, such as Pusan and Taegu. Very few came from rural areas. Nearly all, then, were experi-enced urbanites prior to their emigration. Their exposure to and famil-iarity with urban conditions in South Korea seemed to prepare many of them to adapt well to similar environments in the United States.[6]

Not all of them, however, were urbanites by birth. Only 43 percent of the respondents in the L.A. survey had been born in Seoul. This indi-cates that about half of those who came to the United States from Seoul had been born in other parts of Korea and then migrated to Seoul. In fact, 11.7 percent of the L.A. respondents had been born in provinces of North Korea and made their way south before and during the Korean War (1950–53). If we included respondents whose parents were born in North Korea, the percentage of those with such origins would be even higher.[7] Because of their migration experience within Korea, interna-tional migration did not prove to be a drastically uprooting experience for many Korean immigrant business owners.

Other distinctive characteristics that they shared are more evident from an analysis of their occupational backgrounds in South Korea. As table 3.5 illustrates, approximately 40 percent of the respondents had been engaged in professional, technical, managerial, or other white-collar occupations there. If we consider that these kinds of workers com-prised only 11.7 percent of the South Korean workforce in 1990, it becomes obvious that they are disproportionately represented among Korean business owners in the United States. In contrast, very few of

Table 3.4. Selected Background Characteristics of Respondents

	Chicago			Los Angeles		
Characteristic	Total	Koreatown	Black Areas	Total	Koreatown	Black Areas
Age (mean)	42.0	42.1	41.8	45.6	44.8	46.4
% Women	23.0	32.0	14.0	19.2	17.1	21.5
% Currently married	95.4	93.6	97.0	86.5	87.3	85.7
% Living in extended family[a]	15.0	21.0	10.0	27.5	16.1	39.6
Schooling (years)	15.2	15.0	15.4	16.4	16.7	16.0
% College graduates[b]	67.0	61.0	72.0	62.4	69.2	54.8
% Immigrated from Seoul	82.0	79.0	85.0	85.8	90.4	80.6
% Christian[c]	56.8	67.7	46.6	66.6	69.5	63.4
Length of U.S. residence (years)	10.4	11.2	9.7	14.5	14.5	14.5
Total number	199	96	103	198	105	93

a. Extended family includes near relatives, such as parents, brothers, or sisters, who live in a household in addition to a nuclear family.

b. Graduates of four-year colleges.

c. Christians include both Protestants and Catholics.

these owners (less than 2 percent) came from agricultural or manual labor occupations, which accounted for almost half of employed South Korean workers in 1990 (KEPB 1990).

Korean business owners also include a high percentage of persons with direct or indirect business experience in South Korea. Approximately a quarter of the respondents had run small businesses of their own as their main occupation in South Korea. A still higher proportion (39 percent in the Chicago survey and 32.8 percent in the L.A. survey) had at some time worked in small businesses there. Moreover, 44 percent of the Chicago respondents and 61 percent of the L.A. respondents had fathers who had been self-employed businessmen in South Korea. Of course familiarity with small business is not difficult to acquire in the South Korean economy, in which such businesses are still viable. In 1988, 43 percent of all employed Korean workers engaged in the management of small businesses, either as owners or as unpaid family workers (Korean Ministry of Labor 1989). Thus, participation in small business is not an unfamiliar experience for many Korean immigrants, who are likely to regard it as a realistic alternative when they confront limited opportunities in the U.S. labor market.

Table 3.5. Main Occupations of Respondents in Korea (Percentages)

	Chicago			Los Angeles		
Characteristic	Total	Koreatown	Black Areas	Total	Koreatown	Black Areas
Employed						
Professional	2.0	4.2	0.0	11.9	13.7	9.8
Technical	5.1	7.3	2.9	4.1	5.9	2.2
Other white-collar[a]	35.9	31.3	40.2	25.3	24.5	30.4
Sales or service	1.0	2.1	0.0	2.1	2.0	2.2
Production or labor[b]	0.5	0.0	1.0	2.0	2.0	2.2
Small business owner	23.7	24.0	23.5	22.2	21.6	22.8
Others	3.0	0.0	5.9	1.0	1.0	1.1
Unemployed	5.6	9.4	2.0	5.7	4.9	6.5
Not in the labor force						
Student	17.2	16.7	17.6	21.6	24.5	18.5
Housewife	4.0	5.2	2.9	2.1	0.0	4.3
Total number	198	96	102	194	102	92

a. Other white-collar workers include managerial, executive, administrative, and administrative support workers.

b. Production and labor workers include precision production, craft, and repair workers; operators and fabricators; and laborers.

This is not to say that Korean immigrant business in the United States is simply the natural outgrowth of an entrepreneurial background among the immigrants. As I point out later in this chapter, the postimmigration experience of downward occupational mobility is far more important in explaining their propensity toward small business than their preimmigration experiences. But it is fair to say that the immigrant population includes a sizable number of persons with an entrepreneurial background, and their rapid adoption of entrepreneurship seems to have been facilitated by this socialization.

Partly because of their business background and partly because of their awareness of the limited opportunity for white-collar wage employment in the U.S. labor market, sizable numbers of Korean immigrants— 47 percent of the L.A. respondents—arrived in the United States with an intention to start their own businesses. Although some managed to bring with them huge amounts of capital by selling their homes and other properties in South Korea, many came with only a small amount of money but a strong entrepreneurial orientation. Seventy percent of the L.A. respondents, for example, brought with them less than

$10,000.[8] In this sense, Korean business owners are "intended immigrant entrepreneurs" (Marger and Hoffman 1994).

Such intentions are stronger among more recent arrivals than among old-timers. For instance, 60.5 percent of the L.A. respondents who immigrated after 1980 intended to start a business in the United States, compared to only 36.6 percent of the pre-1980 respondents.[9] This difference is a result of changing expectations about opportunities in the United States. If the pre-1980 Korean immigrants arrived in the United States with vague expectations of realizing the American Dream, more recent cohorts have come with more realistically modest assessments of their positions as immigrants and racial minorities in American society.

A final distinctive characteristic of the business owners is the prevalence of Christian backgrounds (primarily Protestant) and church membership among them. More than half of the Chicago respondents and two-thirds of those in Los Angeles identified themselves as Christians (either Protestants or Catholics), and many of them actively participate in church activities. Given that only a quarter of the South Korean people are reported to be Christians, this group is disproportionately represented among the Korean immigrant business owners.

With their primarily urban, middle-class, and Christian backgrounds, these business owners have tended to be individuals who experienced geographic and socioeconomic mobility in South Korea. Their strong aspirations for upward mobility were the driving force behind their immigration and their high rates of business ownership upon their arrival in the United States.

Motivations for Immigration, Entry Methods, and Support Networks

The push–pull model views international migration as a joint outcome of push factors in the sending country and pull factors in the receiving country (Lee 1966; Jenkins 1977). For Korean immigrants in general and business owners in particular, the pull factors were far more important than the push factors in motivating emigration. According to my surveys, better economic opportunities, unification with family members, and education were the major pull factors that attracted Korean business owners to the United States. Push factors, such as unemployment or fear of social and political instability in South Korea, were rarely cited as

Table 3.6. Respondents' Reasons for Immigrating to the United States (Percentages)

Reason	Chicago	Los Angeles
Better economic opportunities in the U.S.	53.1	31.3
Unification with family members in the U.S.	19.4	21.2
Education for myself	9.7	15.2
Education for children	7.7	11.1
Individual freedom	3.6	4.5
Aspiration for American way of life	1.5	6.1
Social and political instability of Korea	1.5	5.1
Decision made by someone else	1.5	0.0
Others	2.0	5.6
Total number	196	198

Note: In an open-ended question, respondents were asked to cite their three most important reasons for immigrating to the United States and to rank them according to importance. This table shows what they cited as the most important reason.

motivations for their emigration. These individuals, then, were part of a movement of middle-class Koreans who sought comparatively better opportunities in the United States (see table 3.6).

Chain migration is the most common entry method through which these business owners have come to the United States. Two-thirds of the respondents in the Chicago and L.A. surveys entered this country at the invitation of their resident family members (see table 3.7). Most of them did so under the second preference category (spouses and unmarried sons and daughters of U.S. resident aliens and their children) and the fifth preference category (brothers and sisters of U.S. citizens and their spouses and children). Because of this kinship-centered chain migration, many respondents had natural sources of assistance with settlement in the United States.

The most common sources of assistance came from brothers and sisters and friends. Twenty-three percent of the L.A. respondents reported that they had received help from their brothers and sisters in finding a house and a job. Another 24 percent received such assistance from their friends and fellow school alumni and alumnae. Other relatives, such as parents-in-law and brothers- or sisters-in-law, and church members, including ministers, also provided valuable aid during the early stages of settlement.

Korean business owners therefore benefit from two types of social support networks: kinship networks, which are organized around imme-

Table 3.7. Entry Visa Categories of Respondents (Percentages)

Category	Chicago	Los Angeles
Family reunification preferences		
Unmarried sons and daughters of U.S. citizens and their children	1.5	2.6
Spouses and unmarried sons and daughters of U.S. resident aliens and their children	25.0	28.6
Married sons and daughters of U.S. citizens and their spouses and children	3.1	0.5
Brothers and sisters of U.S. citizens and their spouses and children	35.7	28.1
Parents of U.S. citizens	0.0	2.0
Spouses of U.S. citizens	0.0	5.6
Occupational preferences		
Immigrants in professions and with special skills and their spouses and children[a]	26.5	22.4
Businessmen and investors	5.1	1.5
Other categories	0.0	2.0
Nonimmigrant status[b]	3.1	6.6
Total number	196	196

a. Includes the third, sixth, and nonpreference categories.

b. Includes students, temporary visitors, and others who had entered the United States with nonimmigrant status and who changed their status to that of permanent resident through amnesty or a family reunification preference.

diate family members and relatives, and nonkinship networks, which are based on common schooling, occupational experience, and church membership in South Korea and the United States (Yim 1985). As shown by assistance from parents-in-law and brothers-in-law, old-style Korean kinship networks are modified in the United States to fit the new environment. In Korea, the family system is usually organized along the husband's family line. In the United States, however, the wife's family line is equally valued and is incorporated into the husband's social networks. Thus, the working unit of the Korean immigrants' family system is a modified extended family composed of several nuclear families related to both the husband and the wife (Litwark 1960). The purpose of the modified extended family is to increase the range of a person's social network and thus expand the pool of material and emotional support upon which he or she can draw.

Nonkinship networks are also extensively used by Korean immigrants to cope with individual crises. For those who lack family members in the United States, these networks serve as substitutes and allow the exchange of material and emotional support (I. Kim 1981). By combining both types of support networks in an opportunistic manner, Korean immigrants can construct a complex web of social ties in the new land. Such a wide range of networks provides would-be Korean business owners with access to resources (such as financial assistance, information, and training opportunities) from family members, friends, and co-ethnics, thereby increasing their chances of business ownership.

One of the by-products of these networks is the channeling of newly arrived immigrants into the already saturated small business sector. There is an interesting saying in the Korean immigrant community that a new arrival's career in the United States is determined by who picks him up at the airport. If he is picked up by a liquor store owner, he will likely find himself working behind a cash register, selling beer and snacks to black and Latino customers. If he is picked up by a dry cleaner, he will have a good chance of making a living by washing and ironing the clothes of working- and middle-class customers of diverse races. This happens because a new immigrant tends to depend on his or her sponsor for various kinds of assistance, such as getting a social security number, a driver's license, and even a ride from the airport. If the sponsor happens to be a business owner—which is very likely because of the already high rates of business ownership among Korean immigrants—the new arrival tends to find his or her first employment in the sponsor's business. As the newcomer learns business skills and builds networks with clients and suppliers, he or she is likely to enter the same line of business as the sponsor. It is not coincidental that upon immigration, 56 percent of the L.A. respondents received primary assistance from family members or friends who were business owners themselves.

The clustering of Korean businesses is also encouraged by frequent changes of ownership between entrepreneurs and their Korean employees. Korean employees who purchase businesses from their employers often receive some financial assistance in the form of the owner's financing, by which store rent and stock can be paid off on a long-term basis at low interest rates. Such favors definitely lower the initial financial burden for potential business owners. This kind of intraethnic succession of business is facilitated by the personal relationships and ethnocentric bonds between the store owners and their employees. The following case illustrates how such a bond helped Mr. Yun, a 24-year-old high school graduate, get started in his own business:

> I came to Chicago in 1986 with my parents, a sister, and two brothers. At first, I did not know what to do here and missed my friends left in

Korea. I myself did not want to come to the United States, but my sister invited my parents to come here and I had to follow my parents' decision anyway. My first job in Chicago was a helper in a Korean laundry. I found the job advertisement in the classified ads section of the *Han'guk Ilbo* [the *Korea Times of Chicago*]. After being interviewed by the owner, I got hired mainly because I was a Christian; the owner himself was an elder of a Korean immigrant church. Work in the laundry was physically very demanding. I had to work continuously from 7:00 A.M. to 6:30 P.M. without taking any break time. I endured all the difficulties and gave all the money I earned to my parents, in the belief that I should contribute to the family income. I worked for three years at the store and gained the full trust from my boss. As a result, I got promoted to the position of general manager. When my boss opened a new laundry elsewhere, he offered to sell the store to me. The cost of the store was $75,000. I managed to pay $15,000 as a down payment with lump sums of money from a *kye* [a Korean rotating credit association] and paid the balance within two years. Now I am the owner of a laundry with eleven employees, five of whom are my family members. (Personal interview)

As noted previously, intraethnic succession is particularly noteworthy in the dry cleaning and laundry business. According to the Korean Dry Cleaners Association, there were 8,802 Korean dry cleaners and laundry owners in the United States (excluding Hawaii and Alaska) as of June 1990, accounting for 48 percent of the U.S. total of 18,350 (*KTC* 8 November 1990). In Chicago, Koreans owned 2,000 dry cleaning and laundry establishments, accounting for 66 percent of a total of 3,000.

This business is popular among recently arrived Korean immigrants because managing a laundry or dry cleaning store does not require large amounts of capital, formal training, or good English skills. Instead, those immigrants who can call upon family members to work at their store are in an advantageous position in this labor-intensive business. Another attraction of this type of establishment is that it has shorter business hours than grocery and restaurant businesses. Dry cleaners can take Sundays and holidays off and close their stores around 6:00 or 7:00 P.M., whereas grocery store and restaurant owners must work on these days and keep their stores open until late in the evening. The short business hours also make dry cleaning and laundry a business in which theft and robbery are rare.

Korean immigrants began to enter this field in Chicago during the early 1970s by taking over outgoing Jewish immigrants' laundries. Once a Jewish laundry was purchased by a Korean, subsequent changes of ownership tended to occur exclusively between Koreans. Such an intraethnic succession of business was aided by Korean-language immigrant newspapers, in which all of the business opportunities open to Korean immigrants were advertised. Korean buyers and sellers had earlier access to such information than non-Koreans, keeping such opportunities within the community.

Findings from the L.A. survey show that intraethnic succession is strong in other types of Korean businesses as well, such as grocery and liquor stores, gas stations, and garment manufacturing. Out of the 198 respondents, half purchased an already established business rather than starting a new one; 67 percent of those who purchased a business did so from Koreans, 11 percent from Asians, and 7 percent from Jews or other whites. Moreover, 95 percent of the respondents who purchased a business from a Korean reported that the previous owner had also purchased it from a Korean. Thus, once a business is purchased by a Korean, the next owner is highly likely to be a Korean as well.

Such a high rate of intraethnic succession is largely a result of the nature of social networks, which are built around personal ties and Korean ethnicity. Most respondents came to know the previous owners of their stores through their Korean friends and acquaintances, Korean real estate agents, and the Korean mass media. Among the L.A. respondents, these sources accounted for 37 percent, 17 percent, and 13 percent, respectively. American sources of information were rarely used; only 2 percent of the respondents found the previous owner through American friends and acquaintances, 6 percent through American real estate agents, and none through the American mass media. The social and economic isolation of Korean immigrants from the larger American society and economy seems to render them dependent on their ethnic community for information about employment and business opportunities, and this channels them into select lines of business in which Koreans are already concentrated.

Business Formation

Reasons for Getting Into Business

As noted previously, limited opportunity for jobs congruent with their class background seems to be the main force driving Korean immigrants

Table 3.8. Job Trajectories of Respondents (Percentages)

	Chicago			Los Angeles		
Occupation	1st Job	2nd Job	3rd Job	1st Job	2nd Job	3rd Job
Professional or technical	9.6	5.2	5.7	9.1	4.9	2.9
Managerial or clerical	12.7	5.2	3.3	7.6	4.9	4.9
Sales or service	21.3	20.9	11.5	25.9	15.4	10.6
Production or labor	34.5	15.1	7.4	20.8	13.6	8.8
Small business	8.6	19.8	12.3	18.3	23.9	26.2
Others	0.5	4.1	0.0	0.0	0.0	0.0
Current business	12.7	29.7	59.8	18.3	37.4	46.6
Total number	197	172	122	197	163	103

toward self-employment in small business. As table 3.8 illustrates, more than half the respondents started off in the United States as manual, service, or sales workers; only about 20 percent could find professional, technical, or other white-collar jobs. Considering their largely white-collar backgrounds, most experienced some downward occupational mobility in the period immediately following immigration.[10] The jobs initially available were low skilled and poorly paid because the immigrants were disadvantaged in the American labor market.

Because of such disadvantages in the mainstream economy, substantial numbers of the respondents had found their first employment in the Korean ethnic economy. As table 3.9 shows, 42 percent of the L.A. respondents found their first jobs in Korean-owned firms, compared to 21 percent in non-Korean firms and 37 percent in their own businesses. Throughout their subsequent job trajectories, more respondents were hired by Korean employers than by non-Korean employers. As explained earlier, the chain migration and social support networks built on kinship and nonkinship ties seem to be responsible for channeling more respondents into the Korean ethnic economy than into the general economy. Furthermore, many would-be Korean business owners tend to regard employment in a Korean firm as a chance to learn the ropes that will help them start their own businesses. For this reason, the respondents who had worked in such firms had a higher chance of making a transition to self-employment than those who had worked in non-Korean firms.

The entry point to employment in the U.S. labor market, whether or not it was chosen, affected significantly the type of subsequent em-

Table 3.9. Job Transition Patterns of Los Angeles Respondents (Percentages)

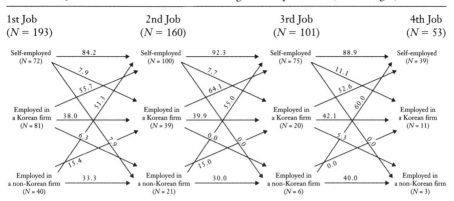

1st Job (N = 193)	2nd Job (N = 160)	3rd Job (N = 101)	4th Job (N = 53)

ployment respondents were able to find. Those who had started their own businesses upon immigration tended to remain in the self-employment sector, although some had to close the first business and start new ones during their careers.[11] Those who had found their first jobs in Korean firms had a higher chance of working in Korean than non-Korean businesses in their second and third jobs, and the same pattern of intrasector job transition held for those who found their first employment in non-Korean firms. Out of 81 respondents who began in Korean businesses, 38 percent also found their second jobs in this sector, whereas only 6.3 percent moved to non-Korean firms. Similarly, 33 percent of the 40 respondents whose first jobs had been in non-Korean businesses stayed in this sector, while 15.4 percent moved to Korean firms.

In a related pattern, job transitions were more likely to involve moving from the non-Korean to the Korean sector than the other way around. Only 6.3 percent of the 81 respondents whose first employment had been in Korean firms found their second jobs in non-Korean firms, whereas 15.4 percent of the 40 respondents moved from non-Korean to Korean businesses. This suggests that job skills and experience acquired in the Korean ethnic economy are more difficult to transfer to the open economy than the other way around, thereby keeping immigrants either self-employed or employed by Koreans. It is also possible, however, that would-be business owners gradually regress toward Korean firms in preparation for opening their own businesses, lowering the likelihood of job transition from Korean to non-Korean firms.[12] I cannot determine at this point which scenario is a more accurate model of job transition among Korean immigrants, because this study is based only on business owners. More research such as that conducted by Nee, Sanders, and Sernau (1994), which examines both self-employed and nonself-employed workers, is needed to answer this question.

Wages for these workers in Korean and non-Korean firms are equally low. Although it is difficult to determine the precise hourly wage rates of the respondents because some received commission or wages on a weekly, monthly, and yearly basis, about half of those who were paid by the hour earned less than $4.40 in Korean firms and $3.50 in non-Korean firms. Partly as a result of such low wages, the duration of employment in both types of businesses was short. Half of the respondents who had found their first employment in Korean firms remained in these jobs for 18 months, whereas half of those who began working in non-Korean firms worked for 30 months. The shorter spell of employment in Korean businesses is most likely a result of respondents' intention to use such employment as a stepping-stone to business ownership.[13]

In the face of low pay and little chance of promotion through employment, the respondents turned to small business to make more money and gain greater independence. Although experience with business management in South Korea motivated some of them to become business owners in the United States, this preimmigration factor was not as influential in the decision to become self-employed as were postimmigration labor market disadvantages (see table 3.10). This highlights again the fact that small business is a situational adaptation of Korean immigrants to limited employment opportunities in the U.S. labor market.

An analysis using data from the 5 percent PUMS of the 1990 U.S. census confirms the income advantages of self-employed Korean American workers over wage or salary workers. As we can see in table 3.11, the ratio of income from self-employment to that from wage employment was greater among Korean Americans than among Asians in general, blacks, Hispanics, and whites. Self-employed Korean workers earned 43 percent more than corresponding wage and salary workers, whereas self-employed white workers earned 21 percent less than corresponding wage and salary workers. The ratio of self-employment to wage employment income was the lowest among blacks at 57 percent.

These patterns hold even when we factor in the educational levels of the workers in each category. Self-employed Korean workers who had graduated from college earned significantly more (19 percent) than corresponding wage and salary workers, while comparably educated black

Table 3.10. Respondents' Reasons for Starting Their Own Businesses
(Percentages)

Reason	Chicago			Los Angeles		
	Total	Koreatown	Black Areas	Total	Koreatown	Black Areas
To make more money	46.5	43.0	50.0	29.8	26.7	33.3
To become my own boss	23.7	21.6	26.0	19.2	17.1	21.5
Disadvantages in the labor market	12.6	17.6	7.3	8.6	3.8	14.0
Influence from family and friends	3.0	3.9	2.1	2.5	1.9	3.2
Prior business experience	3.0	4.9	1.0	8.1	9.5	6.5
Personal preference and talents	u	u	u	20.7	30.5	9.7
Glass ceiling or discrimination	u	u	u	6.1	6.7	5.4
Others	9.1	5.9	12.5	5.0	3.8	6.5
No special reason	2.0	2.9	1.0	0.0	0.0	0.0
Total number	198	102	96	198	105	93

Note: In a closed-ended question, respondents were asked to cite their three most important reasons for getting into business and to rank them according to importance. This table shows what they cited as the most important reason.

u = data unavailable because this category was not included in the interview schedule for the Chicago survey.

workers fared the best in wage employment in the public sector. This intergroup difference seems to result largely from the different values of a college education for Koreans and blacks in the U.S. labor market. Although both groups are racial minorities in American society, affirmative action programs help college-educated blacks secure stable and high-paying jobs in the public sector. However, similarly educated Koreans have great difficulty finding wage employment congruent with their education, partly because of the language barrier and partly because of American employers' tendency to undervalue South Korean education. These labor market conditions seem to attract highly motivated college-educated Koreans to self-employment rather than wage employment, whereas the opposite is true for college-educated blacks.

Self-employment in business is desired among Korean immigrants not only because they can make more money by working for themselves than by working for others but also because it serves as a safety measure against frequent layoffs in American workplaces. Many immigrants believe that they have a higher chance of being fired or laid off than do American workers in times of economic recession. To guard against such

Table 3.11. Median Personal Income of Self-Employed and Wage/Salary
Workers in the United States, 1990

Class of Worker	Koreans	Asians	Blacks	Hispanics	Whites
All levels of education					
Wage/salary workers	14,000	18,141	14,000	13,305	19,000
Private wage workers	14,000	18,000	12,638	12,500	18,156
Public wage workers	17,583	23,000	18,000	18,000	22,000
Self-employed workers	20,000	18,000	8,000	11,000	15,000
Unincorporated	18,000	15,000	7,099	9,354	11,000
Incorporated	25,000	25,000	14,400	19,000	30,000
SE/wage income ratio	1.43	0.99	0.57	0.83	0.79
Total number	15,482	29,098	95,658	101,855	872,462
Non–college graduates					
Wage/salary workers	12,000	15,000	12,750	12,000	16,520
Private wage workers	12,000	14,000	12,000	12,000	16,000
Public wage workers	14,000	19,000	16,000	15,105	18,000
Self-employed workers	17,000	12,740	7,000	10,000	12,000
Unincorporated	15,000	11,592	6,200	8,458	10,000
Incorporated	20,000	17,000	11,000	25,600	24,000
SE/wage income ratio	1.42	0.85	0.55	0.83	0.73
Total number	9,772	25,857	91,773	94,047	770,731
College graduates and over					
Wage/salary workers	21,000	27,000	26,000	25,000	29,247
Private wage workers	20,498	27,000	25,000	24,000	30,000
Public wage workers	23,823	27,000	27,000	27,269	28,000
Self-employed workers	25,000	30,000	20,000	24,200	27,001
Unincorporated	20,000	25,000	15,000	18,000	20,000
Incorporated	35,000	40,000	32,000	40,000	48,000
SE/wage income ratio	1.19	1.11	0.77	0.97	0.92
Total number	5,710	3,241	3,885	7,808	101,731

Source: U.S. Bureau of the Census, 1 percent and 5 percent PUMS of the 1990 census.

Notes: Employed workers who were 25 years old and over in 1990 are included in the analysis. Asians are non-Hispanic Asian Americans (including Koreans) and Pacific Islanders. Blacks and whites are non-Hispanic blacks and whites. As sources of income, wages and salary income in 1989 are used for wage/salary workers, farm and nonfarm self-employment income are used for unincorporated self-employed workers, and wages or salary income plus farm/nonfarm self-employment income are used for incorporated self-employed workers. Persons whose own businesses are incorporated are employees of these businesses and receive wages and salary from them.

possibilities, a husband may work in a factory while his wife manages a
small business. If the husband is laid off or fired, he can work full-time
in his wife's store until he finds a new job. Self-employment in business
is also preferred by Korean immigrants as a retirement plan. Since many
Koreans came to the United States near middle age, they cannot expect

substantial retirement benefits. As long as they make a modest income from their businesses, they can support themselves in their old age.

Reasons for Choosing the Current Type of Business

Once Korean immigrants decide to become business owners, they tend to choose the types of businesses in which they can take advantage of their previous experience as well as their personal interests, talents, and skills. Besides such personal preferences, they also have to take into account situational constraints, such as the requirements of capital and skills and the influence of family and friends who are already in business. While both sets of factors are important in the decision-making process, they have different weights on the two groups of Korean business owners.

As we can see in table 3.12, Korean business owners in Koreatown chose their businesses based on personal factors, whereas those in black areas were strongly influenced by situational constraints. Forty-three percent of the respondents in Chicago's Koreatown, as compared with 20 percent of their counterparts in black areas, cited prior business experience as the most important reason for choosing their current type of business. In contrast, 15 percent of the respondents there, as compared with 21 percent of those in black areas, cited the minimal requirements of capital and business skills as the most important reason. Similarly, about 5 percent of those in Koreatown but 26 percent of those in black areas based their decision on the influence of family and friends. The same patterns were also noted in the L.A. survey.

These patterns seem to be mainly the result of different ranges of business opportunities available in Koreatown and in black neighborhoods. Korean businesses in low-income black areas generally fill economic niches neglected by large department and chain stores because of the small profit margins and high crime rates there. In 1991, for instance, Target had seventy-three retail discount stores in Southern California but none in South Central, and Vons had 300 supermarkets in the region but only two in South Central (Silverstein and Brooks 1991). As a result, Korean businesses tend to be grocery and liquor stores, auto parts and repair shops, general merchandise stores, gas stations, indoor swap meets, and similar types of establishments that meet the daily needs of low-income people for inexpensive consumer goods and services. The NAACP estimates that Koreans own about a third of South Central's

Table 3.12. Respondents' Reasons for Choosing Their Current Type of Business (Percentages)

Reason	Chicago			Los Angeles		
	Total	Koreatown	Black Areas	Total	Koreatown	Black Areas
Prior experience in this type of business	30.8	42.7	19.6	33.5	40.4	25.8
Personal interests and talents	11.6	13.5	9.8	21.8	28.8	14.0
Higher profit margin	u	u	u	7.1	3.8	10.8
Lack of competition	8.6	10.4	6.9	2.5	2.9	2.2
Minimal requirements of capital and skills	17.7	14.6	20.6	16.3	11.5	21.6
Influence from family and friends	15.7	5.2	25.5	11.2	7.7	15.1
Others[a]	14.6	13.5	15.7	6.0	2.0	5.4
No special reason	1.0	0.0	2.0	1.2	1.0	2.2
Total number	198	102	96	197	104	93

Note: In an open-ended question, respondents were asked to cite their three most important reasons for choosing the current type of business and to rank them according to importance. This table shows what they cited as the most important reason.

u = data unavailable because this category was not included in the interview schedule for the Chicago survey

a. Other reasons included safety from crime and unexpected availability of business.

small markets and liquor stores (Cheng and Espiritu 1989). Because business opportunities in such minority areas are heavily constrained by the limited purchasing power of inner-city residents, Korean business owners have a very limited degree of freedom in choosing the types of business in which they have competitive advantages over others.

In contrast, the Koreatown market has reached the stage of institutional completeness in the process of meeting the diverse demands of Korean Americans for cultural products and services. The high economic status of Korean American families (whose average family income in 1990 was $45,760, compared with the national average of $43,803) has allowed even expensive import furniture stores and automobile dealers to prosper there by tapping into the desire of some Korean Americans to display their wealth through conspicuous consumption. The language barrier and the unfamiliarity of Korean immigrants with American formal institutions and their bureaucratic procedures has also created business opportunities for Korean immigrant professionals such as accountants, lawyers, and health specialists. According to the 1993 Korean Business Directory, published by the *Korea Times Los Angeles,* 127 types of businesses were operating in the L.A. Koreatown market. Such opportunities permit Korean business owners to take advantage of their prior experience and personal interests, talents, and skills.

Characteristics of Korean Immigrant Businesses

Though handicapped by limitations of capital, English language ability, and business experience in the United States, Korean immigrants manage to lower the entry-level costs of business by specializing in cheap products and services in low-income minority areas. In Chicago's black neighborhoods, for instance, most Korean businesses are concentrated in sales of such items as general merchandise, clothing, footwear, beauty supplies, and wigs. Because liquor license regulations are tougher in Chicago than in Los Angeles, very few Korean business owners operate liquor stores in these neighborhoods. For unknown reasons, Korean-operated grocery stores are also rare there. In contrast, in South Central and other minority neighborhoods of Los Angeles, Koreans are overrepresented in grocery and liquor stores.[14] As of June 1990, Korean independent beer, wine, and/or liquor retailers accounted for 34 percent of such retailers in Los Angeles County, 23 percent in Orange County, 21 percent in Santa Barbara County, and 24 percent in all eight counties in Southern California (Kern, Riverside, San Bernardino, San Diego, and Ventura in addition to the other three) (KAGRO 1990). These figures do not include chain grocery and convenience stores. If they did, the percentage of Korean retailers would be even higher.

The marginal position of Korean immigrant businesses is also indicated by the racial composition and income level of their customer base. Koreans, blacks, and Latinos constitute major customer groups for these businesses. In Koreatown of Los Angeles, for instance, Koreans comprised 59 percent of their total customers, followed by Latinos and non-Hispanic whites, who each accounted for 14 percent of the customers. In South Central Los Angeles, blacks and Latinos accounted for 50 percent and 29 percent of the total customers, respectively (see table 3.13). White and Korean customers seldom bother shopping in these minority areas.

The majority of the customers in minority areas also have low incomes. Seventy-four percent of the respondents in South Central and 90

Table 3.13. Racial Composition and Income Level of Customer Base among
Los Angeles Respondents (Percentages)

	Total	Koreatown	South Central
Racial composition			
Koreans	35.1	58.6	9.2
Other Asians	3.2	3.5	2.8
Whites	10.9	14.1	7.3
Blacks	25.9	4.6	49.5
Latinos	21.1	14.3	28.6
Others	3.2	4.7	1.5
Total			
Percentage	100	100	100
Number of respondents	198	105	93
Income level			
Lower	19.2	6.0	33.3
Middle-low	26.9	15.0	39.8
Middle-middle	35.8	43.0	28.0
Middle-upper	26.9	39.0	15.1
Upper	7.3	10.0	3.2
Total			
Percentage	116.0	113.0	119.0
Number of respondents	193	100	93

Note: The total percentage of income levels is over 100 because respondents cater to customers of different income levels.

percent of those in Chicago's black areas reported that their customers were lower- and middle-low-income people. As we have seen in table 3.2, the median family income in West Garfield Park, where the largest Korean business concentration area in Chicago is located, was less than $11,000 in 1979, contrasted with the city median of more than $15,000. Almost 40 percent of the residents there lived below the census poverty level. The general unemployment rate exceeded 20 percent; among those 16 to 19 years old, the rate was about 40 percent for those who had graduated from high school and greater than 60 percent for those who had not. More than one-third of all families drew on Aid to Families with Dependent Children (Hansis 1984, 72).

Thus, the fate of Korean businesses in minority areas depends heavily on the economic condition of inner-city black and Latino residents. After the Reagan and Bush administrations began to cut welfare expenditures in the mid-1980s, these businesses experienced a recession because of the deteriorating position of their customers. Regarding the declining purchasing power of black customers, some veteran Korean business owners in Chicago lament, "The good old days have gone."

Despite the small profit margins and high crime rates, Korean immigrants still prefer to establish their businesses in low-income minority areas. The primary reason is the lower level of barriers to entry. But black customers are also perceived by Korean immigrants as impulse buyers and thus easier to serve and make profits off than white and Korean customers. One respondent in Chicago commented, "Blacks, especially black youths, spend money for clothes, shoes, and electronics without any second thought if they have money in their pockets." One Korean American social worker who works as the spokesman for the Korean Merchants Association of Chicago claims:

> It's easier for someone who doesn't speak English well to get by in
> African-American communities. Even if you don't speak English well,
> this is more tolerable in African-American neighborhoods. Merchants
> tell me, on the North Side, people ask us more logical or analytical
> questions. In African-American neighborhoods, it's more gesture.
> Once they see merchandise, they don't ask questions. They just feel
> they want to buy it. (Longworth 1992)

Black customers are also said to be less likely than white and Korean customers to demand an exchange or a refund for defective merchandise. Such consumption patterns attracted many Korean immigrants into black areas in the expectation that they could make easy money despite their limited command of English.[15]

Financial Resources Utilized in Korean Immigrant Businesses

Although minimal capital requirements reduce the barriers to business ownership, the more important cause of Korean immigrants' proliferation in business is their effective utilization of informal financial resources. The majority of the respondents in both Chicago and Los Angeles accumulated capital mainly through personal savings in the United States, loans from family and friends, and Korean rotating credit associations called *kyes* (in English, "contract"). For instance, 62 percent of the respondents in Chicago and 62 percent of those in Los Angeles relied on their personal savings in the United States as one of the three most important sources of capital for their current business (see table

Table 3.14 Sources of Capital for Respondents' Current Businesses
(Percentages)

Source	Chicago	Los Angeles
Money brought from Korea	17.8	25.6
Personal savings in the United States	61.9	61.5
Loans from kin	35.0	19.5
Loans from friends	19.8	10.8
Loans from American banks	18.8	11.8
Loans from Korean American banks	13.7	17.4
Loans from Small Business Administration	u	8.2
Kyes	27.9	7.2
Partnerships	4.6	2.1
Others	4.1	6.2
Total		
Percentage	204.0	170.0
Number of respondents	197	195

Note: The total percentage is over 100 because most respondents utilized more than one financial resource.
u = data unavailable.

3.14). Personal savings, money brought from Korea, loans from kin, and money from kyes accounted respectively for 41.5 percent, 17.5 percent, 8.1 percent, and 4 percent of the total start-up capital among the L.A. respondents.[16]

This heavy reliance on informal financial resources does not prevent Korean business owners from seeking resources from mainstream financial institutions. Between 30 and 40 percent of the respondents in Chicago and Los Angeles obtained loans from either Korean American or American banks. Loans from the Small Business Administration, however, were rarely used. Only 8 percent of the L.A. respondents reported having received an SBA loan. Complicated red tape, insufficient business credit status, and a lack of information about SBA loans were frequently referred to as major factors inhibiting respondents from borrowing from the SBA.

Partnerships were also seldom used by Korean business owners, although they are said to have been prevalent among the early Chinese and Japanese immigrants. Ivan Light (1972) reported that Chinese immigrants from district and surname associations often pooled their capital to establish a joint business. In addition, district officers mediated and settled internal disputes among district members (Ma 1991). Such a collective approach to business might have been possible among the early Chinese immigrants because traditional social relations based on the region of origin, language, and surnames that the Chinese had transplanted from the Old World bound them together in their social and economic lives.[17]

In the Korean community, however, the heterogeneous class and regional backgrounds of the post-1965 immigrants have meant that there are few associations that can exert such strong control over the group as a whole. For this reason, Korean immigrants are generally individualistic in their approach to business, as evidenced in their low rate of participation in partnerships. Only 5 percent of the Chicago respondents and 2 percent of the L.A. respondents used this as one of their three important sources of start-up capital. Of course this is partly a result of the small size of most Korean businesses, which decreases the need for partnerships. But Koreans tend to believe that partnerships will inevitably lead to disputes over profit sharing and the division of labor and consequently bring previously friendly relationships to an end.

The kye is still a viable form of capital accumulation as well as a social association among Korean immigrants. About 60 percent of the respondents in Chicago and Los Angeles had participated in kyes in the United States, and 35 percent were still participating in them. Twenty-eight percent of the Chicago respondents used them as one of their three main sources of start-up capital, compared to only 7 percent of those in Los Angeles. The majority of the respondents in both cities expressed positive opinions about kyes: 79 percent of those in Chicago and 66 percent of those in Los Angeles thought that they were useful for economic purposes, and 52 percent and 48 percent respectively thought that they were useful for social purposes. These findings indicate that many Korean immigrants still perceive kyes as a useful tool for improving their economic and social lives.[18]

The basic purpose of kyes is self-help. People participate in them not only for their individual interests but also for the altruistic purpose of helping other members who need lump sums of money to start their own businesses. The kye has social functions as well as economic ones. Busy Korean business owners can reserve time for recreation among friends, family members, or relatives at occasional kye meetings. In Korea, such meetings are often held at Korean restaurants or at members' residences. Each gathering is a great party with food and drink. Because the active participants are mostly women (wives often participate on behalf of their busy husbands), kye meetings are one of the rare opportunities to vent stress accumulated from daily household chores.[19] The expense of the party is often covered by the person whose turn has come to receive the lump sum of money. However, because of the busy lifestyle of immigrants and the high rates of labor force participation among Korean immigrant women, such gatherings are less frequent in the United States, and the social functions of kyes are less emphasized than the economic ones. A Korean liquor store owner in South Central Los Angeles describes the ways in which she participated in kyes:

> In my kyes, only about half of the members even showed up for the monthly meetings; most were too busy running their businesses. Sometimes when I was busy, I delivered the money to the *kye ju* [leader] on the day of the meeting or on the night before. I didn't even know some of the members. But I joined because I had heard that the kye ju had produced good results for 10 years. (Kang 1992)

The kye operates according to the following principles: several people (often ten to twenty) contribute an equal amount of money to a fund, which is lent to each of them in a rotating order. All kye members, including the borrower, continue to make the monthly payments until everyone benefits from the fund. There are two ways to assign the fund to members. One is the lottery kye, in which people draw lots to determine who will receive the money. The other is the bid kye, in which each member bids for the privilege of taking the early rounds. The bidder who offers the highest interest rate receives the first lump sum of money, and he or she distributes the interest payment to the other members. These interest rates can range from 14 to 20 percent or more. Those who are not in urgent need of money can collect the high interest paid by members in the early rounds. Generally, the bid kye is larger than the lottery kye in terms of the size of the fund and the number of persons involved, and it is more likely to be used for economic purposes than for social ones.

A kye provides three attractions to its members. First, of course, the members can receive lump sums of money to start their own businesses. A person in need of money organizes the kye and receives the first lump sum, and he or she pays the interest to the other members. The kye has a higher interest rate than a commercial bank loan, but it does not require collateral or a formal credit check. Thus, Korean immigrants who are disadvantaged in obtaining bank loans can overcome a shortage of capital. Second, confidence in the kye is secured through close personal relationships. Although the word *kye* means "contract," there is no written agreement involved. Kyes operate on trust. Strong, informal, and moralistic social relations among members dictate that each individual behave in an honorable way. Finally, the kye is based on the spirit of mutual cooperation. If it is successful, friendship and solidarity among its members are strengthened.

Kye loans range in size from $10,000 to $30,000 or more. In one case, an estimated $10 million kye has allowed a group of Korean immigrants to purchase houses, restaurants, and small grocery stores in the San Francisco Bay Area (*Time* 25 July 1988, 62). The average size of kyes described by the Chicago respondents was 16 members, but this number can vary greatly. A kye organized purely for economic purposes tends to be large. However, it should be small enough to ensure the confidence of its members and maintain friendly relationships among them. Thus, kyes consist primarily of friends, family members, or church members among whom personal trust is guaranteed.

Money brought from Korea also contributes to the capitalization of business, but it is less important than the other types of resources. About 18 percent of the Chicago respondents and 26 percent of the L.A. respondents capitalized their current businesses with such money. Some immigrants had gone to Vietnam, Saudi Arabia, Brazil, Argentina, or West Germany before they arrived in the United States, and they brought money from these countries instead of from Korea. Among the L.A. respondents, money from Korea accounted for 18 percent of total start-up capital. This finding runs contrary to the general public's belief that Korean immigrants bring huge amounts of capital to the United States for business investment.

Money brought from Korea has had a limited role in immigrant business formation for two reasons. First, there has been a legal limit set by the Korean government on the amount of money an emigrant can take out of the country. Until recently, the limit was set so low that a Korean could not have brought a substantial amount of money to the United States. In 1981, the limit was $3,000 per adult and $1,000 per child under 14 years of age (Bank of Korea 1981, 395). It increased to $20,000 for the head of the family in 1984 and to $50,000 for the head of the family and $10,000 for each family member in 1986 (Korea Exchange Bank 1987, 283–85). Although some Koreans smuggled huge amounts of money into the United States and invested it in their businesses, this has not been the case for the majority of immigrants. For instance, 70 percent of the L.A. respondents brought with them less than $10,000 upon immigration.

Second, money brought from Korea could not be devoted wholly to business purposes because of housing and living expenses. Recently, the Korean government adopted a liberal policy on foreign currency regulations and permitted up to $500,000 per emigrating family. The upper limit of investment capital was also raised from $300,000 to $500,000 per family. In other words, when a family of four emigrates for investment abroad, it can take out as much as $1 million. Thus, some recent Korean immigrants have brought huge amounts of capital from Korea to invest in large-scale businesses shortly after their arrival in the United States. Despite the growing importance of such imported capital, personal savings and loans from kin and friends are still the primary sources of capital for the majority of Korean immigrants.

As already noted, one of the key reasons for Korean immigrants' proliferation in small business is their effective utilization of class, family, and ethnic resources. Because of their middle-class backgrounds, Korean immigrants often have class resources, such as money brought from Korea, college education, and interpersonal management skills. Kinship and nonkinship social support networks also provide them with family and ethnic resources. As the immigrants establish business credit, they begin to have greater access to loans from formal financial institutions, such as banks and the SBA, and to use these sources of capital to expand their businesses. The rapid growth of Korean American banks in the 1980s has made it easier for immigrants to obtain bank loans when they have difficulty obtaining them from American banks. As table 3.15 shows, the use of such loans was limited among Koreans in the initial stage of business development, but these resources were more extensively used and sought after by those in the later stages.

This happens because as one's business expands, his or her need for resources from outside narrow kinship and friendship networks grows. Financial resources, information, and business advice obtained from kin, friends, and coethnics on the basis of trust or personal ties become either insufficient or inappropriate for the growing business. Moreover, an entrepreneur's enhanced business credit status allows him or her to tap resources from mainstream financial institutions. Thus, although class, family, and ethnic resources are equally important for business formation and management, their relative significance changes over the course of business development (Yoon 1991a). In the same vein, the significance

Table 3.15. Respondents' Changing Sources of Capital (Percentages)

Source	First Business	Current Business	Future Loan
Money brought from Korea	30.8	25.6	0.0
Personal savings in the United States	60.4	61.5	0.0
Loans from kin	13.2	19.5	31.5
Loans from friends	13.2	10.8	20.3
Loans from American banks	9.9	11.8	24.4
Loans from Korean American banks	9.9	17.4	36.0
Loans from Small Business Administration	1.1	8.2	12.2
Kyes	6.6	7.2	9.6
Partnerships	1.1	2.1	2.0
Others	4.4	6.2	3.0
Total			
Percentage	151.0	170.0	139.0
Number of respondents	91	195	197

Note: This table lists the percentages of respondents who cited each source as one of three most important sources of start-up capital for the first and current businesses or for future business loans. The total percentages are over 100 because most repondents utilized more than one financial resource.

of class and ethnicity—the two principal axes of human association—changes as immigrant entrepreneurship becomes larger and more formal and as immigrant entrepreneurs try to go beyond the ethnic economy to tap a wider pool of customers and employees. More systematic discussion of the relationship between class and ethnicity in immigrant entrepreneurship is presented in the conclusion of this chapter.

Business Management

Vertical Integration in Business

Koreans have achieved strong vertical integration in several lines of business. Such integration is defined here as an interdependence among coethnic producers, suppliers, and retailers. For example, 63 percent of the Chicago respondents and 71 percent of the L.A. respondents had one or more Korean suppliers. Retailers in black areas have much stronger integration with Korean suppliers than their Koreatown counterparts do. In Chicago, 82 percent of the respondents in black areas but only 46 percent of those in Koreatown had Korean suppliers. Conversely, only 18 percent of the respondents in black areas but 44 percent of those in Koreatown had non-Korean suppliers. In Los Angeles, too, 78 percent of the respondents in South Central had Korean suppliers, as compared with 63 percent of their Koreatown counterparts. Those in South Central, however, depended as heavily on non-Korean as on Korean suppliers. Twenty-one percent of them had Jewish suppliers, 52 percent had other white suppliers, and 23 percent had other Asian suppliers.

In Chicago's black areas, Korean retailers who depend most heavily on Korean suppliers are concentrated in a few select lines of business in which the suppliers also concentrate. As already noted, these businesses sell such items as clothes, footwear, wigs, handbags and luggage, jewelry and accessories, and other general merchandise items, all of which are manufactured in Asian countries (South Korea, Hong Kong, Taiwan, and mainland China) and imported and distributed by Korean suppliers. Korean retailers in Koreatown depend less heavily on Korean suppliers because of their greater diversity of business types and more frequent transactions with non-Korean suppliers. Retailers in South Central depend as heavily on non-Korean as on Korean suppliers because their businesses are equally diverse.

The vertical integration of retailers and suppliers is one of the strong points of Korean immigrant business. Retailers say that they receive some benefits or special services from Korean suppliers, including extended credit terms, lower prices, and easy access to information. Since these suppliers dominate certain trades, Korean retailers can get early information about which items have recently arrived and which ones are "hot." Those who feel uncomfortable dealing with American suppliers because of language and cultural barriers can deal freely and comfortably with Korean suppliers. The bond of ethnicity helps them build trust and exchange favors, elements missing in their relations with non-Korean business owners.[20]

In recent years, however, this vertical integration has been slowly deteriorating as increasing numbers of importers and retailers have changed their supply sources from South Korea to other Asian countries, such as Hong Kong, Taiwan, and the People's Republic of China. The rising wages of South Korean workers are to blame for the declining popularity of Korean-made products in immigrant businesses. Although such products are said to be of better quality than those made in Taiwan and mainland China, they cannot compete with the latter in price. It remains to be seen how such changes in the product distribution channel will affect the extent of vertical integration among Korean business owners.

In 1991, there were 115 Korean importers and wholesalers in Chicago (*KTC* 1991). A majority of them were concentrated on the North Side of Chicago along Clark Street, Lawrence Avenue, and Lincoln Avenue. Their major clientele, however, consists of Korean retailers in black and Latino areas in Chicago's South and West Sides. Thus, the success of Korean wholesalers is strongly dependent on the performance of Korean retailers in minority areas.

The interdependence of Korean wholesalers and retailers is similar to the concept of the food chain in ecology. Retailers in minority areas are heavily dependent on the economic condition of blacks and Latinos. Those in Koreatown are, in turn, affected by the business sales of those in minority areas, who along with their family members are the major customers of the Korean retail stores in Koreatown. Sluggish sales in minority areas therefore mean reductions in spending in Koreatown. Likewise, Korean wholesalers are affected by the sales of retailers in minority areas: during economic recessions, they have difficulty collecting delayed payments for their supplies from these store owners. Thus, the deteriorating economic conditions of blacks and Latinos hurt first Korean retailers in minority areas, then Korean retailers in Koreatown, and finally Korean wholesalers.

Horizontal integration, however, is not as strong as vertical integration in Korean immigrant business. Severe intraethnic competition is the norm rather than the exception. Eighty percent of the Chicago respondents and 63 percent of the L.A. respondents named Koreans as their primary business competitors. Because of this competition, veteran Korean business owners often advise would-be and novice owners to watch out for Koreans, not for whites or Jews, in order to survive in the merciless business world.

Such intraethnic competition results from the concentration of Koreans in certain business types and from their heavy dependence on a limited pool of customers. Vertical integration, described earlier as one of the strong points of Korean immigrant business, ironically contributes to this form of competition by facilitating the concentration of Koreans in already saturated markets. For this reason, Korean business owners in black areas experience intraethnic competition more severely than their counterparts in Koreatown. Eighty-seven percent of the respondents in Chicago's black areas pointed to Koreans as their primary business competitors, compared to 71 percent of their Koreatown counterparts.

Vertical integration appears to be possible because suppliers and retailers have complementary interests and benefit equally from participation in ethnic business. Suppliers can find outlets for their products, and retailers can obtain a reliable supply of goods at a lower price. But Korean retailers tend to see little mutual interest in assisting one another; rather, they regard one another as competitors with conflicting interests, threatening their survival in business. There have been numerous attempts among Korean business owners in Chicago and Los Angeles to stop the suicidal price wars and to agree upon prices and business hours, but such agreements break down as soon as one person breaches them and others immediately follow suit. Business associations and other community organizations have not been successful in reprimanding these rule breakers, especially when they are not members of the associations.

Size of Korean Businesses

Korean businesses are generally small with respect to initial capital, annual gross sales, store rent and space, and number of paid employees. Half the Chicago respondents and 44 percent of the L.A. respondents started their first businesses with less than $40,000. Only 13 percent of those in Chicago and 20 percent of those in Los Angeles started with $100,000 or more. Since opening their first businesses, the respondents had accumulated savings and business credit and invested additional start-up capital in order to start their current businesses. As a result, the percentage of the L.A. respondents who started their current businesses with less than $40,000 dropped to 33, whereas the percentage of those who invested more than $100,000 increased to 39. If this trend continues in the future, Korean businesses will no longer be typical mom-and-pop stores.

In terms of annual gross sales, 62 percent of the Chicago respondents in 1988 and 68 percent of the L.A. respondents in 1994 handled less than $500,000 per year.[21] However, 8 percent in Chicago and 21 percent in Los Angeles managed to handle more than $1 million. This indicates first that there is wide variation in the scale of Korean businesses and second that the business scale is much larger in Los Angeles than in Chicago. The larger population of Korean Americans in Los Angeles (72,970 in 1990) than in Chicago (13,863 in 1990) seems to allow large firms there to take advantage of economies of scale (U.S. Bureau of the Census 1992, 466–67).

Reflecting such wide ranges of scale, the net income from business (income remaining after paying taxes, wages for employees, insurance, store rents, and other business-related expenses) was also widely spread across income categories. For instance, 12 percent of the L.A. respondents earned less than $10,000 in 1987, 42 percent earned less than $40,000, and 19 percent earned between $40,000 and $60,000, which may be regarded as the average income for a middle-class family. Still, as much as 21 percent of them earned more than $100,000 as annual net income. Thus, small business is a disguised form of unemployment and poverty for some, a fortune for some, and a decent livelihood for the majority in between.

Building ownership, store rent, and store space are other useful measures of the size of Korean businesses. In one sense, they can be more reliable measures than gross and net income because some business owners, fearing that the Internal Revenue Service might investigate them for tax evasion, do not wish to reveal income totals. As a matter of fact, not a single respondent refused to answer my questions about building ownership and store rent and space, whereas 4 percent and 7 percent of the L.A. respondents did not answer the questions about annual gross sales and net income, respectively.

Nineteen percent of the L.A. respondents owned the building in which their store was located, and the remaining 91 percent rented stores from landlords of different races. There was little difference in terms of building ownership between the respondents in Koreatown and those in South Central. The overall average monthly store rent was $2,579; about 60 percent paid less than $2,000. The average was higher in Koreatown ($3,055) than in South Central ($2,026) despite the larger store space (including both floor and outer space) of businesses in South Central (5,072 square feet) compared to those in Koreatown (3,120 square feet). This indicates that land values and competition for space are higher in Koreatown because of the heavy concentration of Korean businesses in a small territory.

The ethnicity of landlords, like that of suppliers, is an interesting variable that illuminates the structure of ethnic hierarchies in immigrant and ethnic entrepreneurship. Among the 159 respondents in Los Angeles who rented their stores, 38 percent had Korean landlords, 30 percent had Jewish landlords, and 12 percent had non-Jewish white landlords (see table 3.16). These ratios differed sharply between the two locations studied, however. In Koreatown, Koreans were the most dominant landlord class, accounting for 55 percent of the total, followed by Jews

Table 3.16. Ethnicity of Los Angeles Respondents' Landlords (Percentages)

Ethnicity	Total	Koreatown	South Central
Korean	38.4	55.4	19.7
Jewish	30.2	24.1	36.8
Other white	11.9	8.4	15.8
Asian (non-Korean)	8.8	6.0	11.8
Latino	2.5	1.2	3.9
Black	5.0	0.0	10.5
Other	3.1	4.8	1.3
Total number	159	83	76

(24 percent) and other whites (8 percent). In South Central, by contrast, Jews accounted for 37 percent of the total, followed by Koreans (20 percent), non-Jewish whites (16 percent), and blacks (11 percent). As explained earlier, many former Jewish store owners in South Central became landlords after selling their businesses to incoming Korean immigrants during the late 1960s and early 1970s. This interethnic succession of businesses explains the high percentage of Jewish landlords among Korean store owners in South Central.

The relationship between Jewish landlords and Korean tenants, like that between Jewish suppliers and Korean retailers (which applied to 24 percent of the L.A. respondents), is a racially hierarchical one in which Jews are on top of Koreans. Disputes over frequent rent hikes are quite common. For instance, 150 Korean clothes wholesalers who rent their stores from Jewish landlords in the L.A. garment district held a series of demonstrations in February 1995, demanding that their landlords reduce store rents up to 30 percent (Hwang 1995c). More than 90 percent of the 500 Korean stores in the garment district, which is commonly called the "Jobber Market" by Koreans, participated in the demonstration by closing their stores (Hwang 1995a). The tenants protested that despite prolonged economic recessions in Southern California, the landlords had increased store rents by 5 or 7 percent annually, and some of them had even demanded $100,000 premiums from the tenants when they renewed their contracts.[22] They also claimed that because of costly store rents, their hard work was enriching only the landlords. The Korean tenants' demonstration was, however, unsuccessful. Only 40 out of 500 Korean tenants won concessions from their landlords to reduce rents by 20 percent for only nine months, and the majority of landlords were not even willing to negotiate (Hwang 1995b).

Table 3.17. Estimates of Coefficients of Independent Variables on Store Rent in Los Angeles

Variable	B	Beta	Sig. T
Space	0.19	0.62	0.000
Location	−1249.74	−0.27	0.000
Jewish landlord	834.71	0.17	0.037
Non-Jewiah white landlord	251.78	0.03	0.621
Korean landlord	−90.52	−0.02	0.821
R-square	69%		
Adjusted R-square	46%		
F	27.23		
Significance of F	0.00		
Number	156		

Note: Location is a dichotomous variable, with 0 representing Koreatown and 1 South Central. The comparison group for the variable of landlord ethnicity, which is not included in the equation, is Asian, black, or Latino.

The relationship between the amount of store rent charged and the ethnicity of the landlord is an interesting litmus test of the strength or relevance of ethnicity in immigrant and ethnic entrepreneurship. As discussed earlier in this chapter, Korean retailers benefit significantly from coethnic suppliers in the form of lower prices, extended credit terms, and earlier access to information and products. The findings of this study also tend to show that store rent is less expensive when the landlord is a Korean than when the landlord is either a Jewish or a non-Jewish white. For instance, the average monthly store rent was $2,171 under Korean landlords, $3,140 under Jewish landlords, and $2,598 under non-Jewish white landlords. However, the store rent under Korean landlords was more expensive than that under Asian, Latino, and black landlords, whose averages were $2,135, $987, and $1,184, respectively. When store space and the location of business (Koreatown vs. South Central) were controlled in a multiple regression analysis, as illustrated in table 3.17, store rent was still the most expensive when the landlord was a Jew, but there was no significant difference between the rent charged by Korean landlords and that charged by landlords of the other races.

Interviews with Korean store owners tend to point to the fact that Jews kept buildings in established and lucrative areas of Los Angeles (in the garment district or at the intersections of major streets) but sold second-rate buildings to Korean landlords. For instance, some successful Korean businessmen had purchased old warehouses and bankrupt department stores and then converted them into swap meets, where Korean retailers comprised the majority of the tenants. Unlike conventional swap meets, in which people trade used and antique items, these Korean businesses sell a variety of brand-new items imported from Asian countries to low-income minority customers. Immigrant business owners with little start-up capital can rent stores or booths in these buildings. For this reason, their rent is more directly determined by the locational value of their stores than by the ethnicity of their landlords, which simply correlates with the market value of the property. Moreover, unlike relations between Korean suppliers and retailers with complementary interests, relations between Korean landlords and tenants have been riddled with violations of contracts, disputes, demonstrations, and even lawsuits.

The number of paid employees is the final indicator of the size of Korean businesses. In the Chicago survey, 15 percent of the respondents hired no employees, and the average number of paid employees was 2.5. In the L.A. survey, 21 percent of the respondents operated their businesses without the help of employees, and the average number of employees was 4.9. In both surveys, those in Koreatown were more likely to have paid employees in their stores, and their average number of employees was larger than that of their counterparts in black areas. In Los Angeles, for instance, 15 percent of the respondents in Koreatown, as compared with 27 percent of those in South Central, had no employees in their store. This indicates that Korean businesses in South Central and other black areas are generally smaller than those in Koreatown.

When Korean business owners hire employees, they do so not only for economic reasons but also for purposes of social control and public relations. In Chicago, Korean business owners in black areas almost invariably hire one or more black employees. In fact, black employees accounted for 70 percent of the 240 paid employees of Korean stores in such areas. Business owners quickly recognized the advantages of having black employees: they protect the stores and the owners from criminal attacks by blacks, they sometimes mediate between Korean owners and black customers in disputes, and they demonstrate that Korean stores contribute to the local economy. In the midst of growing black hostility toward Korean businesses, hiring blacks is a tactic Koreans use to improve public relations.[23] For instance, Jeff Pritchett, a 32-year-old black employee in a Korean-owned grocery store, acts as teacher, mediator, and peacekeeper between owners and customers. He says:

It's like I'm a translator. I'm a middleman. I don't control the neighborhood, but I try to make things go as easy as they can between Mr.
Lee [the store owner] and the neighborhood. (Sokolove 1994)

In the inner city, Korean merchants often find they are able to form
bonds and trusting relationships with the neighborhood's elders, who
respect their work ethic. But finding a common ground with teenagers
is difficult. Jeff Pritchett's role is to ease the tense relations between pro-
vocative black teenagers and his Korean boss. He says:

The kids tease him. They say: "Why don't you go back to school and
learn to speak English? You're allowed in this country; why can't you
speak the language?" I'll step between them, try to change the subject.
I know he finds it hurtful, but in order to keep face he laughs it off.
(Sokolove 1994)

Despite the roles black employees play as guardians, mediators, and
translators, Korean business owners still complain about them. They are
often regarded as lazy and unreliable in their work habits; absenteeism
and high turnover are common problems, as is shoplifting by such employees and their friends. Despite these costs, however, the benefits and
the social pressure to hire black employees are usually overwhelming.

In sharp contrast, in South Central Los Angeles, significantly more
Latino than black employees are hired in Korean stores. According to
the L.A. survey, Latino employees accounted for 54 percent of the 409
employees of these stores, while black employees accounted for only 16
percent. Korean employers strongly prefer Latino employees to black
ones, in part because of their perception that Latinos are more hardworking, obedient, and reliable and less expensive to hire than blacks.
(See chapter 4 for a more detailed discussion of these issues.)

Such impressions of Latinos and blacks as workers cannot, however,
explain why more Latinos are hired in South Central Los Angeles than
on the West and South Sides of Chicago. Korean employers in Chicago
share the attitudes of their counterparts in Los Angeles toward Latino
and black workers. The more important reason for the discrepancy in
numbers is thought to be the greater availability of Latino workers in
South Central Los Angeles than on the West and South Sides of Chicago. These are predominantly black residential areas, and thus the pool
of Latino employees is small. For this reason, Korean employers in these
areas have to depend on black employees even when they prefer to hire

the supposedly more docile and less expensive Latino employees. In contrast, South Central is a racially mixed—or, more correctly speaking, an increasingly Latino—residential area, where in 1990 blacks and Latinos accounted for 25 percent and 46 percent of the population, respectively (Navarro 1993).[24] Thus, it is easier for Korean employers in South Central than for their Chicago counterparts to find Latino workers.

As black and Latino employees are valued for their public relations with their coethnic customers, so are Korean employees in Koreatown. Almost 70 percent of the respondents in Chicago's Koreatown had one or more Korean employees. The average number of such employees was 1.8, whereas the corresponding number in black areas was only 0.7.

But Korean employees are generally preferred over non-Koreans because they are regarded as more trustworthy and hardworking and easier to communicate with. Their shared language and culture is one reason for their intimate relationship with their Korean employers. In some cases, Korean employees have personal relationships with their employers, and these ties command both parties to behave in an honorable manner. Trust based on common ethnicity is another important reason for Korean employers' preference of Korean employees, particularly in managerial and accounting positions. Mr. Yu, who moved from Chicago to Baltimore to take over an import-wholesale business from a relative, explains why he decided to hire Korean employees in his firm:

> When I first arrived in 1991, all ten employees were whites. Because I had worked in a predominantly Korean workplace in Chicago, I thought it would be a challenging opportunity for me to work in this all-white environment. But one day I caught the white manager stealing $75,000 from the bank account. What shocked me more was that no one informed me about this. All white employees tended to think that was none of their business. When I was troubled by this matter, one of the elders of my church advised me to mix white employees with Koreans. . . . Based on my experience, I can say that Korean employees are more responsible and trustworthy than white employees. White employees do only what they are told to do, whereas Korean employees care more about the firm and go extra miles. One problem is, though, they sometimes do not distinguish between the owner and the employees. (Personal interview)

The attitudes Korean employees have about their employment in Korean stores are thus another reason why they are considered more trustworthy and hardworking than non-Korean employees. They tend to regard such employment as a training opportunity for starting their own businesses in the future. This economic interest motivates them to work hard and to maintain a good relationship with their Korean bosses. In contrast, non-Korean employees are less attached to such employment because they are often assigned to low-paid, humble positions and they do not share the common culture or ascriptive ties that bind Korean employees and bosses together.

Unpaid Family Labor

Korean immigrant businesses rely heavily on family labor. About 60 percent of the respondents in Chicago and Los Angeles had family members who work in their stores at least part-time. Unpaid family members, if available, provided between 40 and 45 hours of labor per week. Spouses—especially wives—are the most important source of family labor. About 50 percent of the Chicago respondents and 70 percent of the L.A. respondents had spouses who worked in their stores. In comparison to labor from the spouse, help from children, brothers and/or sisters, and parents is minimal. In the Chicago survey, only 11 percent of the respondents had children, 8 percent had brothers and/or sisters, and 3 percent had parents who worked in their stores. Extended kin and friends may provide financial support or advice for preparing government documents or tax reports at the stage of business formation, but they seldom involve themselves in the daily operation of such businesses. Thus, husband and wife comprise the basic unit of the Korean immigrant business.

Unpaid family labor is beneficial to small businesses in several ways: it reduces the cost of wages, thereby reducing the operating costs; it reduces shoplifting by other paid employees; and it provides a more trustworthy and reliable labor force than paid employees. Because of low wages and the lack of opportunity for promotion in many Korean businesses, it is really difficult for them to maintain reliable employees. (As a matter of fact, it makes little sense to talk about promotion in Korean businesses that have only three or five employees.) Absenteeism and high turnover are chronic problems. One Korean athletic footwear store owner in Chicago's Englewood Shopping Mall complains about his newly hired black employee:

> I paid his lunch, did a shopping for him, and babysat his daughter,
> then the very next day he did not show up. You see [while pointing to

boxes on the pigeonholelike compartments on the wall], these are all shoes. It took me some time to teach him how to find shoes of the right style and right size. If I hire a new employee, I have to start all over again. (Personal interview)

In such an emergency, family members are vital temporary substitutes to keep a business operating.

Family workers perform a wide range of tasks in stores, including sales, tending the cash register, and stock management. In the most common situation, the wife controls the cash register and the husband takes care of running of the store. This reduces shoplifting and prevents cash from disappearing, a real hazard for small businesses (Min and Jaret 1984, 424).[25]

Furthermore, long business hours—a competitive advantage of Korean businesses over non-Korean ones—are possible only with the support of unpaid family members. Like all small businesses, Korean businesses are labor-intensive. Owners put in extremely long working hours and usually work even on Sundays and holidays. The average working hours per week were 62 for the Chicago respondents and 63 for the L.A. respondents. Half of those in Los Angeles worked more than 60 hours per week, and one extremely hardworking respondent worked 126 hours per week, which means that he had to work throughout the week for 18 hours a day and had only six hours left for sleeping, eating, and other basic survival activities. This is a manifestation of either incredible human will or insanity. Although such an extreme case is rare, many Korean business owners, faced with low profit margins and severe competition from fellow Koreans, must work very long hours and use unpaid family labor to keep their businesses afloat.

Business Problems

Korean business owners are most troubled by the following problems: (1) a shortage of financial resources; (2) competition with other Korean business owners; (3) employee management; and (4) security of business and person.

Shortage of financial resources. Korean business owners generally experience chronic problems of cash flow. Since they start with small amounts of capital, they cannot hold enough money in reserve to survive business fluctuations. A high business failure rate results. The throat-cutting price wars among Korean business owners result partially from the desperate need for cash.

Difficulty in getting bank loans is another cause of financial shortfall among business owners. Although their insufficient business credit is the primary obstacle to getting such loans, tax fraud is another contributing factor. A significant number of Korean business owners underreport their annual gross sales to the Internal Revenue Service (IRS) in order to evade taxes. For this reason, store owners often pay their employees' wages in cash, and wholesalers and retailers cooperate to underreport or even hide business transactions between the two parties (*KTC* 19 January 1985).

Tax evasion is quite a prevalent practice among small business owners of all racial and national backgrounds, and in fact it is one of the major attractions of being a small business owner. For instance, self-employed workers in Seoul and other Korean cities are reported to earn more than four times the income they report to the Office of National Tax Administration. In some types of businesses, real income from self-employment is estimated to be twenty-five times greater than reported income (Jung et al. 1991, 416). Because it is more difficult to assess such income than wage or salary income, wealthy self-employed workers tend to contribute less to the national health insurance than they ought to. This problem is regarded the major obstacle to achieving equity among different classes through national health insurance.

In the United States, it is estimated that the underground economy, in which goods and services change hands clandestinely, conceals 9.4 percent of the GNP from taxation, and the Internal Revenue Service estimated that it lost between $60 and $70 billion in taxes on unreported earned income in 1988 (Light and Rosenstein 1995, 14). Because small businesses predominate in the underground economy, the majority of unreported income is likely to come from self-employed workers. Regarding tactics of tax evasion in New York's Chinatown, Peter Kwong (1987, 79) says:

> Restaurants, garment factories, and other businesses operate regu-
> larly with two sets of books in order to underreport income and evade
> taxes; the workers and suppliers are paid off the books. Workers are
> not expected to report their full income either, so they supposedly
> benefit also.

The same arrangement exists among Korean suppliers, retailers, and employees. To accommodate this clandestine collaboration, employees are often paid cash on a weekly or biweekly basis, and customers are asked to pay with cash instead of personal checks or credit cards in order to get discounts.

While such an illegal business practice may bring immediate economic gains to short-sighted Korean business owners, it eventually hurts them when they try to expand their businesses. In fear of investigation by the IRS, they seldom deposit cash in excess of $10,000 in bank accounts. Instead, they keep their cash in secret places, either at home or in their stores. This not only makes them easy victims of robbery and even murder, it also makes it difficult for them to get bank loans because of their insufficient credit history.

Intraethnic business competition. As mentioned earlier in this chapter, the majority of Korean business owners (80 percent of the Chicago respondents and 63 percent of the L.A. respondents) regard fellow Korean business owners as their primary competitors. Competition from white business owners is not perceived to be serious: only 8 percent of those in Chicago and 13 percent of those in Los Angeles regarded Jews and other whites as their primary business competitors. In addition, none of the Chicago respondents and only one respondent in Los Angeles identified blacks as major competitors. Black business owners themselves acknowledge that they cannot compete with Korean retailers who have connections with Korean suppliers and manufacturers. One black woman who is part-owner of a woman's apparel store on Chicago's South Halsted Street says, "Korean wholesalers deliver promptly but give discounts to Korean merchants, who are able to order in larger quantities than blacks" (Longworth 1992).

In Chicago, the sense of threat from fellow Koreans is much stronger among business owners in black areas than among those in Koreatown, primarily because of the limited range of business lines in the former. Despite the growing Korean–black tensions in these areas in recent years, Koreans have not responded on a collective basis because of the competition and the lack of trust among them. They seldom exchange information or ideas of any kind with one another out of fear that in the process, information about the prices and new items in their stores may leak out to nearby Korean store owners and be used against them.

Competition among Koreans lowers the price of merchandise and consequently their profit margins, threatening the survival of their businesses. As Kim and Hurh (1985) point out, such competition is not limited to the sale of their merchandise; it extends to the cost of store rent as well. The following example illustrates how this can happen:

> Mr. Park's apparel store in the "Madison–Pulaski Shopping District" has expanded substantially in the past several years. He decided to purchase the building of his store from a Jewish landlord. Mr. Park and his landlord made an oral agreement about the purchase and the key money was set at $10,000. But just before he was about to sign the contract, his landlord canceled the agreement without any explanation. Several days later, Mr. Park heard that another Korean outbid him with $20,000 for the key money. (*KTC* 4 August 1981)

Intraethnic competition is a structural problem rather than a personality problem of Koreans. Their concentration in limited markets is one contributing factor to the high level of such competition. The limited power of ethnic organizations in business matters is another. It is true that Koreans in the same line of business have established trade associations in order to moderate competition and protect their common interests against white landlords, white suppliers, and government agencies. However, if we examine closely the size of these associations in terms of membership, budget, and participation of members in association meetings, we see that their influence in business conflicts is often limited. Only 18 percent of the Chicago respondents and 24 percent of the L.A. respondents were members of any kind of trade association, including local chambers of commerce.

Ordinary Korean immigrants' attitudes toward self-proclaimed community leaders and organizations are also indifferent at best and cynical at worst. Key positions in community organizations such as the Korean Association of Chicago and the Korean Federation of Los Angeles have been monopolized by successful business owners. This entrepreneurial class is seen by ordinary Koreans to be interested only in social recognition and status in the Korean community, which are not available to them in mainstream society (Choi 1996, 524). Thus, their pledges of community service have been met with apathy, distrust, and contempt. Very few Koreans bother paying their membership dues to local associations or registering to vote in their presidential elections. Previous elections usually had only one candidate, excluding the possibility of free competition.[26] If there were multiple candidates, the election often involved bribes, threats, violations of rules, and lawsuits.

It is true that trade associations and other organizations have contributed to the Korean community by sponsoring Korean culture nights, parades, Korean language schools, scholarships, and so forth, but ordinary Koreans do not feel any tangible benefits of their existence. In other words, the majority of Korean immigrants are either indifferent to or excluded from participation in community organizations. One newspaper article critically diagnoses the leadership problem in such organizations as follows:

> For many years, Koreatown was dominated by an older set of leaders—leaders who squabbled among themselves, whose limited English skills isolated them from mainstream society and who had little savvy at coping with American political institutions. The Korean Federation is a case in point. It was the major civic group in Koreatown, with a sympathetic orientation toward the government in Seoul, until factional rivalry among its first-generation leadership destroyed its ability to serve the local community. Recent elections for the group's presidency have been fiercely contested, with large amounts of campaign money spent and charges of vote-buying raised. Lawsuits by the losers leave it unclear who was the last legitimate leader of the federation. The group, by all accounts, was dysfunctional during several years of crisis over black–Korean ethnic conflict. Its leaders were nowhere in sight during and after the recent rioting. In early June, the federation announced that it was disbanding. It handed the mantle of community leadership to the younger generation of bilingual Korean-Americans represented by such organizations as the Korean American Coalition, which has emphasized voter registration and political activism.(Schoenberger 1992)

Although membership in civic and community organizations is generally low among Korean business owners, membership in informal social clubs is high. About a third of the respondents in Chicago and Los Angeles regularly attended school alumni or alumnae associations. An even higher percentage (more than 60 percent of the respondents in Chicago and Los Angeles) attended church on a regular basis, making the Christian church the most important organization among Korean immigrants. But the function of the church is primarily religious and has very limited influence on business matters. Because of the prevalence of Presbyterianism in the community, many Korean churches are conservative in outlook and focus on spiritual matters and fellowship within their congregations with little involvement in the larger Korean community.[27] Even when the minister and elders of a church try to resolve disputes between members over business matters, they have very little social control because any dissatisfied member can withdraw from the church at any time.

The difficulty in reducing intraethnic competition also lies partially in the absence of long-term commitment among many Korean business owners to their current businesses in minority areas. Many of the respondents regarded their businesses as means of accumulating capital and experience so they could establish larger, more prestigious, and safer businesses outside these areas. Motivations for changing the type and/ or location of their business were much stronger among those in black areas than among those in Koreatown, primarily because of the high crime rates. Fifty-five percent of the respondents in Chicago's black areas planned such a change, compared to only 28 percent of their counterparts in Koreatown. Similarly, 38 percent of the respondents in South Central—as opposed to 22 percent of those in L.A.'s Koreatown—planned such a change. Frequent turnover of ownership among Koreans is thus the rule rather than the exception in black areas, making it difficult to build an intimate relationship and a consensus among business owners. As long as Koreans have these attitudes, it will be difficult for them to take collective action to reduce intraethnic competition.

In my criticism of the leaders, organizations, and members of the Korean community, I may exaggerate internal divisions and conflicts while downplaying ethnic solidarity and cooperation among Koreans. But in order to have a balanced view of the community, we need to look at its negative as well as its positive aspects. Previous research on the Korean community and Korean immigrant entrepreneurship has tended to overemphasize ethnic solidarity and cooperation while neglecting internal class divisions and conflicts. If we continue to focus on ethnic solidarity and to portray the Korean community as a unified and self-governing body, we grossly oversimplify a complex reality.

Employee management. The relationship between Korean employers and employees is still paternalistic from the American standpoint. Koreans are often hired through personal relationships with employers or through recommendations by other Koreans. About 60 percent of the

Chicago respondents had personal relationships with the Korean employees in their stores, who were nephews, nieces, or children of their own or of their parents' friends. Once hired through these informal channels, employees are expected to work hard and often to work overtime or even on holidays. In return, they usually take managerial positions in stores and are better paid than non-Korean employees. Employers cannot exploit fellow Korean employees for their selfish interests because by so doing they may destroy personal relationships or may earn a bad reputation in the Korean community. Thus, both employers and employees are governed by social norms as well as economic interests.

But many signs of the weakening of such paternalistic relationships have now been observed. For example, employers often complain about the high turnover rate of Korean employees, who leave the stores as soon as they find better employment opportunities elsewhere. Out of the 108 respondents in the L.A. survey who reported that they did not prefer Korean to non-Korean employees, sixty-three (58 percent) cited such turnover rates as one of the three important reasons for their preference. Moreover, Korean employees are disliked because they are perceived to demand special favors or to fail to distinguish between public and private matters. In this sense, Korean employers' attitudes reflect a double standard: Korean employees are regarded as more trustworthy and reliable than non-Korean employees, but they are simultaneously thought to expect and demand more than what they are entitled to.[28] Few employers think they are obliged to help their long-time Korean employees establish their own stores, a practice said to be prevalent among the early Chinese and Japanese entrepreneurs (Light 1972).[29]

As noted earlier, Korean employers often complain of the frequent absenteeism and shoplifting of black employees. In expectation of their unpredictable work habits, Korean employers assign them only marginal positions. If both Korean and black employees are hired in the store, the former are usually put in charge of the managerial and accounting tasks and are paid higher wages than the latter. Black employees often respond by shoplifting or by not working hard, which they justify as compensation for their low wages. Chapter 4 discusses in greater detail Korean employers' attitudes toward black and Latino employees.

Business security. Business security problems endanger not only businesses but also the physical safety of their owners and workers (Kim and Hurh 1985). Such problems are more critical in black areas than in Koreatown. While 24 percent of the respondents in Chicago's black areas reported security as one of their four primary business problems, only 3 percent of their Koreatown counterparts did so. Similarly, 36 percent of the respondents in South Central, as opposed to 9 percent of their Koreatown counterparts, cited security concerns and the lack of police protection as one of their three most serious business problems.

The fear of crime among Korean store owners is based on frequent incidents of shoplifting, burglary, armed robbery, and other serious crimes against them and their employees. About 60 percent of the respondents in South Central Los Angeles reported that they suffered from shoplifting, burglary, arson, looting, and damages to equipment during the 1992–93 period, as did about 42 percent of the respondents in Koreatown.

A Korean American reporter for the *Los Angeles Times*, who has covered various walks of life in the Korean community, illustrates the level of crime committed against helpless business owners in South Central:

> Just seven months after Joong Kun Lee reopened Cat's Liquor, which was ransacked but not burned during the Los Angeles riots, his South Central business was closed again Monday as his stunned family tried to cope with his death at the hands of a gun-wielding killer or killers. Lee, 55, was shot to death Saturday morning as he was opening his store at 7213 S. Broadway, the victim of an apparent robbery, said Los Angeles Police Detective Sal Labarbera. . . . Lee's killing, coming within weeks of three other shooting deaths of Korean-American business operators in Los Angeles County by robbers, has rekindled a fear of violent crime among Korean-American merchants. . . . This year alone, more than two dozen Korean Americans have been killed or wounded during robberies in Southern California, according to statistics compiled by Korean-American community agencies and the Korean language media. . . . After Lee was shot during a robbery five years ago, Kim [a friend of Lee] urged him to move out of South Central. "The last time I talked with him [a day before he was killed] he told me he would like to get out of the liquor store business," Kim said. "He was a good Christian—a deacon at the church. His conscience bothered him to sell alcoholic beverages." (Kang 1993)

Korean store owners have become particularly easy targets of black gangs because they are known to carry cash with them and not report minor incidents to police. Despite frequent robberies and even the murder of some Koreans, they try not to make an issue of such problems for fear of provoking anti-Korean business protests by blacks. In self-defense, many Korean store owners arm themselves, and this often results in accidents involving firearms. The Soon Ja Du and Tae Sam Park cases in Los Angeles that escalated the level of tension between Koreans and blacks before the destructive civil unrest in 1992 started after the shooting deaths of black customers. These cases, which are discussed in the next chapter, involved two store owners who had been repeatedly robbed and had to protect themselves in the absence of proper police protection.

Such fear of crime, whether real or imagined, makes relations between Korean store owners and black customers abrasive and frustrating. After several Koreans were murdered in South Central, increasing numbers of store owners there installed bulletproof glass as a divide between them and their customers. All the business transactions are now made through a small revolving door underneath the wall of glass. This transparent wall gives them a sense of security, but it nonetheless makes their relations with customers purely economical, impersonal, and full of distrust.

For some business owners in South Central, isolation and loneliness are the nature of their businesses and their lives, which are not easily separated. They open their stores at 7:00 A.M. and close at 11:00 or 12:00 P.M. They eat breakfast, lunch, and dinner at the store. During my interview with an old Korean liquor store owner in Inglewood, California, I saw a cup of Korean instant noodle sitting next to the cash register. It was his lunch, and it was already too cold and sodden to eat. He could not finish eating because his customers continued to come. He was listening to Korean news and songs aired by a Korean-language radio station in Los Angeles while he served his customers. Pages of Korean-language newspapers were scattered on his desk, and a Korean O.B. Beer calendar picturing a seductive Korean female model hung on the wall. All these scenes reminded me of a typical street-corner store in a low-income neighborhood of Seoul. This several-square-foot space, walled in by bulletproof glass, was his place of work and life. He created this space and literally lived there. Since Paul Siu wrote his dissertation about Chinese laundrymen in Chicago in 1953, little has changed in regard to the social isolation of Asian immigrant shopkeepers in urban America.[30]

Because of their belief that black customers are frequently shoplifting, Korean store owners and their Korean employees watch more closely when black customers walk into the store and often follow them down the aisles. Although store owners may justify these actions as an effective way to curtail shoplifting, which threatens the survival of their fragile businesses, they nonetheless make many black customers feel that they are treated as criminals. The alleged shoplifting and consequent disputes have become one of the major sources of Korean–black conflict.

Summary and Discussion

Korean immigrants came to the United States seeking better economic opportunities but instead found limited opportunities in their new land. Because of the language barrier and their less transferable education and occupational skills, many of them could not find jobs in the white-collar occupations for which they had been trained. Disadvantaged but still strongly motivated to achieve upward economic mobility, many of them became self-employed business owners. Typically, after experiencing downward occupational mobility upon their arrival, these immigrants, by virtue of hard work and thrift, could save a small amount of seed capital to start their own businesses. They often supplemented this capital with loans from kin and friends or lump sums of money from rotating credit associations. With this money in hand, they established their businesses either in minority areas or in the Korean community, where the barriers to entry were low with respect to capital, business skills, and English-speaking ability. As a result, self-employment became the livelihood of many Korean immigrants in large cities where Koreans and blacks were concentrated.

   Class, family, and ethnicity are three important variables in explaining the formation and evolution of Korean immigrant entrepreneurship. The middle-class background of many immigrants has been the driving force behind their entrepreneurial aspirations. They have responded to bleak employment prospects in the American secondary labor market by turning to self-employment in business, whereas other minority groups have not. They have tried vigorously to reestablish their premigration social and economic status in American society. After recognizing that small business is the only and best way for them to "make it," they have mobilized all the resources at their disposal to start their own businesses. Their willingness to work harder and longer than others and to risk their safety in crime-ridden minority neighborhoods all derive from their class background and their strong motivations for upward economic mobility.

Class is also an important resource in business formation. A high percentage of Korean immigrants have received a college education. Although most did not major in business-related fields such as business administration or accounting, their advanced education equipped them with general managerial skills and a strong work ethic, preparing them to learn and adapt quickly to a new entrepreneurial role in a new environment. Moreover, a significant percentage of Korean business owners had experience with business management in South Korea, either by having engaged in business themselves or by having had parents who operated businesses. Thus, for many of them, small business was not an unfamiliar occupation. Such early exposure might have prepared them to view small business as a viable option to limited employment opportunity in the general labor market.

Similarly, family (both nuclear and extended) represents an important resource for Korean immigrant entrepreneurs. A high rate of marriage, a large average household size, and access to unpaid family labor are important assets for the survival and success of their businesses. Moreover, kinship-centered social support networks, which are the products of chain migration, provide would-be and novice business owners with financial assistance, business advice and information, training opportunities, and favorable terms of business acquisition. These kinds of aid are originally intended to help only close family members and relatives, but they quickly reach other Koreans. New business opportunities and innovations discovered by a few Koreans are shared first with immediate family members and relatives, then with individuals who are distantly related and finally with virtually all Koreans in the community by virtue of the complex web of social networks. In this manner, small business becomes an ethnic matter rather than merely an individual initiative.

Ethnicity builds trust and solidarity among business owners, employees, and customers and oils interpersonal relations that are prone to conflict. For instance, Korean retailers receive benefits and special services from Korean wholesalers in the form of extended credit terms, lower prices, easy access to information, and comfortable communication. These wholesalers, in turn, find outlets for products that are not in big demand among non-Korean retailers. Korean employers find Korean employees more trustworthy and dedicated than non-Korean employees and expect them to work harder and longer than is minimally necessary. In return, such employees occupy supervisory and managerial positions in the firms, whereas their non-Korean counterparts usually occupy service and labor jobs. Korean customers who are still unfamiliar with American lifestyles, bureaucratic procedures, and formal institutions patronize these businesses, which deliver more personal and culturally sensitive services than non-Korean businesses can.

In the face of external political and economic crises that threaten the survival of Korean businesses—such as the black boycott of two Korean grocery stores in New York City in 1990–91 and the Los Angeles civil unrest in April 1992—Korean Americans from all classes and walks of life united and supported financially and emotionally the targeted Korean businesses.

As such, class, family, and ethnicity are the foundations of Korean immigrant entrepreneurship. However, the three factors are not always in harmonious relationship. As Korean businesses become larger and more diversified with regard to the ethnic composition of the workforce, customer base, and sources of financial and technical resources, they inevitably encounter problems associated with formal and bureaucratic organizations. For instance, Korean employers—whose actions, like those of all capitalists, are governed by the principle of profit maximization—seek to replace Korean workers with more docile and less expensive Mexican workers. According to the L.A. survey, Mexicans and other Latinos represent 43 percent of a total of 960 employees in Korean firms, and this percentage is even higher in South Central, where they constitute 54 percent of the total employees. As the workforce becomes larger and more heterogeneous, formal and bureaucratic relations gradually replace informal and personal relations between previously benevolent employers and loyal employees.

At this stage, Korean business owners seek financial and informational resources not only in the Korean community but also in mainstream society, since their improved credit status and expanded social networks allow them to do so. Their dependence on family and ethnic resources for strictly economic purposes is then likely to decline because these resources become either insufficient or inappropriate for growing businesses.

As the Korean ethnic economy continues to expand, capital is increasingly concentrated in the hands of the few, who build more spacious and stylish stores to attract customers away from smaller independent stores. For example, as a result of merciless price wars, extended sales, free gifts, and advertising in the Korean mass media by "super" grocery stores such as California Market (the first large-scale grocery market in Koreatown, opened in September 1987), Plaza Market, Han Kook Super Market, and Hannam Chain, small mom-and-pop Korean grocery stores have virtually disappeared in Koreatown of Los Angeles.[31] To make matters even worse, the giant grocery stores have been establishing branch stores in such suburbs as Northridge, Van Nuys, Gardena, and Hacienda, places where Koreans are concentrated and small grocery stores used to find small but protected markets. These developments have led to the formation of the Southern California Korea Grocery Association, an association of twenty-seven such stores outside the city of Los Angeles that seeks to protect their interests against those of big businesses.[32] Members of the association have held demonstrations in front of the big grocery stores, demanding that they stop unethical business practices and allow small stores to coexist.

Similarly, relations between Korean landlords and vendors in approximately 130 indoor swap meets in Los Angeles, Orange, and San Bernardino Counties have been tainted by charges of violations of initial contracts, frequent rent hikes, harassment, and lawsuits. The vendors claim that the Korean landlords promised them low or discounted rent and exclusive rights on certain items when the swap meets first opened in 1985. As the businesses prospered, however, they asked for a higher premium (or key money or goodwill money) for continuations of leases, raised rental rates, and allowed unauthorized vendors to sell popular items. The vendors also claim that some landlords do not return the premium, which is usually worth two months' rent, when they close their stalls. Such unethical business practices led to the formation of the Southern California Swap Meet Vendors' Association in 1991 to protect their interests against those of the powerful Korean landlords. The association, which had 2,000 members in 1993, hired lawyers to successfully file lawsuits against several landlords who had violated their contracts.

These class divisions in the Korean American community ironically became more visible in the aftermath of the 1992 L.A. unrest, which on one level enhanced Korean ethnic solidarity. The losses and plight of the Korean victims prompted a national donation campaign among Koreans in the United States and South Korea. As of April 22, 1993, $4.5 million had been collected in South Korea and $5.1 million in the United States for a total of nearly $10 million.

But conflicts arose over the issues of how to use the relief fund and who was eligible for it. At first, business owners (but not swap meet vendors, who were included only when they protested vigorously) received the relief money whereas dislocated Korean employees did not, even though they were victims of the unrest just as their bosses were. Some workers were able to receive $500 from the Koreatown Emergency Relief Fund Distribution Committee in May 1992. This money was supposed to be distributed to Korean business owners as well as their Korean and non-Korean employees (H. Lee 1994, 6–7).

But Korean workers were excluded from the relief fund without an explanation when the Koreatown Emergency Task Force, which later became the Korean American Relief Fund (KARF), decided to distribute the money to business owners only. Angered by KARF's unfair policy, Kyung Kuen Lee and forty-nine other displaced workers, with the help of the Los Angeles-based Korean Immigrant Workers Advocates (KIWA), formed the Employee Victims Association (EVA) in July 1992 to claim an equal share of relief funds. They argued that the funds were donated by concerned fellow Koreans to help victims meet the costs of such everyday necessities as water, telephone, mortgage, and car payments and that all victims, whether employers or employees, should receive the relief money.

The Koreatown Emergency Task Force (KETF), composed of business owners, then received additional funds from South Korea and distributed $2,500 apiece to the affected business owners. KETF again excluded the workers by requiring each recipient to show a business registration as well as a police report documenting his or her loss. After KETF exhausted all its funds, it passed the baton to KARF, which provided $2,500 apiece to those business owners who were unable to receive money from KETF. After facing protest from the workers, KARF proposed a compromise payment of $1,500 pér worker, but this amount was scheduled to be distributed in three stages instead of all at once. This dragged-out process has made the workers tired and caused some of them to give up the fight.

At this time, Kyung Kuen Lee, who had worked as a laborer for sixteen years in the United States and served as the vice-president of EVA, again sought help from KIWA, a community service organization that provides job-related legal assistance and services to Korean immigrant workers. In early July 1993, KIWA began the 4.29 (April 29) Displaced Workers Justice Campaign with a community-wide petition drive calling for fair distribution of relief funds (KIWA 1994, 3). In December 1993, KIWA took the campaign to the Los Angeles County Small Claims Court. To date, four displaced workers have each won a judgment of $3,000. Meanwhile, KIWA and the workers have continued to embarrass the KARF board members by attending their monthly meetings and demanding that fair distribution of the relief fund be put on their agenda.

Contrary to the wishes of the workers, however, KARF has decided to use the remaining relief fund of $1.7 million to build a Korean community center for the long-term interest of the community rather than satisfying the short-term needs of the victims. This decision is viewed by the workers as a deviation from the original purpose of the relief fund and a self-interested ploy by the KARF board members, most of whom are business owners and could make real estate profits from the building of the community center. The workers, who are excluded from the decision-making process in the Korean American community, feel that KARF was unsympathetic toward them in the first place and represents only the interests of business owners (KIWA 1994, 11).

This series of events illustrates that Korean immigrant entrepreneurs and the Korean American community are not as internally harmonious or as united as they appear to the general public but rather increasingly stratified and competitive. This does not mean, however, that class has completely replaced ethnicity as the organizing principle of Korean immigrant entrepreneurship. Rather, at least at the community level, Koreans will continue to organize themselves on the basis of ethnicity and to transcend class differences when external forces challenge their businesses and their community on racial and ethnic grounds. But internally, Korean immigrant entrepreneurs and the Korean community will be further stratified and divided as people of different classes compete for their interests and rights. The growing immigration of Koreans from lower- and working-class backgrounds in the past decades is expected to make the community more heterogeneous and stratified along class lines. It will therefore increasingly resemble the larger American society, in which a person's identity and group loyalty are determined by his or her race, ethnicity, and class.

Thus, the concentration of Koreans in small businesses does not always enhance their intraethnic solidarity. In fact, it can increase internal conflicts and class divisions among them. In other words, two contradictory forces—the centripetal force at the ethnic-group level and the centrifugal force at the individual level—seem to operate simultaneously in the Korean community. This insight can help answer the puzzling question of how Koreans maintain a high level of ethnic solidarity while they suffer from severe intraethnic conflict. Koreans become ethnic and united in relation to non-Koreans. In this sense, Korean ethnicity is a relative rather than an absolute concept, existing only in relation to other ethnicities in a pluralist society such as the United States. It is also a situational and defensive contrivance that arises, grows, and weakens in response to external threats that affect Koreans from all walks of life. Such threats tend to strengthen group ties and create a sense of solidarity that might not otherwise exist. Conflicts with other ethnic groups also unify in-group members and postpone internal conflicts, at least temporarily.

When the external threats are gone, however, the internal conflicts resume, and interpersonal relations among Koreans are governed principally by individual interests and characteristics. Social networks are formed largely around immediate family members, relatives, friends, church members, school alumni, neighbors, and people from the same region. These are the kinds of people with whom individual Koreans feel trust and exchange favors. Those outside these primary relations are at first mistrusted and ill-treated, even when they are Koreans. But trust and mutual support gradually expand and spill over to other Koreans adjacent to the initial circle.

Thus, Korean ethnicity is not a static and absolute concept that commands unconditional loyalty to the Korean community. Rather, it is an evolutionary concept that is initially segmented along the lines of primary relations and then expands outward through a complex web of social networks.[33] Through this process, a sense of personal accountability, acceptance, and social control can be gained in a wider circle of Koreans, and this sense is the building block of progressively more inclusive Korean ethnic solidarity.

FOUR

WHO IS MY NEIGHBOR?: KOREAN–BLACK
RELATIONS IN CHICAGO, LOS ANGELES,
AND NEW YORK CITY

Race relations in the United States have undergone significant changes during the last three decades. In the 1960s, blacks claimed and to a large extent gained full citizenship and meaningful participation in American society through the Civil Rights movement. But the zeal for civil rights and equal opportunity for all met a major setback during the 1970s, as whites feared that their social and economic positions would be undermined by liberal reforms such as affirmative action programs and expressed resentment about black advancements (Wilson 1978; Rieder 1985; Omi and Winant 1986). In the 1980s, racial conflicts intensified between members of different minority groups, particularly when recent immigrants from Latin America and Asia established their residences and businesses in the black neighborhoods of central cities and began to compete for social and economic resources. Tensions between blacks and Latinos in Miami (Oliver and Johnson 1984; Johnson and Oliver 1989; Portes and Stepick 1993) and between blacks and Koreans in Los Angeles, New York City, Chicago, and Philadelphia (Cheng and Espiritu 1989; Chang 1990; Yoon 1991b; Jo 1992; H. Lee 1993; Min 1993; 1996) are good examples of such deteriorating relations between minority groups.

This new pattern represents a departure from traditional race relations, in which minorities were usually the victims of racial oppression by majorities. By fighting among themselves for social and economic resources and thereby breeding misunderstanding, prejudice, and hatred, members of different minority groups have failed to acknowledge their shared disadvantages and to collectively advance their common interests. Only majority group members seem to gain from this conflict, which has divided minorities and hindered them from challenging the status quo that created racial inequality in the first place.

Despite the growing importance of relations between minority groups in the United States, theories and empirical research on this subject are still scarce. Conventional theories have limitations in explaining such relations because they tend to focus on majority–minority relations, particularly those between whites and blacks. Accordingly, the need for systematic theory and research on minority–minority relations is greater than ever, especially in light of the recent tensions.

Conflicts between Koreans and blacks in major American inner cities are one example of these tensions. Such conflicts surfaced in the early 1980s and attracted particular attention among the public and the mass media after the destructive urban unrest in Los Angeles in April 1992. Despite this mass media coverage, however, only a few scholarly studies have been conducted on the subject, mostly by Korean American scholars (Cheng and Espiritu 1989; Yoon 1991b; Chang 1990; 1993; Jo 1992; H. Lee 1993; Ong, Park, and Tong 1994; Abelmann and Lie 1995; Min 1996). Strangely, black American scholars have not shown serious interest in the subject to date and have produced very little scholarly research on it. Thus, it is difficult at this point to compare how Korean and black American scholars view and interpret Korean–black relations.

In addition to the relative dearth of scholarly research, current approaches to the Korean–black conflict seem to suffer from a lack of scientific methodology and analytical interpretation. Many existing studies are based on indirect or conjectural evidence collected from the media or other popular portrayals of minorities. While some scholars have employed sample surveys to study racial tensions between Koreans and blacks, findings from these surveys usually have limited generality because of their small sample size, use of nonprobability sampling methods, and geographical specificity.

Moreover, current approaches to the subject remain at the descriptive level. They discuss a series of plausible causes of the racial conflict (including economic competition, prejudice, differences in political power, and biased media coverage) but fail to analyze the relative significance of each factor and the relationships among them. What is generally missing in the existing literature is a systematic discussion of the interdependence of social, economic, political, and psychological processes that affect Korean–black relations. For a complete understanding of this conflict, we need to know first how macrostructural changes in the American economy and society have affected the socioeconomic conditions of blacks and their neighborhoods. Second, we need to know how these changing conditions have affected the attitudes of blacks toward immigrants in general and Koreans in particular. Third, we need to know how psychological and situational factors, such as attitudes and the nature of the ghetto economy, have strained relations between black customers and Korean store owners. Finally, we need to know how political factors such as black nationalism have mobilized individual blacks' grievances toward individual Korean merchants into collective actions such as boycotts of Korean stores.

To these ends, I have examined the racial conflict between Koreans and blacks in Chicago, Los Angeles, and New York City as a case study of contemporary relations between minority groups. In this chapter, I first survey major incidents of this conflict in the three cities to demonstrate how it starts, progresses, and subsides. These incidents include the yearlong black boycotts of two Korean grocery stores in Brooklyn, New York; similar but short-lived black boycotts of Korean stores on the South Side of Chicago; and the Soon Ja Du and Tae Sam Park cases in South Central Los Angeles. Second, I introduce a theoretical framework that explains the Korean–black conflict from a broad racial/ethnic stratification system perspective. This involves examining four dimensions of the conflict (structural, psychological, situational, and political) with a special focus on how they interdependently affect Korean–black relations. Third, I compare the different perceptions Korean store owners have of blacks and Latinos as employees, customers, and neighbors. By so doing, I try to assess the roles of race, class, and nativity in Korean-black–Latino relations and to explain why Korean businesses experience greater rejection and hostility from the black community than from the Latino community. Finally, I summarize my research findings and make some policy recommendations for improving Korean–black relations.

Major Events of the Korean–Black Conflict

Black Boycotts in Chicago

The Korean–black conflict surfaced in the early 1980s in major U.S. cities, but its tension level remained low until the late 1980s and early 1990s. In Chicago, there have been several black boycotts of Korean businesses on the West and South Sides, but they have been relatively small-scale and short-lived. In August 1981, the opening of a Korean-owned apparel store (Jo Kim Fashions) between two existing black-owned apparel stores provoked a demonstration and boycott. The site of the dispute was the 47th Street shopping district, which is located at the intersection of 47th Street and Roosevelt Road. Since Kang Sok Chung had opened his sports store there in 1971, the number of Korean stores in the area had grown to twenty, accounting for 40 percent of a total of fifty stores in 1981. Blacks and Jews owned twenty and ten stores, respectively (*KTC* 7 August 1981).

This dispute began when Hyo Kwan Kim (Jo Kim is his American name) started a grand-opening sale on August 1. As a result of the new competition, the daily sales at Flora & Lorenna's next door dropped in half. The female black store owner went to the 47th Street black merchants' association, of which she was the treasurer, and asked for its assistance, claiming that the opening of Jo Kim Fashions was not simply her problem but a threat to all black businesses (*KTC* 10 August 1981). The association held an emergency meeting on August 6 and claimed that Koreans and Jews were making 90 percent of the profits earned in the business district. It proposed to drive out all Korean and Jewish stores so as to allow black-owned businesses to make money from black customers. The boycott started on August 10, with participants calling Koreans "Korean Jews" and urging black customers not to buy from them. On the following day, the targeted Jo Kim Fashions was set on fire by a boycotter; the fire spread to Flora & Lorenna's and to an adjacent Korean wig shop (*KTC* 11 August 1981). As the situation deteriorated, the Korean merchants' association in the area held a meeting during which Kang Sok Chung, its president, claimed that the boycott was not simply Jo Kim's personal problem but a serious threat to all Korean businesses and that the simplest solution to the crisis would be Jo Kim's withdrawal from the area. The dispute subsided after Jo Kim decided to leave. He was compensated for his business losses by his fellow Korean merchants (*KTC* 20 August 1981).

Another black boycott of Korean businesses took place in the 87th Street shopping district in September 1988. This one was organized by Karen Summerfield, president of a local black organization (Black Women for Economic Parity), who had tried unsuccessfully to launch a boycott against Korean stores in 1984 after forming an alliance with the Muslims. She ran for city alderman in 1988 and was accused of taking advantage of anti-Korean sentiments among black residents in her political campaign. The boycott was joined by the black chamber of commerce in the neighborhood in the expectation of collecting annual membership fees from Korean business owners (*KTC* 2 September 1988).

A more threatening boycott was organized by a local chamber of commerce in Roseland (RBDC) in cooperation with a black city alderman, Robert Shaw, in June 1990. The site of the boycott was the Roseland shopping district located on the South Side, where more than forty Korean businesses accounted for 60 percent of all stores. The RBDC and Alderman Shaw accused Korean business owners of not paying annual membership fees to the RBDC, being discourteous to black customers, and not exchanging or giving refunds for defective merchandise. The first boycott took place on June 30, with the boycotters demanding that Korean merchants hire more black employees, use black banks, and be more respectful to black customers.

As the boycott intensified, Korean merchants held an emergency meeting and selected a spokesperson to unify their channels of communication with the protesters. When the mass media turned the blacks' demands into headlines and viewed the boycott not as a personal dispute but as a racial conflict, the Korean community sent a strong message to them that this was a serious mistake and started collecting facts and data that could challenge the boycotters' claims. For instance, on July 11, the task force announced that the Korean merchants in Roseland employed 176 blacks, who accounted for more than two-thirds of all their employees (*KTLA* 23 March 1991). The boycott ended peacefully when Korean business owners raised $6,300 for unpaid membership fees along with $3,000 for local charity organizations and promised to exchange or give refunds for defective merchandise in the future (*KTC* 13 July 1990). Although Alderman Shaw applauded these efforts, he was still unhappy that it was Koreans or Arabs, rather than blacks, who were running the stores. But he added that the real culprits were not the immigrants but lenders who wouldn't help blacks buy into the American dream:

> "I'm talking about black banks, too," said Mr. Shaw. "They loan somebody $80,000 in a blink to buy a new Mercedes, but they won't come up with $18,000 to make a down payment on a food market." Unless black small business is encouraged, said Mr. Shaw, the situation will never change. "Except," he said, "that 20 years from now, it will be some other immigrant running the store where black people will still be spending their money" (Schmidt 1990).

Since the 1990 boycott in Roseland, there have been a number of black boycotts and violent acts against Korean businesses, but all of them have been small-scale and short-lived. For example, on June 14, 1992, Korean businesses in Chicago's black neighborhoods were victimized by the so-called Chicago Bulls' riots immediately after the Bulls' NBA Championship victory. According to the *Korea Times of Chicago* (16 June 1992), thirty Korean stores were looted and set on fire. However, these were not viewed as racially motivated riots against Korean stores because the looters indiscriminately hit white, black, and Arab stores as well. The extent of the property damages and losses was also modest, partly because of the close cooperation between the Chicago Police Department and the Korean Merchants' Association beforehand. After seven Korean stores were looted and set on fire in the aftermath of the Bulls' 1991 victory, the Korean community of Chicago had formed an emergency task force to coordinate prevention efforts in 1992. Moreover, various Korean community organizations—such as the Korean Association of Chicago, the Korean Community Service Center, the Korean Merchants' Association on the South Side, the Church Federation–Chicago, and the Korean Consulate—had established the Korean–Black Goodwill Association to mediate between the two communities and to do charity work in the black community (such as delivering food baskets on Thanksgiving Day or offering scholarships to high school students) (*KTC* 18 June 1992).

The Korean merchants on the South Side went further to diffuse tensions with their black customers. They hired a black woman to go undercover in their stores and hang out among the racks and shelves. She was not looking for shoplifters but watching how the merchants interacted with their black customers. She reprimanded the merchants who were rude to blacks and offered them advice on how to deal with these customers. This was all part of the Korean merchants' efforts to help themselves become more sensitive to their customers and more involved in the inner-city communities where their shops were located (*KTLAEE* 31 March 1993). Partly because of such efforts, and partly because of the weak influence of militant political organizations in Chicago's black community, Korean–black relations there have been kept under control without the long-term boycotts and riots that have taken place in New York City and Los Angeles.

The Black Boycott in Brooklyn, New York

On January 18, 1990, an incident that occurred at a Korean-owned fruit and vegetable store in the Flatbush section of Brooklyn, New York, prompted a yearlong black boycott of two Korean grocery stores. This boycott is remembered as the most controversial and agonizing event in the history of Korean–black relations in urban America.[1]

Family Red Apple Inc. and Church Fruits, Inc., were two Korean-owned stores on Church Avenue in Flatbush, which is a predominantly black neighborhood occupied mostly by new immigrants, such as those from Haiti. At the time of the incident, Koreans owned more than one-third of the small businesses in the neighborhood, whereas blacks owned only one-fifth of them, mainly beauty salons and cosmetics stores (Lee 1993). This apparent disparity in business ownership ultimately provided the boycott leaders and participants with the opportunity to justify their actions as means for achieving economic self-determination in their own community.

The incident occurred when Ghislain Felissaint, a Haitian woman who lived nearby, was shopping for a few items at the Red Apple store. She says that when she was leaving the store, she was asked to open her bag by the manager, who suspected that she was shoplifting. When she refused, he pushed her back and slapped her three times. One Korean employee joined him and punched her on her left side, and after another Korean employee kicked her under her stomach, she fell to the floor. Heon Cheol Lee (1993, 76), who interviewed the store manager and the Korean employees, described the situation as follows:

> The police were then called to the store. The customer told the police that she could not get up because of a pain in her back. Soon an ambulance arrived, a stretcher was brought in, and she was carried out and taken to the hospital. According to Captain Vincent Kennedy, Executive Officer at the 70th Precinct, who visited Caledonian Hospital where she was "awaiting treatment for apparent superficial injuries," she had just "a scratch on her cheek" and was released the same day.

After the incident, Felissaint claimed that she had frequent headaches, developed serious gynecological problems, and was unable to work for five months. Her attorney further alleged that the Korean female cashier at the Red Apple pronounced such racial slurs as "I'm tired of black people" in English. The police officer who interviewed Felissaint, however, stated that the cashier spoke little or no English (U.S. Commission on Civil Rights 1992, 35).

The cashier, who was the manager's wife, and the store's Korean employees gave quite a different account of the incident. According to the cashier, Felissaint paid only two dollars for plantains and limes that cost three and did not respond to the cashier's request to pay the full price. Because the line of customers behind Felissaint was long and the customers were complaining about the delay, the cashier returned the money to Felissaint and put her bag behind the counter. Felissaint then threw a handful of hot peppers in the cashier's face, and the cashier threw them back at her. Felissaint threw the peppers again and spat in the cashier's face. At that moment, the store manager, who was the owner's brother, intervened, holding Felissaint by the shoulders and asking her what the problem was. According to the Korean employees, she became so upset and furious that she couldn't control herself. She swung her arms around while stepping backward, screamed something like "Mother fuckin' Chinese, Korean, no more business, go back to your country," and laid herself down on the floor (Lee 1993, 76).

A crowd quickly grew outside the store after police cars and an ambulance arrived and Felissaint was carried out on a stretcher. Within an hour, approximately forty persons assembled in front of the store to protest the assault upon the Haitian woman by the Korean employees. They became violent and threw rocks, bottles, and pieces of fruit at the store. In fear of his safety and that of his employees, the manager closed the store earlier than usual and asked his employees to get in his truck for a ride home or to nearby subway stations. One employee missed the truck and ran to Church Fruits across the street for protection (77–78). While crossing the street, he was hit by bottles, rocks, and pieces of fruit thrown by the angry demonstrators (U.S. Commission on Civil Rights 1992, 35). Because he took refuge there, the demonstrators thought that Church Fruits was related to the Red Apple and targeted it for boycott as well. As a matter of fact, the owners of the two stores had been competitors and had not visited or talked to each other before the incident. The owner of Church Fruits later deplored the fact that his store was targeted for black boycotts simply because he was a Korean.

On the next day, a demonstration by about twenty-five persons was held in front of the two stores. The demonstrators demanded that they be closed permanently, claiming that a woman had been beaten and was now in a coma. The following day, approximately 150 protesters began to demonstrate in front of the stores, and by the afternoon the crowd had grown to about 400 persons. In this manner, the boycott gathered momentum (U.S. Commission on Civil Rights 1992, 36).

At the beginning, the protesters were local residents who reacted spontaneously to what they perceived to be an assault upon a black woman. But within a week, the December 12th Movement, a New York-based black nationalist organization led by Sonny Carson, took control of the boycott. Carson is a militant black activist who had intervened in all five major black boycotts of Korean stores in New York City in the previous ten years (Min 1996, ch. 6). Although some local residents subsequently participated in the demonstrations, those who led the boycott were outsiders who were brought into the area by the boycott leaders. These were native blacks, not immigrant groups such as the Haitians, who later complained that their community had been taken over and used by outsiders. From the outset, in fact, a large number of Haitian community organizations denounced the boycott because they thought it was counterproductive to the interests of black people (Lee 1993, 197).

As the politically motivated black outsiders took control of the boycott, its stated goals expanded from punishing several Korean business owners who were mistreating and disrespecting black customers to giving control of the black community to blacks. On January 27, a black power street rally was organized by the December 12th Movement, and the boycott leaders urged participants to "boycott all Korean stores and not to shop with people who don't like us" (Lee 1993, 74). On February 3, the African People's Farmers Market opened at the corner of East 18th Street and Church Avenue, and on March 3, it reopened at St. Paul's off Church Avenue to demonstrate blacks' ability to do business. On May 20, a Black Unity Rally in the Spirit of Malcolm X and Jean-Jacques Dessalines was held at Church Avenue and St. Paul's Place. The slogans chanted during the rally included "Whose streets? Our streets," "Black power," "What time is it? Black nation time," and "Too black, too strong," clearly indicating that the ultimate goal of the boycott was to achieve black self-determination economically and politically by eliminating nonblack businesses from the community (188).

The prolonged boycott caused tremendous financial damage to the targeted stores. Red Apple's average weekly sales of $25,000 declined to a few dollars within a couple of days. Because of harassment by the gatekeeper demonstrators, most customers were scared away from the stores. When the news of the black boycott spread in the New York Korean community, other grocers felt that they could be the next targets and decided to help the affected grocers withstand the boycott. During the summer of 1990, more than $12,000 came in monthly to the stores as donations through the Korean Produce Association of New York and a group of Korean fruit and vegetable store owners. Ordinary Koreans in

New York, other U.S. cities, South Korea, and Japan also participated in this donation campaign, which raised a total of $150,000. They also wrote letters to the two grocers, encouraging them in their battle against what they viewed as black racism against a powerless minority group. The owner of the Red Apple, Bong Jae Jang, even toured several U.S. cities to speak at meetings. In this manner, his struggle against the black boycott became a symbol of courage among Koreans, and if he had sold or closed his store, it would have affected all of them. As the boycott became a showdown between Koreans and blacks, winning the battle became more important than resolving the conflict (Lee 1993, 177).

After a year, the fervor of the boycotters waned. On January 30, 1991, Bong Ok Jang, the manager of the Red Apple, who had been arrested and charged with third-degree assault, was acquitted of all charges by a grand jury in Brooklyn. The number of picketers declined further. The boycott finally came to an end when Bong Jae Jang sold his store to another Korean merchant on May 30 and opened a new business in the Bay Ridge area of Brooklyn with an SBA loan of $500,000, which was arranged by the Department of Justice.

Black Boycotts in South Central Los Angeles

In 1991, two incidents that involved the murder of black customers by Korean grocers in South Central Los Angeles exacerbated simmering racial tensions between the Korean and black communities. The first incident, which took place in March, was the murder of 15-year-old Latasha Harlins by Soon Ja Du, a 49-year-old Korean grocer who operated the Empire Market in South Central. Three months later, Lee Arthur Mitchell, a 42-year-old former boxer, was shot to death by Tae Sam Park, a 46-year-old Korean grocer and owner of John's Market in South Central, during an alleged attempted robbery. The subsequent black boycotts and individual acts of violence against the two Korean stores paved the way for the massive destruction of Korean businesses during the L.A. civil unrest in 1992.

The Soon Ja Du case. On March 16, 1991, Latasha Harlins entered the Empire Market owned by Soon Ja Du and her husband, Hong Gi Du. She picked up a bottle of orange juice from the store's refrigerator and put it in her backpack. When she approached the counter, Du thought that she was going to steal the orange juice, so she grabbed Harlins's sweater and tried to pull the bottle from the backpack. The two women tussled, and Harlins punched Du in the face four times, knocking her down to the floor behind the counter. Du responded by throwing a stool at Harlins and grabbing a handgun from behind the counter. Harlins, who did not know that Du had a gun, placed the orange juice on the counter and turned to walk away. As she did so, she was shot in the back of the head by Du, who claimed that she was unconscious after the assault and accidentally pulled the trigger (Mydans 1991). The whole incident was videotaped by the store's security surveillance camera, and the brutal scene was repeatedly played on TV news programs.[2]

Although the jury ultimately convicted her of voluntary manslaughter, Du was initially charged with first-degree murder on March 19 (Hager 1992).[3] Understanding the significance of the incident, the Los Angeles Police Department immediately held a press conference and defined the incident as "a simple homicide" involving "a dispute" between a store owner and a customer, not "a racially motivated incident" (Moon 1991a). Representatives of both Korean and black organizations—such as the L.A. chapter of the NAACP, the Southern California Christian Leadership Conference, the Black–Korean Alliance, and the L.A. Korean Chamber of Commerce—and officials of the mayor's office and the L.A. County Human Relations Commission held an emergency meeting on March 19 and declared that "this incident is tragic, but it should not exacerbate the Korean–black conflict." The Korean Federation of Los Angeles also held an emergency meeting to discuss the incident and decided to send its representative to influential black organizations to express the community's wish for racial harmony and its condolences to the Harlins family (Cho 1991a).

Unlike New York City Mayor David Dinkins, who had been reluctant to intervene in the 1990–91 black boycott, Los Angeles Mayor Tom Bradley involved himself more actively in the reconciliation efforts of the Korean and black communities. On March 22, he stated that he did not want the killing of a black teenage girl to escalate tensions between the two communities, and he urged the establishment of cooperation among diverse ethnic and racial groups on the basis of mutual trust and respect. He highly praised the reconciliation efforts of the two communities and urged them to quickly establish countermeasures to all potential crises and problems. On that day, twenty leaders of the Black–Korean Alliance, the L.A. County Human Relations Commission, and the NAACP had a closed-door meeting at an office of the Southern California Christian Leadership Conference to discuss solutions that could minimize the tensions. In this meeting, they decided to hold a large-scale reconciliation session on April 2 in which 400 leaders of the two communities would participate. More important, they decided not to interpret the shooting incident from a racial perspective. In the meantime, the mayor's office announced that it was considering purchasing the Empire Market through a joint investment between Koreans and blacks if Du were not willing to keep it open (*KTLA* 24 March 1991).

Despite the swift response and early coalition efforts of the Korean and black communities, anti-Korean feelings and violence spread among blacks in South Central. On March 21, the *Los Angeles Sentinel*, the largest black newspaper in the city, reported that Latasha had been killed by a Korean grocer for a bottle of orange juice. The day before, four blacks had entered a Korean-owned liquor store (Jack's Bottle Bar & Jr. Liquor) in South Central, made racial slurs about "money-sucking Koreans" and "killer Koreans," hit the female store owner in the face, and then ran away. The assaulted store owner said that it became really difficult to do business after the shooting incident (*KTLA* 22 March 1991).

On March 21, the Brotherhood Crusade held a press conference in front of the Empire Market with 150 black residents and community activists and claimed that Du frequently made racial slurs against black customers and treated them as if they were thieves. Danny Bakewell, president of this group, urged black residents not to buy from Korean stores that treated black customers rudely and pledged to continue a boycott until the Empire Market closed. During the press conference, the participants shouted such slogans as "Send Koreans home," "Get rid of Koreans," "Stop murdering our young children," and "We want justice" (Moon 1991b; 1991c). One week later, the Brotherhood Crusade announced at another news conference that it would drive unkind and undesirable store owners out of black neighborhoods and start a fundraising project to enable blacks to own stores in their neighborhoods (Moon 1991d). As this proposal illustrates, the militant black organization was concerned about not only customer rights but also economic issues within the black community.

This demonstration spilled over onto other innocent Korean businesses in South Central. On March 22, about 100 blacks in Watts staged a violent protest in front of the Watts Market to express their anger over the killing of Latasha Harlins. The demonstration lasted for five hours, and some excited demonstrators threw bottles at the store and at Mr. Lee, its owner. The placards displayed during the demonstration read, "Don't spend money on Koreans who disrespect blacks," "Join if you are with us," "Darryl Gates stand up," and "It's time to join" (Moon 1991e). More than ten other incidents of black retaliation against Korean businesses occurred within a month after the killing of Latasha Harlins (*KTLA* 30 March 1991).

The Korean–black conflict reached a new stage on October 11, 1991, when L.A. Superior Court Judge Joyce Karlin sentenced Du to prison for voluntary manslaughter in the fatal shooting of Harlins. Karlin rejected the probation department's suggested sixteen-year sentence and instead ordered a ten-year suspended sentence with five years of probation, 400 hours of community service, and a $500 fine. She said that Du was subjected to a "violent attack" before she fatally shot Harlins and that the crime would not have occurred if the trigger of the gun had not been altered to make it fire more easily. Mentioning that Du had been living in a "state of terror" because her store had been robbed repeatedly prior to the shooting incident, Karlin stated that Du's action was inappropriate but understandable under the circumstances.[4] She granted Du probation on the grounds that Du did not have a criminal record and was not likely to kill again. Finally, she hoped that the tragedy would be used to further understanding and tolerance rather than revenge:

> Latasha's death should be remembered as a catalyst to force [blacks and Koreans] to confront an intolerable situation and to create solutions. This is not a time for rhetoric. It is not a time for revenge. It should be a time of healing (Wilkinson and Clifford 1991). . . . The parties involved in this case and anyone truly interested in what caused this case can make sure that something positive comes out of this tragedy. (Gibbs 1991)

Contrary to the judge's wish, this sentence added fuel to the fire of Korean–black relations. After it was announced, the 10-year-old sister of Latasha Harlins ran out of the court crying, and some blacks expressed their dissatisfaction with the sentence by shouting "Koreans, see you at South Central" and "Go back to Korea." One member of the Harlins family even shouted that he would drive all Korean businesses out of black neighborhoods (*KLTA* 17 November 1991). Gina Rae, representative of the Harlins family and head of the Latasha Harlins Justice Committee, claimed that the verdict was unfair and that she would protest it as long as she lived. The responses of black politicians were equally harsh. Danny Bakewell called the sentence a "travesty of justice in the absolute highest order." Los Angeles City Councilman Mark Ridley-Thomas called it "another assault on the quality of life and the dignity of African-Americans" (Katz and Clifford 1991). Joseph H. Duff, president of the L.A. chapter of the NAACP, thought it represented "a sign of institutional racism at work." Maxine Waters, a congresswoman representing the 29th District, which includes South Central Los Angeles, said that it implied that black lives are worth less than others and called for Judge Karlin's defeat in the next year's election (Perez-Pena 1991).

Although many Koreans were delighted with the outcome of the case, some were critical about the sentence and concerned about its impact on Korean–black relations. For instance, in an article published in the Readers' Column of the *Los Angeles Times* (25 December 1991), one member of the community made the following comment:

> As a Korean-American, I was stunned by the light sentence announced by Judge Karlin for the death of Latasha Harlins. The value of her life was not validated. This is no longer a Korean–African American problem. As an American citizen, I question our social values and justice system. Also since my immigrant parents have established some economic security here, I have the luxury to wonder what I can do personally to support and invest in the South Central community, a community where many Koreans earn their livelihoods.

Jerry Yu, executive director of the Korean American Coalition, cautioned the mass media that not all in the Korean community offered unconditional support for Du. He said, "We can relate to her as a Korean and we can pray for that she does not suffer, but, on the other hand, just because we are Korean, that doesn't mean we wanted her to get off. There has to be justice" (Katz and Clifford 1991). Angela Oh (1991), a Korean American lawyer and the undeclared spokesperson of the Korean community after the 1992 civil unrest in Los Angeles, thought that the sentence was too lenient for a person convicted of voluntary manslaughter. She cautioned both the black and Korean communities about the repercussions of the sentence:

> The anger of the African-American community is real and justified. [But] the greatest challenge facing that community is to resist seeking vengeance in the name of "justice." . . . The fear of Korean-American

immigrants is also real and justified. Within the past six years, more than a dozen merchants have been killed in their own shops. . . . Token political gestures, such as finding 100 jobs in Korean-owned shops for African-Americans, miss the point. The void in genuine leadership signals danger and self-destruction for both communities.

The mass media's reaction to Judge Karlin's verdict was generally negative. For instance, the *Los Angeles Times* conducted a random survey of 1,831 Los Angeles County Superior Court sentences in the summer of 1990 and found that only two of the 247 defendants sentenced for violent crimes received straight probation with no jail time. Both of these probations were granted in assault cases. In the one murder and ten manslaughter cases reviewed, no defendants received straight probation; ten were sentenced to prison and one to jail (Wilkinson and Clifford 1991).

While emotionally outraged by the sentence, leaders of the black community tried to channel this anger into a campaign to increase black political and economic strength in the community. On November 16, more than 300 activists gathered at the Bethel African Methodist Episcopal (AME) Church in South Central, and a number of the city's black leaders emphasized that the best response to the sentence was to elect more black representatives, develop more black-owned businesses, and devote more resources to action. Danny Bakewell, real estate developer turned community leader, told the gathering that he was seeking the support of thirty community groups willing to devote their resources one day a month to inflict "economic paralysis" on any merchant who dealt with blacks in bad faith. Archbishop George A. Stallings Jr. hoped that Harlins's death would raise the consciousness of the black community. He said, "It is time to wake up Los Angeles and take destiny into our own hands" (Katz and Chavez 1991).

While such leaders tried to channel their anger into constructive directions, other black residents were more direct in their protest. On the morning of November 26, some of them threw five Molotov cocktails into a Korean liquor store (Ace Liquor Store) in South Central. The store owner, Mr. Kwon, said that he had not had a dispute with residents in the three years since he had opened his business and that this act seemed to be committed by some blacks dissatisfied with Du's sentence (*KTLA* 27 November 1991).

Some retaliatory acts even spilled over to affect other innocent Asian Americans. On December 4, a 36-year-old woman of Japanese descent was pulled out of her car and beaten with baseball bats by two black gang members who mistook her for a Korean. One of them was arrested by an off-duty RTD policeman and tried for a hate crime. This incident prompted the Japanese American Citizens' League and other Asian American community organizations to hold a press conference at the Compton Municipal Court to discuss the threat to all Asian Americans. Although they had been and continue to be indifferent to the Korean–black conflict, this incident reminded them that they, too, could become victims of hate crimes because of mistaken identity (*KTLA* 20 December 1991).[5]

The black community's protest against Du's light sentence was directed at Judge Karlin as well as at the Korean community. Denise Harlins, an aunt of Latasha, pledged to lead an effort to recall Karlin in the next year's election and demanded a federal civil rights investigation of the killing (Hager 1992). Danny Bakewell organized a demonstration in front of the Compton Municipal Court where Judge Karlin worked. Five hundred blacks, including the mayor of Compton, attended the demonstration, criticizing Karlin's verdict and racism against blacks (S. Kim 1991b). Bakewell said that he planned to lead a protest in front of Karlin's home in Manhattan Beach to disrupt her activities and make her life miserable (Katz and Chavez 1991).

A bigger threat to Judge Karlin, however, came from her white superior. Los Angeles County District Attorney Ira Reiner announced on November 26 that he would ask the 2nd District Court of Appeal to overturn her decision and sentence Du to state prison. He argued that the sentence was more appropriate for someone convicted of involuntary than of voluntary manslaughter. He even pledged to use an unusual California law to bar Karlin from trying criminal cases. Although his move received some praise and support from the black community, he was accused by trial lawyers and judges of assaulting the independence of the judiciary. Attorney Charles E. Lloyd, who represented Du, denounced the appeal as an effort to pander to people's emotions. Many people suspected that Reiner's move was politically motivated: in 1991, he ran for California Attorney General but failed to advance past the Democratic primary. Facing a reelection campaign in 1992, Reiner took a hard line against plea bargaining and criticized judges who imposed anything less than maximum sentences on convicted criminals (Perez-Pena 1991).

To the disappointment of the district attorney and the black community, the state appeals court held 3 to 0 in April 1992 that Karlin had not exceeded her authority, noting that judges have broad discretion in sentencing (Hager 1992). In July 1992, the state supreme court refused to review a subsequent appeal by the district attorney. Another disappointment came to black activists who had tried to remove Karlin from the bench. Instead, she defeated three challengers and won reelection by a narrow margin in June 1992. The publicity of the Soon Ja Du case, although much of it was negative, helped her get more attention from voters than the other candidates. In addition, the black community's campaign to recall a white judge provoked a backlash from white voters and motivated them to give heavy support to Karlin. In contrast, the black community's protests against Karlin did not translate into action because of low voter registration and turnout in black neighborhoods (Stolberg and Muir 1992). The failure to remove Karlin from office raised again the problem of political apathy in the black community and prompted calls for more effective political mobilization.

The Tae Sam Park case. Almost three months after Latasha Harlins's death, Lee Arthur Mitchell was killed on June 4 by Tae Sam Park, owner of John's Market, during an attempted robbery. According to the police, Mitchell did not have money to pay for the beer that he was trying to purchase. He reached into his pocket, pulled out a gold chain, and asked Park's wife how much she would give him for the necklace. When she answered that she would not give him anything for this piece of jewelry, Mitchell reached into another pocket and pretended to point a pistol at her. He then ordered her to empty the cash register and went behind the counter. Park's wife began to scream. Park, who was taking a nap in a back room, heard the noise and came to the counter to discover a black man shouting "Hands up!" while apparently pointing a pistol concealed in his jacket at him. He pleaded with Mitchell not to shoot and walked to the cash register to give him the money. While he stood there, a gun wrapped in newspapers sitting next to the register caught his attention. He grabbed the gun, lowered himself below the counter, and shouted back at Mitchell to drop his weapon. Despite this warning, Mitchell rushed at Park, who shot him. Mitchell, who was a former boxer, still dashed ahead and knocked Park down. The two men wrestled for a while until Mitchell abruptly collapsed because of the gunshot wound in his chest. Park himself was injured in the battle, with three of his ribs broken. The police determined that he had acted in self-defense and said that it would not press charges against him (*KTLA* 6 June 1991; J. Kim 1991a).[6]

The black community, however, did not accept the police report. Robert Jackson, a longtime friend of Mitchell, argued that Park had killed his friend for 20 cents. According to Jackson, Mitchell and Park knew each other well because Mitchell lived in a neighborhood near Park's market. He also claimed that Park's use of the gun was an overreaction and a sign of disrespect for human life (Moon 1991f). Richard Allen, president of Urban Housing Consultants, Inc., and owner of the Hoover Street Gymnasium where Mitchell trained other boxers, said that he had known Mitchell for more than ten years and in that time he had always been a nice, level-headed gentleman. He added that unless Mitchell had another side to him, he could not have done the things that he was accused of doing (Mitchell 1991). The *Los Angeles Sentinel* commented on June 13 that it was incomprehensible why Park was released with no criminal charges despite the fact that he had shot Mitchell to death. The story added that the police report was not reliable because it was based on consultations with only Park, his wife, and a Korean employee, and the security surveillance camera in the store was not operating at the time of the murder.

Following the shooting incident, John's Market was subjected to a 110-day boycott from June 17 to October 3. The boycott was organized by Danny Bakewell and the Reverend Edgar Boyd of the Bethel AME Church. Reverend Boyd's church was located across the street from John's Market, and his congregation was said to have had bad feelings toward Park, who often called a towing company to remove their cars that were parked in front of the market.

During the boycott, which was initially expected to end in three months, Park had to endure tremendous financial and mental suffering. The boycotters harassed him and the customers who dared to cross the picket line. For instance, on August 3, a black female patron was insulted by several boycotters irritated by her shopping at Park's market. She engaged in a bitter argument with them and went home safely after the police arrived. In the afternoon of the same day, a black customer entered the store and threw down cans stacked on the shelves while yelling at Park for killing Mitchell (*KTLA* 6 August 1991). On August 17, arson occurred in John's Market and the Empire Market simultaneously. Although the fire was put out in seventeen minutes by firefighters and caused only minor damage, the Korean community was deeply concerned that other Korean businesses could become the targets of arson (Moon 1991g).

In his time of trials, Park received some moral support from fellow Koreans. Some wrote him letters of encouragement, and some went out of their way to visit his store and make small purchases. For instance, on August 3, the Korean Buddhist Businessmen's Association purchased $145 worth of merchandise for its golf tournament from Park. Such individual support expanded to a national-level donation campaign as the black boycott persisted. On July 2, Korean American professionals and directors of community service organizations formed the Korean American Race Relations Emergency (KARE) association to support Park financially and to help ameliorate racial conflicts between ethnic communities through communication and cultural exchange.[7] This organization, led by a young generation of Korean Americans, was to represent the Korean community to other ethnic groups with the financial support of organizations such as the Korean Grocers' Association that were led by first-generation immigrants. In cooperation with the KARE, the Korean American Grocers' Association (KAGRO) asked members of its twenty-two chapters across the country to send donations. By August 4, they had collected $27,210 and delivered $6,000 to Park.

As the entire Korean community backed Park, the black boycotters became more determined in their efforts. In an interview with the *Korea Times Los Angeles* (Moon 1991h), Reverend Boyd said that he would continue to boycott even if John's Market were operated by another Korean who was fluent in English and knowledgeable about black culture but did not live in or contribute to the black community. He added that the only way to end the boycott would be to close John's Market, and he vowed to continue until that goal was achieved.

As the situation did not seem to improve, Mayor Tom Bradley arranged a meeting on August 30 between the police department and the leaders of the boycott to find a solution to the black–Korean conflict. The mayor, who was concerned about the repercussions of the black–Jewish conflict in Brooklyn, New York, on the situation, tried to end the boycott by explaining to its leaders the truth of the shooting incident in John's Market. He said that he would serve as the permanent "bridge of peace" between the Korean and black communities and emphasized the importance of creating an atmosphere in which anyone could do business without fear of boycotts. He added that people shouldn't attempt to close business because they did not like the owner's business style. Despite the mayor's plea and warning, the black leaders claimed that the boycott was a peaceful way of expressing their concerns about "nonresident" store owners who treated all black customers as if they were criminals, did not contribute to the local community, and did not hire local residents. Reverend Boyd renewed his vow to continue the boycott until Park closed his store or was brought to trial. Other black leaders criticized the mayor because he did not console the family of Latasha Harlins but did appear at a Korean store to condemn anti-Korean arson (*KTLA* 31 August 1991; Sahagun 1991).

A big demonstration took place on September 10 in front of John's Market to show the boycotters' persistence in their cause. Fifty people participated in this demonstration, which was a big increase from the five or six participants in previous protests. But the demonstrators were thought to be outsiders who came from Gardena, Hawthone, Lynwood, and Hollywood, not local residents. Boyd and Bakewell restated the boycott's goals as the reopening of the police investigation of Mitchell's death, the closing of John's Market, and the development of black businesses in black neighborhoods (Jung 1991).

As there appeared to be no clear resolution to the boycott, which had dragged on for four months, a complete reexamination of the Korean community's strategies became necessary. The KARE's donation campaign had proved to be ineffective, and even its members, who were from the younger generation, were critical of this approach. By September, the KARE had collected $43,281 and delivered $16,794 in financial assistance to Park. While such assistance helped him continue his fight against the boycott, some members expressed a concern that it would expand a store-level dispute into a continuing racial conflict between the Korean and black communities. Citing the 1990–91 black boycott in Brooklyn, in which winning the battle rather than resolving the conflict became the main goal of both sides, younger members of the group demanded that the financial assistance to Park be stopped. The first-generation members countered that the KARE should continue to support Park financially because the donations had been collected for that purpose.

Debates among the KARE members extended to the very nature of the organization. Some members argued that it should be dissolved, and others supported the idea of transforming it into a permanent dispute-prevention center. In accordance with the overwhelming opinion, the

KARE announced on September 10 that it would end financial support to Park and use the balance of the fund for solving future racial conflicts. This decision was received with dissatisfaction by first-generation Korean community leaders, who complained that the KARE should have not started the donation campaign in the first place if John's Market were to be sold now and that the group had wasted Koreans' money without any tangible results. One leader pointed out that Koreans had donated the money to help Tae Sam Park, not the KARE, and thus it should be used for Park alone (Cho 1991b; Moon 1991i; *KTLA* 12 September 1991).

The KARE's decision to end its financial assistance to Park expedited negotiations to end the boycott. On October 3, the Brotherhood Crusade, the KARE, and the KAGRO reached an agreement that the Brotherhood Crusade would suspend the boycott for thirty days while the Korean and black communities searched for a black buyer for John's Market. If that effort failed after two months, they agreed to search for a Korean buyer instead. Finally, they agreed that the new owner could not sell liquor or beer on the premises.

The boycott leaders did not hesitate to call the agreement a victory for the black community. Reverend Boyd described the boycott as the cornerstone of blacks' self-defense against external economic pressure. He added that beginning in November 1991, he would establish educational and economic centers to boost blacks' economic self-sufficiency. Bakewell, after praising the efforts of the boycotters, declared that he would establish a dispute-resolution center to solve problems between Korean store owners and black customers, and he demanded that L.A. County and KAGRO each donate $25,000 for this cause (J. Kim 1991b).

Although the black community was pleased with the agreement, the Korean ethnic newspapers called it a "fruitless compromise" conforming completely to blacks' demands. Tae Sam Park, who had been excluded from the negotiation process, expressed dissatisfaction with the terms of the agreement, under which he was essentially forced to sell his market. Because the new owner would be prohibited from selling liquor, Park would lose his $20,000 liquor license premium (Paik 1991). He even said that he felt betrayed by the KARE, which had decided to end its financial assistance to him after the boycott of his store had already become a community-level issue, not just an individual matter (S. Kim 1991a). Faced with no choice but to sell his store, and not knowing what to do next, he decided to return to Korea permanently on March 20, 1993. In an interview with a Korean reporter from the *Korea Times Los Angeles* (*English Edition*), he said:

> I believe that America was a land where you could always find a job and earn a lot of money if you worked hard enough. I had nothing but hope when I first came to this country, but now I don't see anything. . . . I want to say thank you to the Korean community for helping me when my troubles began and apologize for leaving without repaying them, but I am relieved because I feel as if I am leaving a war zone. (Hwang and Ki 1993)

A Multivariate Analysis of the Korean–Black Conflict

The Korean–black conflict is a complex social phenomenon composed of multiple dimensions. We often think that prejudice, language barriers, and cultural differences between Koreans and blacks cause this conflict. But personal and psychological factors alone cannot explain why and how over-the-counter disputes between individual black customers and Korean store owners often develop into collective actions such as boycotts. This does not explain either why black boycotters state that their ultimate goal is to achieve economic and political self-determination in their community, not simply to punish individual Korean store owners who mistreat and disrespect black customers. Thus, it is important to understand that the ways in which Korean store owners and black customers perceive and relate to one another are affected not only by personal and psychological factors but also by impersonal structural and situational forces beyond the control of individuals.

The Structural Dimension

The structural dimension of the Korean–black conflict consists of large-scale social and economic forces that affect the relationship between members of the two groups. The primary structural cause of the conflict is the racial/ethnic stratification system of U.S. society, which distributes society's resources unequally among different racial and ethnic groups. In this system, blacks and Koreans, as disadvantaged racial minorities, are denied opportunities in the mainstream economy and society and have to compete for limited resources in ghetto areas. This economic competition in turn provides motivations and rationales for sustaining conflict between Koreans and blacks.

The ethnic stratification system. Gerhard Lenski (1966) has offered a theoretical framework useful for our analysis of the Korean–black conflict. He thinks that a society's stratification system consists of several class hierarchies, which he calls class systems, each based on such key social criteria as wealth, occupation, political authority, and ethnicity. He distinguishes four class systems: political, property, occupational, and ethnic. These four systems together make up what he calls the distributive system, which is the total socioeconomic structure of society (Marger 1991, 40). In most multidimensional societies, majority and minority group members each occupy similar ranks across the class systems.[8] For instance, whites in the United States occupy higher positions than blacks in the political, property, occupational, and ethnic class systems. But hierarchies among different minority groups in the class systems are not consistent.

By applying Lenski's model to Korean–black relations, I can make the following three observations. First, Koreans and blacks occupy similar class positions in the ethnic stratification system, and this proximity increases the probability of contact and competition between the two groups for society's resources. Because Koreans interact more directly than whites with blacks in low-income inner-city neighborhoods, they can become more direct competitors to blacks.

The same explanation can be applied to racial conflicts between blacks and Jews. Jews have traditionally been sympathetic toward black interests and supportive of blacks' efforts to secure civil rights. But paradoxically, Jews have become the target of blacks' jealousy and hostility.[9] Although there are multiple factors responsible for the continuing anti-Semitism among blacks, one root cause seems to be the class position of Jews, which is immediately above theirs in the ethnic stratification system. Blacks keep bumping into them when they try to advance themselves. Black novelist James Baldwin ([1967] 1994) attributes black anti-Semitism to the circumstances under which blacks and Jews engage in stressful and competitive interactions with unequal status. As blacks moved into Jewish neighborhoods, they became the customers of Jewish shopkeepers, the tenants of Jewish landlords, the employees of Jewish employers, the domestic workers of Jewish housewives, and the students of Jewish teachers. When middle-class blacks began to enter the govern-

ment agencies that provide the most secure employment for the upwardly mobile, they again came into contact with Jews, who had gotten
there before them. Baldwin describes as follows the bitter feelings blacks
had toward Jews in the 1960s, which are parallel in many respects to the
feelings they have toward Koreans in the 1990s:

> When we were growing up in Harlem our demoralizing series of land-
> lords were Jewish, and we hated them. We hated them because they
> were terrible landlords and did not take care of the building. . . . The
> grocer was a Jew, and being in debt to him was very much like being
> in debt to the company store. The butcher was a Jew, and yes, we cer-
> tainly paid more for bad cuts of meat than other New York citizens,
> and we very often carried insults home, along with the meat. We
> bought our clothes from a Jew and, sometimes, our secondhand
> shoes, and the pawnbroker was a Jew. . . . Not all of these white
> people were cruel—but all of them were exploiting us, and that was
> why we hated them. . . . It is bitter to watch the Jewish storekeeper
> locking up his store for the night, and going home. Going, with *your*
> money in his pocket, to a clean neighborhood, miles from you, which
> you will not be allowed to enter. Nor can it help the relationship be-
> tween most Negroes and most Jews when part of this money is do-
> nated to civil rights. In the light of what is now known as the white
> backlash, this money can be looked on as conscience money merely,
> as money given to keep the Negro happy in his place, and out of
> white neighborhoods. (31–32, 34)

As Glazer and Moynihan (1970, 73) state, the relationship between
inferior and superior in a hierarchy is inevitably tension-producing, and
the conflict between individuals is always subject to interpretation in
group terms. By the same logic, the relationship between blacks and Koreans is likely to develop into racial conflict because the two groups occupy class positions in U.S. society that increase the chance of direct and
competitive interaction. When blacks pursue greater economic autonomy and growth in their community, they are likely to compete with
Koreans, who dominate blacks as merchants, employers, and landlords.

The second observation about the class positions of Koreans and
blacks is that the two groups have attained different levels of status in the
different class systems. Blacks achieve higher status in the political class
system but lower status in the economic class system than do Koreans.
The political weakness of Koreans originates from the following factors:

(1) the majority of Koreans are recent immigrants; (2) they have limited English proficiency and are not familiar with American customs and institutions; (3) the number of naturalized Koreans who can vote and be elected to office is still small; (4) they have a strong mistrust of and apathy toward politics and political participation; (5) their interest in politics in the homeland hinders them from channeling their energies and resources toward political empowerment in the United States; and (6) their political affiliations are divided between the Democratic and Republican Parties, making it more difficult to elect Koreans into office (Takami 1988; Wang 1991).

In contrast, blacks have strengthened their political power through the Civil Rights movement and the Voting Rights Act of 1965, and they have learned how to accomplish their goals through collective actions such as boycotts. They also have the demographic advantages of a relatively large population size and concentration in a few large cities. Residential segregation has created disadvantages for blacks in many aspects of life, but it has had the unintended consequence of building up a protected power base for middle-class black politicians. Beginning in the mid-1980s, blacks began to constitute more than half of the population of major cities, in which black political candidates have gained the upper hand over other candidates.

For these reasons, blacks have produced many politicians and high-ranking government officials, whereas Koreans have elected a very tiny number of coethnic representatives to positions of power and influence. For instance, as of 1994, the number of black U.S. congressional representatives was thirty-eight, compared to one Korean congressman, Jay Kim from Southern California. Blacks' political power is stronger than that of Koreans in the Democratic Party, in which Jesse Jackson ran for the presidency in 1984. Ron Brown became the chair of the party in 1989 and led its 1992 presidential election campaign. After Bill Clinton won that election, he appointed four black cabinet members while selecting no Asian Americans to high-ranking government positions. But blacks' political power is the strongest at the city level. In the late 1980s, 300 U.S. cities had black mayors—including, by 1989, the six largest cities except for Houston. In these cities, blacks also dominate lower-ranking positions, such as those on the city council and various advisory committees. In contrast, Koreans' participation in the U.S. political system became noticeable only after 1992, when six Koreans became state assembly members and one became a congressional representative.

Although Koreans are weaker than blacks in political power, they are stronger in economic power. For instance, in 1990, blacks' median family income ($22,429) was only two-thirds of that of Koreans ($33,909). The intergroup difference in economic power is more noteworthy in the rate of business ownership. About a quarter of adult Koreans were self-employed in 1990, compared to only 4 percent of adult blacks. In 1987, the number of black-owned businesses nationwide was 424,165, which was six times that of Korean-owned businesses (69,304). However, because blacks were thirty-seven times more numerous than Koreans, the business–population ratio was higher for Koreans. The average annual gross sales of Korean businesses was $100,859 in 1987, which was 2.4 times the corresponding figure for black businesses ($46,593).

Apart from these objective criteria, Koreans' economic superiority is especially visible in the low-income inner-city neighborhoods in which their businesses are concentrated. There Korean merchants are viewed as the wealthy, propertied class, giving blacks a sense of relative deprivation. Some black nationalist leaders have attempted to overcome such economic disadvantages through their political advantages, a strategy that is often expressed in boycotts against Korean businesses.

My third and final observation is that the criteria for determining ranks among minority groups in the ethnic class system are often subjective, self-centered, and inconsistent, unlike those in the political and economic class systems. For this reason, Koreans and blacks have contradictory viewpoints about their relative ethnic ranks in U.S. society. Blacks claim that they have a higher ethnic status because they have been in the country longer than Koreans and have better English skills and greater familiarity with American culture and lifestyles. In contrast, Koreans think they have a superior ethnic status because of their lighter skin color, higher socioeconomic status, and greater acceptance by whites. They tend to view blacks as the hopeless underclass, trapped in poverty and joblessness. Such contradictory views seem to increase prejudice and widen the social distance between Koreans and blacks.[10]

Economic restructuring. Economic restructuring is another external structural force that has made blacks hostile toward immigrants, including Koreans. In Los Angeles, more than 70,000 workers lost their jobs because of plant closures between 1978 and 1983, and almost 75 percent of these losses occurred in the auto, tire, steel, and civilian aircraft sectors (Soja, Morales, and Wolff 1983, 217). Major U.S. auto and tire makers, such as General Motors, Goodrich, Firestone, Goodyear, and Uniroyal, led this deindustrialization trend. Plant closures had particularly adverse effects on blacks living in central cities since they were concentrated in areas and industries that had employed large numbers of blacks.

The massive job loss in the heavy manufacturing sector was accompanied by a sharp growth in the light manufacturing (for example, garment manufacturing), service, and retail industries, but this trend did not provide blacks with alternative employment opportunities. These industries employ primarily women and Latino immigrants, allow only short working hours, pay low wages, and are not protected by union agreements and benefits. Latino immigrants filled more than two-thirds of the new low-wage jobs created between 1969 and 1987 in these peripheral industries of Los Angeles (Schimek 1989, 38).

This economic restructuring has widened income inequality between blacks and whites in Los Angeles and increased unemployment, poverty, crime, and other forms of social illness among inner-city black residents (Ong 1989). According to the 1990 census, the unemployment rate in South Central Los Angeles was 13.4 percent, more than twice the rate for California (6.6 percent) and the United States as a whole (6.3 percent). The average family income in South Central was $30,746, only 69 percent of California's average ($51,198) and 80 percent of the U.S. average ($43,803). The poverty rate in South Central was 27.2 percent, more than twice the rate for California (12.5 percent) and the United States (13.1 percent) (CACI Marketing Systems 1991, 22-B; 1992, 22-B–23-D).

Another consequence of the restructuring of Los Angeles as a global city was the massive influx of Asian and Latino immigrants into the economy. When U.S. capitalists faced declining profits at home and stiff competition from newly industrialized countries in Asia in the 1960s and 1970s, they employed two strategies to increase profitability. One was cutting labor costs; the other was increasing efficiency through reorganization and investment in new technology and industry. Cutting labor costs involves laying off redundant workers, lowering wages, lengthening the workday, and using immigrant workers from low-wage, Third World nations. By employing such workers, U.S. capitalists created a "Third World within in Los Angeles" to compete against producers in these nations (Ong, Bonacich, and Cheng 1994). Increasing efficiency through innovation and investment involves decentralization, subcontracting, and expansion of professional services in finance, communications, health, education, and the like. When the sudden expansion of the professional and business service industry created a labor shortage, highly trained foreign professionals and managerial workers in such fields as health, engineering, and education were imported. Thus, the economic restructuring has involved two strands of immigration: "Latino immigrants generally perform the role of low-wage labor as part of the cheap labor strategy, and Asian immigrants both join whites in the professional and managerial stratum as part of the 'investment-in-innovation' strategy and join Latino immigrants in the cheap labor strategy" (19).

As a result of the rapid influx of Asian and Latino immigrants into Los Angeles, the city is now 40 percent Latino, 37 percent white, 10 percent Asian, and 13 percent black, with the last of these percentages shrinking (Meyer 1992). In particular, the Latino population has doubled over the past decade, replacing blacks in Watts and other traditionally black neighborhoods of Los Angeles. These recent demographic, social, and economic changes seem to have made inner-city blacks more hostile than ever toward immigrants, who have been encroaching on their neighborhoods and competing with them for jobs and housing (Stengel 1985; Regalado 1994, 228).

According to a *Los Angeles Times* poll (20 August 1993), in which 1,232 adults in Southern California were surveyed by telephone from August 7 to 10, 1993, blacks' attitudes toward Asian immigrants in general and toward Koreans in particular are generally unfavorable. Fifty-nine percent of the black respondents thought that new immigrants from Asia were a burden on the economy of Southern California, whereas only 11 percent of them thought that Asian immigrants were a boost for the economy. Among white, black, Latino, and Asian respondents, blacks were the most likely to think that Asians were getting more economic power than was good for the region. Another important result of the poll that is relevant to the Korean–black conflict is that blacks were more likely than respondents of other races to think that of all Asian immigrant groups, Koreans were particularly responsible for the problems in Southern California. The concentration of Korean businesses in black neighborhoods and the frequent clashes between black customers and Korean store owners discussed throughout this book seem to be primarily responsible for these negative attitudes.

In summary, the deteriorating socioeconomic conditions of inner-city blacks, the influx of Asian and Latino immigrants, and the concentration of Korean businesses in black neighborhoods all provide the context in which competition for jobs, businesses, and housing among different minority groups is likely to lead to racial conflict.

The Psychological Dimension

The attitudes that members of two minority groups have toward one another are shaped by suspicion, mistrust, and fear of being treated the same. In U.S. society, whites establish the major norms and values, and members of minority groups apply these standards to one another.[11] Thus, when whites discriminate against members of a particular minority group, members of other minority groups tend to follow suit. This tendency to identify with whites is stronger among members of those groups with a stronger motivation for achieving upward mobility and acceptance by whites.

The desire for acceptance by whites is often expressed as the desire for dissociation from American blacks, whom whites try to avoid. Portes and Stepick (1993, 183) describe the process by which Cubans in Miami adopt whites' attitudes toward American blacks as follows:

> Cubans are afraid of blacks. Their experience in the United States has made them more racist than they were, and this gets translated into fear. . . . As they go up the totem pole trying to become successful, many Cubans find out that these white Anglos don't like colored folks, so if I'm going to progress, I must take on some of the same behaviors of the Anglos. You don't discriminate, but as a way of doing business you begin to laugh at racist jokes, you talk about those niggers over there in Overtown . . . because you're surrounded by racist people and because it is more important in this moment of your life to pursue your own agenda.

The desire for dissociation from American blacks is also evident among less upwardly mobile Haitian refugees. Although they accept black American support in their struggles against racism, they do not wish to be identified with what they see as the poorest and most downtrodden group in the host society. As Portes and Stepick explain, "They resist being pulled down to the economic level of native blacks and of having their distinct immigrant identity submerged into that of the urban underclass" (190). American blacks are, for their part, ambivalent about Haitians, who are brothers in color but see themselves as somehow above native blacks. Thus they do not extend their acceptance unconditionally to Haitians, whom they view as "newcomers who must learn about their new society and adapt to its culture."

The nativism of American blacks has a long history.[12] In his famous Atlanta address, delivered at the opening of the Cotton States Exposition in September 1895, Booker T. Washington admonished the white leaders in his audience not to "look to the incoming of those of foreign birth and strange tongue and habits for the prosperity of the South" (Fuchs 1990, 295). He thought the Chinese particularly objectionable because, unlike blacks, they "lacked moral standards and could never be assimilated to occidental civilization" (296). His sentiments were no different from those of whites toward the Chinese and Japanese before World War II, who were excluded from immigration for this reason. The black press and black leaders repeatedly expressed the nativist sentiments of Frederick Douglass whenever waves of immigrants came to take over jobs that they thought should rightfully go to black Americans. From 1900 to 1930, African-American newspapers opposed the immigration of Greeks and Italians, and they strongly endorsed proposals to bar Mexicans from entering the United States during the late 1920s and early 1930s. A black writer captured these general attitudes as follows: "Negro labor is native labor and should be preferred to that of the offscourings of Europe and Asia. Let America take care of its own."

Significant changes in the attitudes of American blacks toward immigrants came in the 1960s, when black leaders struggled against racial oppression by launching the Civil Rights movement. In order to be consistent with their goal of achieving basic human rights for blacks, they had to be cosmopolitan and humanitarian toward immigrants and refugees. Thus, under the leadership of Martin Luther King Jr., many black civil rights leaders opposed restrictions on the entry of Indo-Chinese, Cuban, and Haitian refugees into the United States. But not all civil rights leaders shared these views. In spite of his creation of the Rainbow Coalition, Jesse Jackson opposed the entry of Vietnamese boat people into the United States after the fall of Vietnam. He justified his action by saying that American blacks should be taken care of first before the U.S. government turned its attention to the boat people or any other immigrant groups. He later changed his position toward the Vietnamese and favored all types of immigration, but many blacks still share his original sentiment (Jo 1992, 404).

Korean–black relations do not differ significantly from general patterns of interaction between minority groups. One of the psychological dimensions of the Korean–black conflict centers on mutual feelings of prejudice and wide social distance and on different attitudes about social and economic assimilation into white-dominated American society. Because of their middle-class backgrounds and strong aspirations for upward mobility in the United States, which inspired their immigration, Korean immigrants tend to distance themselves from blacks, who are seen to have the lowest social and economic standing. Such attitudes cause resentment among blacks, who feel that Koreans have a free ride because of the social and economic justice that they achieved through the Civil Rights movement (Jo 1992).

The nativistic sense of seniority blacks have toward immigrants is another important psychological dimension of this racial conflict (Cheng and Espiritu 1989; Chang 1990, ch. 5). Because they have been in the United States longer than immigrant groups, blacks tend to think that they deserve social and economic enhancement ahead of new arrivals. For this reason, they are likely to perceive Korean businesses in their neighborhoods as a hindrance to their own economic mobility and to oppose strongly any signs of disrespect and mistreatment they receive as customers.

In contrast, both Latinos and Koreans are predominantly immigrant groups and are not therefore in a position to claim seniority or superiority over each other. Their common nativity status also enables the two groups to share an "immigrant mentality" and to feel closer to each other culturally, psychologically, and ideologically (Uhlaner 1991). For this reason, Koreans' success in small business does not arouse jealousy and hostility among Latinos, who instead try to emulate them. Such differences in attitude are one of the major reasons why there are fewer conflicts between Latinos and Koreans than between blacks and Koreans. (This issue is discussed in greater depth later in this chapter.)

The Situational Dimension

Interpersonal relations between Korean store owners and black customers are greatly constrained by situational factors such as the characteristics of Korean businesses, customers, and neighborhoods. As described throughout this book, Korean stores in minority neighborhoods cater mainly to low-income black and Latino customers. Because of the paucity of decent employment in these neighborhoods, the temptations for shoplifting, burglary, and other crimes are greater among poor and unemployed customers than they would be among middle- and working-class patrons. According to my survey of Korean business owners, about 60 percent of the respondents in South Central Los Angeles suffered from such crimes during the 1992–93 period.

Korean stores in minority neighborhoods are also generally small in terms of start-up capital, annual gross sales, and number of paid employees. Because of their high debt/equity ratio, store owners are under tremendous pressure to generate fast cash flow. The easiest and only available ways to achieve this goal are to extend business hours, to reduce the number of paid employees, and to use the labor of unpaid family members.

However, the long business hours, which often extend to 10:00 or 11:00 P.M., make the stores more vulnerable to shoplifting and burglary. In an effort to reduce shoplifting, Korean store owners and their Korean employees watch black customers closely, causing many of them to feel treated as if they were criminals. The constant fear of crime, close surveillance of customers, and long working hours all combine to cause Korean store owners mental and physical exhaustion and to reinforce their earlier prejudice against blacks. Under these conditions, it is difficult for them to sustain friendly and courteous relations with customers on a constant basis.

In this context, the rude and disrespectful words and behaviors of some black customers cause Korean store owners to respond in a similar manner. Some of them intentionally act tough in order not to be seen as weak and thus easily exploitable by troublemakers. The alleged mistreatment of black customers by Korean store owners is, then, not merely a reflection of their prejudice against blacks but also a coping mechanism necessary for survival in the ghetto economy.

The Political Dimension

Structural, psychological, and situational factors make Korean–black relations prone to conflict, but they do not automatically lead to concrete incidents of confrontation. Most disputes that flare up in Korean stores are not violent. They are of the type that always take place in mom-and-pop stores: clashes over prices, demands for refunds or exchanges, and the like. Store owners who deal with these over-the-counter disputes on a daily basis say that they are manageable and do not pose a serious threat to business. They also tend to believe that most disputes are not racially motivated since their customers care more about prices and service than about the race of store owners. So what causes minor disputes and clashes between individual black customers and Korean store owners to become racial conflicts between the Korean and black communities?[13]

It is through political mobilization on the part of black nationalist activists and their organizations that blacks' personal experiences of mistreatment by Korean business owners are linked to a larger notion of Koreans' economic exploitation of blacks. Specific actions against Koreans are also devised and implemented through such mobilization. The Korean–black conflict is therefore an essentially political phenomenon, not merely an economic competition or a cultural clash.

Contrary to the general public's perception, only a small percentage of blacks display strong anti-Korean sentiments and support black boycotts against Korean businesses. Min's survey in New York in 1992 shows that only 26 percent of the black respondents supported the 1990–91 boycott in Brooklyn, and an even smaller 14 percent agreed to the statement that blacks should not buy from Korean stores (Min 1996, ch. 6).

Despite the limited community support for such anti-Korean campaigns, a few militant black nationalist activists make the Korean–black conflict look widespread and devastating to the outside world. A small number of picketers in front of targeted Korean stores is often enough to draw the attention of the mass media, which is quick to respond to violent aspects of life. In some cases (such as the boycott in Brooklyn), the picketers were not even local residents but outsiders brought into the community by activists.

As noted in the previous section of this chapter, local activists, such as Sonny Carson of the December 12th Movement in New York City and Danny Bakewell of the Brotherhood Crusade in Los Angeles, have played important roles in the Korean–black conflict. Carson once told news reporters that his ultimate goal was to drive all Korean businesses from black neighborhoods. Because of his extreme position, he was even expelled from David Dinkins's camp during the mayoral election campaign.

Thus, the visibility of the Korean–black conflict seems to be largely determined by the organizing capacity of black nationalist organizations. In cities in which local organizations have greater influence in the black community than do national organizations, black boycotts of Korean businesses are more numerous, longer-lasting, and more violent than elsewhere. This is because local organizations can take militant stances to protect "black-only" interests, whereas national organizations such as the NAACP, Operation PUSH, and the Urban League cannot resort to chauvinistic actions against a specific minority group. Another major difference is that the national organizations try to work out solutions to racial problems within the political system, while the local organizations do not trust the system itself and hence are not restrained from resorting to violent means to achieve their goals.

The militant stance of black nationalists and their organizations toward immigrants stems from their ideology of self-reliance, which was advocated by Booker T. Washington, Marcus Garvey, Elijah Muhammad, Malcolm X, Stokeley Carmichael, and Charles Hamilton. Black nationalism generally refers to a philosophy that encourages blacks to see themselves in a positive light as blacks first, not Americans. It means that they wish to control their own destiny and resist any attempts to continue their own subordination (Schaefer 1988, 244). The advocates of this philosophy interpret black poverty as a result of the failure of society to provide education and employment for blacks rather than a result of loose morals and lack of effort on the part of blacks. They also believe that social and economic mobility in the United States can be achieved through the social and economic self-reliance of blacks in their own communities. Thus, they are more likely to believe that the expulsion of nonblack businesses from these communities through political means such as boycotts is an important step toward this goal. As such, Koreans are rejected not simply because they are Koreans but because they are part of larger system that creates and maintains injustice against blacks. This is the same logic for anti-Semitism among blacks. Baldwin ([1967] 1994) says, "Blacks are anti-Semitic because they are anti-white."

Koreans' Perceptions of and Feelings toward Blacks and Latinos

Lucie Cheng and Yen Espiritu (1989) developed the "immigrant hypothesis" to explain why Korean store owners in Los Angeles have not encountered the same hostility from the Latino community that they have from the black community. According to these researchers, Koreans and Latinos share an "immigrant ideology" that endorses hard work and frugality as the keys to success in American society.[14] In the eyes of immigrants, America is "the land of opportunity," although it may be seen as "the land of opportunity denied" in the eyes of native blacks. As mentioned earlier in this chapter, Koreans' success in small business does not arouse jealousy and hostility among Mexicans and other Latinos, who instead try to emulate them. As fellow immigrants, Koreans and Mexicans also cannot claim a nativistic sense of superiority over each other. By contrast, native-born blacks are in a position to harbor feelings of seniority over Koreans, and for this reason they are more likely than Latinos to get angry when they feel they are disrespected and mistreated by people they consider foreigners:

> Black folks are angry . . . because here are a bunch of foreigners, a bunch of folks who don't speak English, who can't vote, who come here with money, and that is how it is perceived. (Cited in Cheng and Espiritu 1989, 528)

In a similar fashion, Koreans feel that they are racially and socioeconomically superior to blacks. As Jo (1992, 403) explains, "Many Koreans associate American blacks with Africans in Africa and their culture. Africans are inferior people and so are American blacks." Koreans also take pride in the success they have achieved despite their language barrier and short residence in the United States. Their self-esteem is enhanced further when they compare their socioeconomic status with that of American blacks, who are seen to be trapped in poverty despite their better English skills and American citizenship.

Chen and Espiritu's immigrant hypothesis seems to hold for Korean–black–Latino relations in Los Angeles. However, their data and methodology reflect their heavy reliance on newspaper articles, and thus their interpretations are based mostly upon indirect and conjectural evidence. Moreover, the viewpoints of community leaders cited in the mass media may not necessarily represent those of ordinary people. Rather, these leaders may exaggerate the level of prejudice and racial tension among Koreans, blacks, and Latinos for their own political purposes.

In this study, I attempt to fill these gaps through the data I gathered in my survey of 105 store owners in Koreatown and 93 store owners in South Central Los Angeles. As discussed in chapter 3, these two areas represent different business environments in which owners interact with racially different clienteles. The two areas are also markedly different in crime rates and socioeconomic status of customers. About 60 percent of the Korean businesses in South Central but only about 42 percent of those in Koreatown experienced shoplifting, burglary, arson, looting, and damages to equipment during 1992–93. Seventy-four percent of the

Table 4.1. Preferences for Employees of Different Races (Percentages)

Preference	Total	Koreatown	South Central
Prefer Koreans to non-Koreans			
Yes	52.0	63.6	38.7
No	40.0	29.8	50.5
Don't know	9.0	6.7	10.8
Total number	197	104	93
Prefer Latinos to blacks			
Yes	80.0	83.3	75.8
No	10.0	2.9	18.7
Not applicable	10.0	13.7	5.5
Total number of respondents	193	102	91

Note: The "Not applicable" category refers to those who do not have need or preference for either Latino or black employees.

businesses in South Central have members of the lower classes as their customers, whereas only 21 percent of those in Koreatown depend on these groups for customers. Such differences are expected to have a significant impact on the relations of owners in these two areas with their employees, customers, and neighbors.

Perceptions of Blacks and Latinos as Employees

As mentioned earlier, Korean store owners have a strong preference for Latino employees over black ones. In response to my question, 80 percent of the respondents said they would rather hire a Latino than a black employee, whereas only 10 percent gave the opposite answer (see table 4.1).

This preference was stronger among the respondents in Koreatown than among their counterparts in South Central, in part because of the different racial composition of local residents and customers in the two areas. Although Koreatown is an economic center for Koreans, it is not their residential area. The largest ethnic group there consists of Mexicans, who along with other Latinos accounted for 36.7 percent of the local residents in 1980. Koreans accounted for only 10.5 percent of the total (Min 1993, 189). The proportion of Koreans in Koreatown increased to 19.3 percent in 1990, but Latinos remained more numerous, accounting for 51.6 percent of the residents (U.S. Bureau of the Census 1993b, 1057–58).

Reflecting this distribution, more Korean businesses in Koreatown cater to Latino customers than to black customers. About half of the businesses there depend on Latinos as one of their three most important customer groups, whereas only 17 percent rely on black customers. Store owners in Koreatown also seem to have a stronger motivation for hiring Latino employees: 83 percent of the respondents there preferred Latinos to blacks as employees, whereas only 3 percent preferred blacks.

In contrast, Korean store owners in South Central seem to feel greater social pressure than their counterparts in Koreatown to hire black employees. Blacks account for half the customers of such businesses, 84 percent of which cater to them. By comparison, Latinos represent 29 percent of the customers of these businesses, 70 percent of which cater to them. More respondents in South Central (19 percent) than in Koreatown (3 percent) preferred to hire black employees. Yet an overwhelming majority of the respondents in both areas still preferred Latinos to blacks as employees. Thus, the racial composition of the customer base is not the determining factor of Koreans' preference for Latino employees.[15]

The more important reason offered by Korean store owners for their preference is their perception that Latinos possess a more desirable work ethic and personality traits than do blacks. More specifically, Latinos are perceived by Koreans as more hardworking, docile, honest, prompt, responsible, and trustworthy than blacks. However, the other side of such positive perceptions is the idea that Latinos are easier to control and fire without fear of being sued for workers' compensation. As table 4.2 shows, 46 percent of the respondents who favored Latino employees cited their work ethic and personality traits as the primary reason for this preference. By comparison, only 15 percent of the respondents who favored black employees mentioned their work ethic and personality traits. The majority of these respondents cited instead the situational consideration that blacks were their major clientele.

These negative perceptions of blacks as employees are not unique to Korean employers. According to Joleen Kirschenman and Kathryn Neckerman (1991), white employers in Chicago's inner-city area also maintain negative stereotypes about blacks and prefer Latinos to blacks as employees. According to the stereotypical images, blacks are "unskilled, uneducated, illiterate, dishonest, lacking initiative, unmotivated,

Table 4.2. Reasons for Preferring Employees of Different Races (Percentages)

Reason	Prefer Latinos	Prefer Blacks
Work ethic and personality traits	45.9	15.0
Racial composition of customer base	19.0	75.0
Cultural similarity[a]	18.9	5.0
Lower wages	10.1	0.0
Job-related skills and ability	4.1	5.0
Others	2.0	0.0
Total number of respondents	148	20

Note: Respondents were asekd in an open-ended question to cite three reasons for preferring Latino employees to black ones or vice versa. Their responses were later coded into the above five broad categories. This table shows what they cited as the most important reason for their preferences.

a. Similarity in culture, values, mentality, and ways of thinking, which leads to a sense of affinity and affection.

involved with drugs and gangs, did not understand work, had no personal charm, were unstable, lacked a work ethic, and had no family life or role models" (208). The following quotation from that study illustrates whites' preference for Latino and Asian employees over black ones:

> [W]hen we hear other employers talk, they'll go after primarily the Latinos and Oriental first, those two, and, I'll qualify that even further, the Mexican Latinos, and any Oriental, and after that, that's pretty much it, that's pretty much where they like to draw the line, right there. (228)

Thus, Korean and white employers alike prefer not to hire inner-city black employees.

However, Korean employers consider an additional status marker when hiring employees: nativity. Nativity is usually a constant in relations between white employers and black employees, but it is a variable in relations between foreign-born Korean employers and native-born black employees. Past research on relations between whites and blacks has mostly focused on race, with little attention to nativity. However, nativity affects very significantly the nature and pattern of relations between minority groups, regardless of the race and class of the groups involved.

The common nativity status of Koreans and Latinos tends to reduce the feelings of social distance between the two groups, whereas the different nativity status of Koreans and blacks tends to increase the distance between them. Because of their similar skin color, immigrant status, and language barrier, Koreans feel emotionally closer to and more sympathetic toward Latinos than they feel toward blacks. One respondent described this feeling with the Korean word *Jung*, which refers to the force that bonds humans to one another. It is not exactly the same as love but more like affinity, empathy, sympathy, and affection. Latinos—especially Mexican immigrants—remind some Koreans of the naive, innocent, and simple-minded countrymen in the old days of Korea. Some Korean employers also say that they have fewer language barriers with Latinos than with blacks, although Korean is by no means closer to Spanish grammatically or phonetically than it is to black English. As a matter of fact, Koreans and Latinos should have a greater language barrier because of their equally limited English proficiency. But at least psychologically, Koreans are more comfortable and confident communicating with less fluent and thus less threatening fellow immigrants. This greater confidence puts Korean employers in a commanding position over their Latino employees.

In contrast, Koreans feel less secure about their status in relation to American blacks. In particular, the nativity difference between Koreans and blacks seems to conflict—at least in the eyes of Koreans—with the roles expected of employers and employees. With Latino employees, Korean employers can maintain a seemingly proper hierarchy of race, nativity, and class. It is not difficult to observe in Korean stores (particularly grocery stores) that Korean employers order Latino employees in Korean, and these employees understand simple Korean words and expressions. This kind of employer–employee relationship is rare between Korean employers and black employees.

During an interview for this study, one Korean dry cleaner in South Central said that he feels emotionally closer to Latinos than to blacks because he and his Latino employees share the same *minority* status. By this he meant immigrant status, because of course blacks are also racial minorities in the United States. However, his remark suggests that he does not regard blacks as minorities. It also suggests that blacks are perceived to have greater power than Koreans or Latinos.

Another important reason for the preference for Latino employees is their willingness to accept low wages and menial positions in Korean stores. Ten percent of the respondents cited this as one of the three most important reasons for their preference. Because of their immigrant status (for some, illegal immigrant status) and disadvantages in the general la-

Table 4.3. Race of Employees of Korean Businesses

	Total		Koreatown		South Central	
Race	N	%	N	%	N	%
Korean	450	46.8	336	61.0	114	27.9
Asian (non-Korean)	11	1.1	8	1.5	3	0.7
White	15	1.6	10	1.8	5	1.2
Latino	413	43.0	191	34.7	222	54.3
Black	70	7.3	5	0.9	65	15.9
Other	1	0.1	1	0.2	0	0.0
Total	960	100.0	551	100.0	409	100.0

bor market, Latinos are in a weak position to bargain for higher wages and better working conditions. In contrast, native-born blacks object more strongly to being used as cheap and docile labor, partly because of the availability of government assistance programs and partly because of their sense of honor. They tend to use the white standard of living as their frame of reference and are not willing to accept low wages and menial positions in immigrant-owned businesses. Service-oriented jobs as dishwashers, helpers, and laborers in Korean stores are perceived to be too demeaning to take.

Immigrant Latinos are in a different situation. They still compare their economic status in the United States with that in their home countries, and wages and work conditions in Korean stores are perceived to be better than or at least similar to those at home. Moreover, some of them have only a short-term goal of making money in the United States and returning to their home countries. Any jobs that accomplish their goal are acceptable, even if they are not desirable. Immigrant Latinos eager to find work often walk into Korean stores and ask for jobs. This kind of job hunting is less common among blacks. Thus, both the supply of and demand for Latino employees are greater than those for black workers, resulting in the hiring of far more Latinos than blacks in Korean stores. Latino employees account for 43 percent of a total of 960 employees in Korean stores in Los Angeles, and their proportion is even higher in South Central, where they constitute 54 percent of the total (see table 4.3).[16]

The kinds of jobs that Latino and black employees can get in Korean stores are often limited to low-skilled, menial, and dead-end positions as cashiers, service workers, and laborers. Higher-level jobs as managers, technicians, and clerical workers are usually reserved for Korean employees. However, one noticeable difference in this area separates Latinos from blacks. Latino employees are highly represented in precision production, craft, and repair jobs (such as auto repair, manufacturing, and installation) and in operation and fabrication jobs (sewing, pressing, and welding), whereas black employees are nearly absent in these jobs (see table 4.4). Some Korean employers claim that this is the result of blacks' tendency to avoid dirty and physical labor.[17] However, it is also possible that such preconceptions cause employers to screen potential black employees out of these jobs in the first place.

Although some Korean employers are attracted to Latino employees as a source of relatively cheap labor, members of both groups, once hired, receive almost the same wages. This is primarily because the wage rates for low-skilled, entry-level jobs are more or less flat, with little regard to such personal attributes of workers as their race. As table 4.4 shows, very few workers earn less than the minimum wage, and the majority earn between $4.25 and $6.99 per hour. The number of weekly work hours is also almost the same for the two groups, although Latino employees are slightly more likely to work full-time (40 or more hours per week) than their black counterparts. The typical monthly wages of Latinos and black employees cluster in the range of $800 and $1,500. These findings suggest that more Latinos are hired in Korean stores not because they demand lower wages than blacks for the same kind of work but because they are more willing to take low wages for the menial jobs offered in the stores.

Perceptions of Blacks and Latinos as Customers

As stated earlier, most disputes between Korean store owners and their customers are trivial and not violent. As table 4.5 shows, out of the 198 respondents asked to rate the level of clashes with their customers on a seven-point scale, only eight (4 percent) said that they had very serious or somewhat serious clashes. The majority of respondents said that they had some clashes with their customers but mainly over prices, short-changing, shoplifting, and returned items, all of which could be resolved through better English-speaking ability and greater patience with customers. Although the respondents in South Central reported a slightly higher level of disputes than their counterparts in Koreatown, 96 percent

Table 4.4. Type of Work, Hourly Wages, and Weekly Work Hours of Employees of Different Races

	Korean		Latino		Black	
	N	%	N	%	N	%
Type of work						
Managerial	25	15.9	0	0.0	3	8.1
Professional	4	2.5	1	0.8	1	2.7
Technical	9	5.7	1	0.8	0	0.0
Sales	45	28.7	23	18.0	10	27.0
Clerical	9	5.7	1	0.8	1	2.7
Service	20	12.7	20	15.6	7	18.9
Precision production, craft, and repair	22	14.0	27	21.1	2	5.4
Operator and fabricator	5	3.2	17	13.3	1	2.7
Transportation	1	0.6	1	0.8	0	0.0
Laborer	17	10.8	37	28.9	12	32.4
Total	157	100.0	128	100.0	37	100.0
Hourly wage ($)						
Less than 4.25	1	0.7	2	1.8	0	0.0
4.25–6.99	49	35.8	72	66.1	24	75.0
7.00–9.99	40	29.2	25	22.9	5	15.6
10.00–12.99	29	21.2	9	8.3	3	9.4
13.00 and over	18	13.1	1	0.9	0	0.0
Total	137	100.0	109	100.0	32	100.0
Weekly work hours						
Fewer than 20	4	3.3	3	3.1	3	9.7
20–29.99	9	7.4	4	4.1	1	3.2
30–39.99	8	6.6	11	11.2	5	16.1
40–49.99	53	43.8	59	60.2	18	58.1
50–59.99	28	23.1	15	15.3	3	9.7
60 and over	19	15.7	6	6.1	1	3.2
Total	121	100.0	98	100.0	31	100.0

Note: Because some kinds of information about employees are highly sensitive (for example, wages and legal status), I asked the respondents to report only the *typical* types of work, hourly wages, and weekly work hours of employees of different races rather than detailed information about each employee. Information collected this manner is not as precise as that collected from each employee.

Table 4.5. Perceived Level of Clashes with Customers

Level	Total		Koreatown		South Central	
	N	%	N	%	N	%
1 Very serious	0	0.0	0	0.0	0	0.0
2	3	1.5	3	2.9	0	0.0
3	5	2.5	1	1.0	4	4.3
4 Not toward one end or the other	65	32.8	21	20.0	44	47.3
5	19	9.6	9	8.6	10	10.8
6	64	32.3	39	37.1	25	26.9
7 No clashes at all	41	20.7	32	30.5	9	9.7
8 Don't know	1	0.5	0	0.0	1	1.1
Mean	5.31		5.68		4.90	
SD	1.28		1.28		1.15	
Balance[a]	−59.1		−72.3		−44.2	
Number of respondents	198		105		93	

Note: The "Don't Know" category is not included in the computation of the mean scores, standard deviations, and balance.

a. Balance is the percentage difference between those who reported scores of 1 through 3 (serious levels of clashes) and those who reported scores of 5 through 7 (not serious). The negative sign of the percentage difference means that more respondents thought the level of clashes with the customers was not serious than thought it was serious.

of them still reported having only a moderate level of clashes or none at all.

Despite the generally low overall levels, Korean store owners still experienced more frequent clashes with black customers than with Latino customers (see table 4.6). About 40 percent of the respondents reported this trend, compared with less than 5 percent who reported having more frequent clashes with Latino customers. In South Central, where the respondents depend more heavily on both black and Latino customers, 65 percent reported more frequent clashes with black customers and only 3 percent with Latino customers. Thus, frequent contact increases the level of clashes with black customers but not with Latino customers. It is also interesting to note that even the respondents in Koreatown conformed to this pattern, although blacks are a marginal customer group there (3 percent of the total). If more frequent contact increases the potential for intergroup clashes, these respondents should have reported more frequent clashes with Latino customers. The fact that they did not suggests that different levels of intergroup clashes result from something other than different levels of intergroup contact. Differ-

Table 4.6. Perceived Differences in the Frequency of Clashes with Black and Latino Customers

	Total		Koreatown		South Central	
Frequency	N	%	N	%	N	%
More frequent clashes with						
Black customers	83	42.1	23	22.1	60	64.5
Latino customers	9	4.6	6	5.8	3	3.2
No difference	26	13.2	11	10.6	15	16.1
Don't know	20	10.2	14	13.5	6	6.5
Not applicable	59	29.9	50	48.1	9	9.7
Total	197	100.0	104	100.0	93	100.0

Note: The "Not applicable" category refers to those who have no interaction with black and Latino customers.

ent sets of attitudes and behaviors among Koreans, blacks, and Latinos seem to be a more important cause of this pattern.

The most frequently cited reason for the more frequent clashes with black customers is the perception of Korean store owners that blacks are more demanding than Latinos in their requests for better prices, credit, and refund and exchange of merchandise (see table 4.7). Blacks, who are more fluent in English and more aware of customer rights than Latinos, are seen to be more assertive in these demands.

Merchandise sold in Korean stores is cheap and thus not built to last. Store owners expect that their customers accept this risk when they purchase the merchandise. In addition, because of their small profit margins, store owners either deny refunds and exchanges entirely or allow only a three-day or one-week warranty period. This is the most frequent source of disputes between Korean store owners and black customers. Accustomed to the lenient refund and exchange policies of larger department stores, blacks expect the same services at smaller Korean stores. When their requests are rejected, they engage in verbal disputes with the owners that often involve the exchange of racial epithets between the two parties.

Refund and exchange policies are not widely practiced in Korean stores partly because they are not part of business practices in South Korea and immigrant store owners are therefore not accustomed to them. Although it may sound exaggerated, store owners are the king in South Korea, whereas customers are the king in the United States.

Table 4.7. Reasons for Frequency of Clashes with Black Customers (Percentages)

Reason	Total	Koreatown	South Central
Blacks are major customers	23.8	4.5	31.0
Blacks are more demanding and assertive[a]	55.1	63.7	51.7
Blacks' more frequent misbehaviors[b]	33.8	27.3	36.2
Blacks' worse economic conditions	7.5	9.1	6.9
Greater cultural difference with blacks	10.0	0.0	13.8
Greater language barriers with blacks	11.3	0.0	13.8
Blacks' prejudice against and mistreatment of Koreans	13.8	13.6	13.8
Koreans' prejudice against and mistreatment of blacks	3.8	9.1	1.7
Mutual prejudice, distrust, and disrespect	2.5	4.5	1.7
Others	1.3	4.5	0.0
Total			
Percentage	163.0	136.0	171.0
Number	80	22	58

Note: In an open-ended question, respondents were asked to cite three reasons for having more frequent clashes with black customers than with Latino customers or vice versa. Only the respondents who reported having more frequent clashes with black customers were included for analysis in this table. The total percentage is over 100 because the respondents cited more than one reason.

a. In their requests for better prices, credit, and service.

b. More likely than Latinos to lie, shoplift, and use bad language.

American standards of customer rights and protections are much different from those in South Korea. There customers are annoyingly chased by store owners and employees and often pressured to purchase unwanted merchandise, which they must then keep whether they like it or not. Korean immigrant business owners who were instructed in this practice in South Korea tend to think that black customers assume they have no duties, only rights.

Blacks' more demanding stance toward Korean store owners is also seen as a reflection of their sense of seniority.[18] In the words of many Koreans, blacks tend to think of themselves as hosts and Koreans as strangers who were not invited into this country. Some Koreans coined the term "master consciousness" to describe this attitude. The story of a Korean liquor store owner illustrates his contrasting feelings toward black and Latino customers:

> Blacks often come in with the attitude that they are the king and feel
> superior to the store owner. They feel that as customers they are enti-

tled to good quality service; no matter how badly they treat the store owner, they are always right. Since blacks have the advantage over language, they look down on me. However, Mexican customers would come in with a more friendly attitude. Many times a group of Mexicans would come in and say, "¿Qué pasa amigo" or "Hi, my friend!" They expect someone on the other side to be friendly and be on an equal level. With many Mexican customers I am able to build friendly relationships. As a gesture of respect, many Mexican customers try to learn Korean or teach me a couple of easy Spanish phrases that would be useful to them. Even though we have language barriers, we are able to communicate adequately with broken English. Since blacks speak fluent English, they are less patient in communicating. (Personal interview)

Another factor contributing to the more frequent clashes with black customers is, as mentioned earlier, their alleged shoplifting. Although Latino customers are also said to shoplift, Korean store owners tend to believe that black customers do so more frequently in their stores, leading to greater intergroup tensions and potential for conflict.

Perceptions of Blacks and Latinos as Neighbors

It is not clear whether their more frequent clashes with black customers are a cause or a symptom of Koreans' greater prejudice against blacks. In my judgment, the two factors are closely related in such a way that an initial prejudice against blacks increases the likelihood of clashes with them, which in turn reinforces the prejudice.

Probably because of this reciprocal relationship, Korean store owners have more unfavorable attitudes toward and greater feelings of social distance from blacks than they do from whites, Asians, or Latinos. As table 4.8 indicates, blacks were perceived by the respondents as the least hardworking, the most prone to violence, the least intelligent, and the most dependent on welfare. Although Latinos were perceived unfavorably in terms of their personality traits, they were still seen as superior to blacks in terms of their work ethic, aversion to violence, intelligence, and self-sufficiency. For instance, 78 percent of the respondents thought that blacks were lazy, whereas 44 percent thought that Latinos were lazy. Similarly, 76 percent believed that blacks lived off welfare rather than supporting themselves, while 58 percent said that Latinos did likewise.

Table 4.8. Korean Store Owners' Perceptions of Four Racial Groups (Percentages)

Trait Dimension	Whites	Asians	Blacks	Latinos
Diligence				
1 Hardworking	10.2	28.1	0.5	0.0
2	17.9	43.9	0.5	4.6
3	27.0	16.3	1.0	10.7
4 Intermediate	31.6	7.1	13.3	38.3
5	2.6	1.0	24.5	25.5
6	1.0	0.5	41.0	13.8
7 Lazy	0.0	0.0	12.2	5.1
8 Don't know	9.7	3.1	6.1	2.0
Mean	3.0	2.1	5.5	4.5
Balance[a]	51.5	86.8	−75.7	−29.1
Number of respondents	196	196	196	196
Violence				
1 Violence-prone	1.5	1.5	21.4	6.6
2	5.6	3.1	32.1	14.8
3	9.2	8.7	19.4	26.5
4 Intermediate	25.0	26.0	13.8	29.6
5	11.7	14.8	2.0	8.2
6	18.4	20.4	1.5	5.1
7 Not violence-prone	9.7	16.8	2.6	1.5
8 Don't know	18.9	8.7	7.1	7.7
Mean	4.7	5.0	2.5	3.4
Balance[a]	−23.5	−38.7	66.9	33.2
Number of respondents	196	196	196	196
Intelligence				
1 Intelligent	6.2	10.8	0.0	0.0
2	27.2	38.5	1.0	1.0
3	25.6	25.1	3.1	5.1
4 Intermediate	25.6	15.9	19.5	23.6
5	1.0	1.0	25.1	29.7
6	0.0	0.5	30.3	23.1
7 Unintelligent	0.5	0.0	10.3	8.2
8 Don't know	13.8	8.2	10.8	9.2
Mean	2.9	2.6	5.3	5.0
Balance[a]	57.5	72.9	−61.5	−54.8
Number of respondents	195	195	195	195
Dependency				
1 Self-supporting	25.0	17.9	0.0	0.5
2	38.3	39.3	2.6	3.6
3	13.8	20.4	3.1	4.6
4 Intermediate	14.8	12.2	11.3	26.7
5	0.5	4.6	22.6	28.2

Table 4.8. *Continued*

Trait Dimension	Whites	Asians	Blacks	Latinos
6	0.0	0.0	39.0	24.1
7 Live off welfare	0.0	0.0	14.4	5.6
8 Don't know	7.7	5.6	7.2	6.7
Mean	2.2	2.4	5.5	4.9
Balance[a]	76.5	73.0	–70.3	–49.2
Number of respondents	196	196	195	195
Summary ratings[b]				
(Undesirable–Desirable)				
Mean	20.4	21.9	10.4	13.1
Number of cases	135	166	164	166

Note: Respondents were shown a seven-point scale on which the characteristics of people in a group could be rated. A score of 1 meant "almost all of the people in that group" had a given positive (negative) trait; a socre of 7 meant "almost all of the people in that group" had a given negative (positive) trait; and a score of 4 meant "the group was not toward one end or the other."

a. Balance is the percentage difference between positive responses and negative responses. When the mean scores and percentage difference are used together, they yield more reliable results than when used alone. The "Don't know" category was not included in the calculation of the mean scores and the percentage difference.

b. Summary savings were computed by summing up the scores of the four trait ratings. They range from 4 (most undesirable) to 16 (intermediate) to 28 (most desirable). Traits one, three, and four were reverse coded.

The respondents in Koreatown were slightly more favorable toward blacks than their counterparts in South Central, but the difference between the two groups was negligible. For example, the summary trait ratings of blacks, which ranged from 4 (the least desirable) to 28 (the most desirable), were 10.6 for the respondents in Koreatown and 10.1 for the respondents in South Central. In addition, the two groups were almost equal in their attitudes toward Latinos. These findings indicate that the respondents' prejudice toward blacks and Latinos was not determined by the business environment. In other words, the respondents in Koreatown, who interact less frequently with black and Latino customers than their counterparts in South Central, have essentially the same attitudes toward the two minority groups.

The respondents also displayed greater feelings of social distance from blacks than from any of the other racial groups. Eighty percent of them were opposed to the idea of living in a neighborhood in which half the residents were black and 72 percent of them to the idea of having a close relative marry a black person. In contrast, 39 percent were opposed

Table 4.9. Korean Store Owners' Social Distance Feelings of From Members of Four Racial Groups (Percentages)

Social Distance Category	Whites	Asians	Blacks	Latinos
Residential Integration[a]				
1 Strongly favor	24.7	8.6	0.0	0.0
2	37.4	29.8	1.5	5.6
3 Not favor or oppose	36.4	52.0	16.7	25.3
4	1.5	8.6	49.0	46.0
5 Strongly oppose	0.0	1.0	32.0	23.2
Mean	2.2	2.6	4.1	3.9
Balance	60.6	28.8	−79.5	−63.6
Number of respondents	198	198	198	198
Intermarriage[b]				
1 Strongly favor	1.0	4.5	1.0	0.0
2	2.5	16.7	0.5	2.0
3 Not favor or oppose	49.0	47.5	24.7	34.8
4	27.3	19.7	34.8	36.4
5 Strongly oppose	20.2	11.6	38.9	26.8
Mean	3.6	3.2	4.1	3.9
Balance	−44.0	−10.1	−72.2	−61.2
Number of respondents	198	198	198	198

a. Living in a neighborhood in which half the neighbors are from the given racial group.

b. Having a close relative marry a member of the given racial group.

to living in a predominantly white neighborhood and 44 percent to having a close relative marry a white person (see table 4.9).

Interestingly, Korean store owners seem to be more prejudiced against blacks than are whites. According to Bobo and Kluegel (1991), who used data from the 1990 General Social Survey, 44 percent of 1,150 white respondents thought blacks were lazy and 56 percent thought they lived off welfare. (In contrast, 78 percent and 76 percent of the 196 Korean respondents in my study held these views, respectively.) Similarly, 47 percent of the white respondents in the GSS survey (compared to 81 percent of my Korean respondents) were opposed to living in a predominantly black neighborhood and 65 percent (compared to 74 percent) were opposed to having a relative marry a black person.

What, then, are the sources of Korean store owners' prejudice against blacks? It is often said that Koreans were prejudiced against blacks prior to their immigration to the United States (Jo 1992). Coming from a culturally and racially homogeneous society, they are said to be ill prepared to deal with racial diversity in the United States. To make matters worse, their images of blacks were negatively shaped by Hollywood movies and TV programs that stereotyped blacks as lazy, unintelligent, prone to violence, and inferior to whites.

Their postimmigration experiences seem to have reinforced rather than changed their initial attitudes toward blacks. This has happened primarily because of their limited and biased interaction with the black population. As Korean immigrants established their businesses in inner-city black neighborhoods, their contact with low-income blacks increased, and a growing number of them and their employees became the victims of assault, harassment, and murder by black criminals. In addition, because of their great social and economic isolation in the United States, Korean immigrants have tended to rely on the ethnic mass media and on institutions such as the church for information about the larger society.[19] These ethnic institutions are essentially nationalistic and conservative, making divisions between "us" and "them," between "the Korean community" and "the American community," and justifying the actions of Koreans while blaming others for any troubles. Such events and processes have tended to solidify Koreans' initial stereotypes about blacks.

Their tendency to maintain a wide social distance from blacks also results from their perception that blacks have a significantly different attitude toward upward mobility in American society. Like all immigrants, Koreans have strong motivations for such mobility and believe in the American Dream. Eighty percent of the respondents in this study agreed to the statement that everyone in America can achieve whatever he or she wishes through hard work. Yet 85 percent of them also agreed to the statement that racial discrimination makes it difficult for members of minority groups to achieve the same level of success as whites. These findings may sound contradictory, but in fact they show Korean immigrants' belief that although the United States is not a perfect society, it still provides opportunities for upward mobility for hardworking persons.

From this viewpoint, Korean immigrants find it difficult to comprehend why many American blacks—who were born in this country, are fluent in English, and are familiar with American customs—remain unemployed and poor. A veteran Korean business owner on the South Side of Chicago commented on his initial difficulty in understanding the lack of motivation and work ethic among low-income blacks:

"There are things my employees and customers can learn from me,"
says Mr. Ku. "My employees spend $3 a day on lunch. But I don't
spend my money on lunch. I bring a bag lunch. That means I save
$18 or $20 a week." He pauses for a moment and points to his blue
polyester trousers. "Look at these pants. They're seven years old. My
shoes cost $10. I don't spend money on clothes; I save money for spe-
cific reasons. We know why we are here—for a better education for
our children, the second generation. This country is the best. It offers
us golden opportunities for economic success." He laughs and
blushes, acknowledging that his enthusiastic recital sounds immodest.
Most of his customers, Ku adds, do not share his optimism about the
potential for success and achievement in this country. It took him a
while to understand that. (Joravsky 1987)

The strong aspirations of such immigrants for economic mobility
and for acceptance by whites discourage them from associating with
blacks. Instead, they tend to identify themselves with whites and to ad-
here to the negative stereotypes whites have about blacks. Such an orientation, of course, causes resentment among blacks. Thus, the prejudice
Koreans and blacks have toward each other and the different attitudes
they have toward social and economic assimilation prevent them from
acknowledging their common status as disadvantaged minority members
and from taking collective approaches to advance their common interests.

Summary and Discussion

Attitudes and feelings of social distance between members of different
minority groups in American society seem to be affected by two contradictory forces. On the one hand, the members of such groups may acknowledge their common status as the disadvantaged and the oppressed
in a white-dominated society and join together to challenge the system
that created inequality and racism in the first place. On the other hand,
members of one group may attempt to be accepted by the majority group
and to distance themselves from the other minority group. Moreover,
when the two groups compete for society's scarce resources, this may
reinforce the prejudice and hatred between them.

Findings from this study consistently show that Koreans do not
identify with blacks but rather try to distance themselves from them.

They discriminate against blacks in hiring practices, experience frequent clashes with them as customers, and exhibit negative stereotypes about them as neighbors. By comparison, they maintain smoother relations with Latinos, strongly preferring them as employees and experiencing few clashes with them as customers.

These differences in Koreans' relations with blacks and with Latinos result from several factors. First and foremost, the common nativity status of Koreans and Latinos makes the two groups feel emotionally and culturally close to each other. As immigrants, both groups suffer from similar disadvantages and are not in a position to assert a nativistic sense of seniority over each other. Consequently, Koreans' success in small business is perceived not as a threat to Latinos but as a desirable path to success they want to follow. In contrast, the difference in nativity status between Koreans and blacks makes Korean store owners feel less confident in their relations with blacks, who are seen to be more assertive than Latinos toward Koreans. Blacks are also seen to claim seniority over and entitlement to social and economic advancement ahead of immigrants. Because of these attitudes, blacks are perceived as resenting more strongly than Latinos any signs of disrespect and mistreatment they receive as customers.

The next important factor is the different level of political mobilization among blacks and Latinos. Historically, blacks have used political means, such as boycotts, to correct discrimination and economic injustice against their community. Locally based black nationalist organizations have been most active in organizing anti–Korean business boycotts. However, a similar level of political mobilization has not been reached in the Latino immigrant community. Thus, even when Latinos feel mistreated and exploited by Korean store owners, their grievances are not likely to develop into collective actions against these businesses.

Solutions to the Korean–black conflict are not simple, for it is caused by a myriad of psychological, situational, and political factors. Moreover, it cannot be solved by grassroots efforts of individuals or by the Korean and black communities alone. Individual store owners' efforts to improve their communication skills and their service to their customers can reduce to a certain degree over-the-counter disputes and clashes, but these are still partial solutions. Korean businesses in inner-city neighborhoods that are plagued by joblessness and poverty can provide some jobs to local residents, but they cannot change the overall economic conditions of such neighborhoods. Thus, effective solutions to the conflict should involve multifaceted and coordinated efforts of individuals, communities, and the government.

Although there is no panacea, I would like to make some practical policy recommendations that could prevent destructive conflicts from developing between Koreans and blacks. First, at the government level, more funding should be allocated for dispute-prevention and -resolution centers in areas with a high probability of group conflict. The function of these centers is to mediate between Korean store owners and black customers in disputes and to provide them with appropriate counseling and assistance, including translation. Staffed by social workers, business owners, local residents, community leaders, scholars, politicians, and government agents, these centers could effectively prevent minor disputes and accidents from developing into destructive group conflicts. Both the Korean and black communities and the city and federal governments should provide funding sufficient to hire qualified, full-time staffs who could devote their time and energy to education, counseling, mediation, and coalition building between Koreans and other racial minority groups.

More effective police protection should also be provided to small businesses in high-crime areas. Many Korean store owners in South Central complain that the police do not respond to their calls promptly, and criminals receive penalties too lenient for their crimes. Out of fear that they will be the victims of revenge by the arrested criminals, store owners are discouraged from filing police reports, which in turn makes them easy and safe targets of criminal activities. In self-defense, many store owners arm themselves, and this often results in accidents involving firearms. The Soon Ja Du and Tae Sam Park cases in Los Angeles grew out of this context. Both store owners had been robbed numerous times and had to protect themselves in the absence of proper police protection. Twenty-five Korean store owners had been murdered by blacks in South Central during the previous two years. To stop these tragic incidents from occurring, more bilingual Korean American police officers should be hired to facilitate communication with Korean store owners, and branch police stations should be established in Koreatown and South Central for more reliable protection.

At the community level, more cultural and educational programs should be established to bridge the cultural and ideological gap between the Korean and black communities. Art festivals, seminars, scholarships for needy black students, essay and speech contests, sponsored trips to

South Korea, joint church worship, and the like could promote better understanding and greater appreciation of each group's history, culture, lifestyles, and living conditions. In particular, Korean store owners who are too busy to attend English language courses would benefit from educational videotapes that teach practical, business-related English words and expressions as well as black culture. This information would help them communicate more effectively with black customers and treat them more appropriately. The Korean and black communities should join together in the production and wide distribution of such videotapes.

Political empowerment of Korean store owners and Korean Americans in general is another strategy to protect the community from being victimized in the Korean–black conflict. Although there are many ways to accomplish this goal, one practical means would be to consolidate various Korean community organizations. United, these organizations could mobilize community resources more effectively than they can through the uncoordinated efforts of individuals and organizations, and they could also represent and protect more forcefully the interests of Koreans in times of political crisis. The Korean American Inter-Agency Council (KAIAC), which was formed during the 1992 civil unrest in Los Angeles by coordinating the resources and services of nine Korean American voluntary associations, exemplifies the collective approach that the Korean community should pursue in its relations with other ethnic communities and the government.[20] Store owners have traditionally donated money individually to local black charity organizations, but their donations have not received attention from the mass media and the black community because of the lack of publicity. If united Korean organizations could collect donations from the owners and deliver them to influential and respected organizations, Koreans could make more effective use of their money by improving their public relations with the black community. The same strategy could be applied to political donations. By consolidating votes and donations, Korean Americans could put more effective pressure on politicians and get more tangible returns from their support.

United Korean organizations could fulfill several functions that would help improve Korean businesses and race relations between Koreans and members of other minority groups. One is coalition building between the Korean and black communities. By participating in and supporting responsible black political organizations, such as the NAACP, the Urban League, or the Rainbow Coalition, Koreans could in return get their support in times of political crisis and could prevent political demagogues from using Koreans as convenient scapegoats for their selfish political interests. In collaboration with such mainstream organizations, Koreans and blacks could work out solutions to racial problems within the system and deny militant black nationalist organizations any opportunities to use violent means to advance "black-only" interests.

Another important function this coalition could fill is market research and social service delivery. Staffed by experts in marketing, banking, and social service administration, the united Korean organizations could explore new business markets and business types beyond the narrow range of those in South Central. By informing Korean business owners of new opportunities outside black neighborhoods and helping them get the bank and SBA loans necessary for relocation, they could lower the concentration of Korean businesses in such neighborhoods, thus reducing the potential for conflicts between Koreans and blacks.

Finally, at the individual level, Koreans should make a Copernican change in their business philosophy and attitudes toward blacks. Obsessed with the goal of quick upward economic mobility, Korean immigrants have developed what Max Weber called a dual ethic, featuring one morality for in-group members and another for the out-group. As Light and Bonacich (1988, 433) poignantly highlight, many Koreans have been indifferent to the impact of their businesses on the local community. Liquor stores in low-income minority neighborhoods illustrate the case. When such businesses become a target of opposition from local residents, Koreans need to consider changing to more socially and morally acceptable businesses, such as dry cleaning. In short, public relations should be more seriously considered in their accounting of costs and profits.

Finally, Koreans should ask themselves, "Who are my neighbors?" By definition, neighbors are those who live close by and suffer from problems similar to ours; thus blacks and Latinos—not whites, by whom Koreans strive to be accepted—are their neighbors. Only when they begin to accept blacks and Latinos as neighbors and to participate in collective approaches to challenge discrimination against racial minorities can true racial harmony be achieved among Koreans, blacks, and Latinos.

FIVE

CONCLUSION

Immigration, entrepreneurship, and race relations are three foundational issues in the contemporary Korean American community. They affect significantly the family structures and relations, the cultural, social, and economic incorporation, and the political participation of Korean Americans in American society. They are also closely interrelated. Thus, a complete understanding of the community requires systematic analyses of the origins, patterns, and consequences of these three issues.

In this book, I have explained under what conditions and with what motivations middle-class Koreans have come to the United States, why and how small business has become the major economic activity of these immigrants, and finally how their businesses in minority neighborhoods have intensified racial tensions with such minority groups as blacks and Latinos. In this concluding chapter, I summarize the major findings of each chapter; predict the future directions of Korean immigration, immigrant entrepreneurship, and race relations; and propose an agenda for future research.

Korean Immigration to the United States

Korean immigration to the United States has evolved in the context of the American military, economic, and cultural involvement in Korea. The early Korean immigration (1903–44) was initiated by Hawaii's sugar planters, who wanted to recruit Korean laborers to work in their plantation fields. More than 400,000 immigrant laborers from thirty-three countries had been recruited in this way since the 1830s (Patterson 1988, 2–3), and 7,226 Korean immigrants arrived between 1903 and 1905. Among Asians, the Chinese had begun to arrive in 1852, and the Japanese began to arrive in 1885 because of restrictions on the entry of Chinese laborers. Koreans were recruited to break a strike by these Japanese laborers, but when their immigration was abruptly halted because of the Japanese government's opposition in 1905, Filipino laborers began to enter the market. As such, Asian immigration to the United States before World War II involved an ethnic succession of labor (Bonacich 1984), and early Korean immigration was part of this larger trend.

The U.S. military involvement in Korea after World War II paved the way for the immigration of large numbers of Korean women and children to the United States. At the conclusion of the war in 1945, the United States and the Soviet Union had become the superpowers in Asia competing for political hegemony. During and after the Korean War (1950–53), the United States provided military and economic aid to South Korea to prevent the spread of communism in Asia. The presence of U.S. troops resulted in a sizable number of intermarriages between Korean women and American military servicemen, and these women later entered the United States as spouses of American GIs.

The political and military dominance of the United States over South Korea has extended to cultural dominance. Between 1945 and 1965, about 6,000 Korean students came to the United States to seek higher education at colleges and universities. They did so in expectation of achieving social prestige back in South Korea with their American diplomas. Many of them, however, settled in the United States after finishing their studies and laid the foundation for chain migration from their homeland.

After the Korean War, the United States provided greater economic aid to South Korea to strengthen its economic stability and thus to help the country withstand communism. The United States also became Korea's primary supplier of capital and technology as well as its largest overseas market, helping it build economic infrastructures and foundations for a free market economy that were essential for its continuing economic growth. The economic linkage between the United States and South Korea thus paved the way for large-scale immigration of professional, managerial, and technical workers to the United States in the 1960s and 1970s.

From the beginning of its involvement in South Korea, representatives of the United States tried to inculcate the American concept of democracy among the Korean population through school reforms. American missionaries representing Protestant denominations also built many high schools and universities throughout the country as part of their mission. As many Korean elites were educated in these private schools, Christianity became a symbol of modern ideas and spread rapidly among the educated urban classes. Such assistance from the American public and private sectors made it possible for South Korea to expand its educational system even when its economy would not have permitted it. A strong desire for higher education has also motivated Koreans to invest in education with little specific reference to its economic returns. The outcome has been an oversupply of highly educated workers in the domestic economy.

Rapid expansion of higher education and export-oriented economic development produced a new urban middle class in South Korean society. The members of this class maintained strong motivations for upward social and economic mobility, but they could not realize their goals in South Korea because of its limited resources and opportunities. After the United States opened its door to all immigrants in 1965, they began to immigrate in search of better economic and educational opportunities.

The first wave of post-1965 immigrants included a high proportion of professionals, particularly medical practitioners. These highly educated and skilled workers were preferentially admitted to the United States until 1976 via occupational visa categories. Economic recessions of the early 1970s and lobbying by U.S. medical schools finally forced Congress to reduce the annual number of occupational immigrants by placing various hurdles before them. Prospective Korean immigrants then began to use family reunification preference categories more intensively, and the majority of them now obtain their U.S. permanent residency through such categories (90 percent in 1989).

As more Korean immigrants have come to the United States through family networks, the proportion of them who come from working-class backgrounds has been increasing. Now, Korean immigrants come in almost equal numbers from middle-class and working-class backgrounds. This trend has made the Korean American community more diverse and heterogeneous in terms of occupations, socioeconomic status, and class positions in American society.

The future of Korean immigration to the United States is difficult to predict, yet we can make several projections of its future size and characteristics by examining past and present trends. First, unless drastic upheavals take place in the Korean peninsula, the annual number of immigrants to the United States will not exceed the current level and will probably decline. The improving standard of living in South Korea will make immigration less and less attractive. Second, the proportion of Korean immigrants from lower- and working-class backgrounds will increase, as immigration will continue to be more attractive to them than to the members of the middle and upper-middle classes. Third, the annual number of immigrants who return to South Korea will increase as the expanding Korean economy provides them with greater employment opportunities and security than the U.S. economy. In particular, the return migration of American-educated professionals and technicians will increase as South Korea competes more intensely with other industrialized nations in the global economy and needs an internationally competitive workforce.

Finally, the volume of Koreans who migrate between South Korea and the United States will continue to grow as a result of expanding economic and cultural ties between the two countries. However, their migration will be more bidirectional and temporary than unidirectional and permanent. Thus, the annual number of temporary workers, visitors for business or pleasure, students, and intracompany transferees will increase, whereas the number of permanent immigrants will decrease.

Korean Immigrant Entrepreneurship

The rapid proliferation of Korean businesses in large American cities has attracted the attention of many scholars. However, they have not reached a consensus on what constitutes the social origins of Korean immigrant entrepreneurship. Alejandro Portes and Robert Manning (1986, 56) said, "The origins of Korean enterprise may be uncertain but its existence is indisputable." Illsoo Kim (1981, ch. 10) claimed in the conclusion of his now-classic *New Urban Immigrants* that the value congruence between Confucianism and the Protestant ethic, both of which emphasize self-control and self-abnegation, explains the success of Korean immigrants. "An emphasis on economic motivation and mobility," he wrote, "has contributed to acculturation in the new land because it was already a deep part of contemporary Korean culture and values" (295). Such character, according to Kim, motivates these immigrants to work hard and succeed in small business. Ivan Light and Edna Bonacich (1988, ch. 11) disagreed with Kim's attribution of Korean entrepreneurship to the character of individual immigrants and instead emphasized class culture (for example, educational background and values) as its likely source. Pyong Gap Min (1988), on the other hand, proposed that the status inconsistency of Korean immigrants in American society is the primary cause of their propensity toward small business.

In short, it is not easy to pinpoint the basic social origins of Korean immigrant enterprise, but as discussed in chapter 1, an interactive model that takes into account immigrants' employment and business opportunity structures as well as their ability to mobilize resources seems to provide the best explanation.

For many Korean immigrants, self-employment in business is a situational adaptation to limited opportunities for white-collar wage employment in the U.S. labor market. Although the majority of post-1965 Korean immigrants have received a college education and have come from white-collar occupational backgrounds in South Korea, the positions initially available to them in the United States have been low-skilled and low-paying manual, service, and sales jobs. The language barrier and their Korean education and occupational skills, which are not easily transferable to the American labor market, are largely responsible for their difficulty in obtaining the types of employment for which they have been trained. Under such circumstances, they have turned to small businesses to earn more income and gain more independence than they would have working for others.

In addition to aspirations for upward economic mobility, the economic development of South Korea has been crucial for the growth of Korean immigrant businesses. Since 1962, South Korea has experienced export-oriented development that is highly dependent on foreign markets, especially that of the United States. The international trade linkage among Korean manufacturers, importers, and retailers provided immigrants with initial business opportunities in minority neighborhoods of central cities, where inexpensive Korean-made products were in great demand among low-income customers.

The interracial succession of residence and business in these areas during the 1960s also facilitated the entry of Korean immigrant businesses. As blacks moved into previously white-dominated neighborhoods, the white population moved out, frequently followed by white business owners. By increasing the number of vacated businesses in these racially transitional areas, such changes enabled Korean immigrants to establish their businesses in minority neighborhoods without great resistance.

Korean immigrant businesses are generally small in size with respect to start-up capital, annual gross sales, and the number of paid employees.

Half of the Korean business owners in Chicago and Los Angeles started their first businesses with less than $40,000, and more than 60 percent of them handle less than $500,000 in annual gross sales. About 20 percent of these businesses do not hire any paid employees, and those that do usually have between three and five.

Handicapped by limited capital, the language barrier, and the lack of prior business experience, Korean immigrants tend to concentrate in labor-intensive retail and personal service trades, such as produce, grocery, liquor, apparel, accessory, and general merchandise retail; dry cleaning and laundry; and the restaurant business. Establishing such businesses in low-income minority neighborhoods lowers their entry-level costs further. Businesses in these neighborhoods fill a marginal market that is neglected by large retail stores because of the low profit margin and the high crime rates.

Recently, however, there has been a noticeable movement toward more capital- and technology-intensive businesses. According to the U.S. Bureau of the Census's Survey of Minority-Owned Business Enterprises (1985; 1991), 6,494 new Korean-owned businesses were established in construction, manufacturing, wholesale trade, finance, insurance, and real estate from 1982 to 1987, representing a 197 percent increase. In contrast, retail trade posted only a 104 percent increase, from 12,831 to 26,161 businesses. As a result of this upgrade in business types, the average receipts per business increased from $9,480 (in 1987 dollars) to $110,859.

While Korean immigrants will continue to engage in such businesses at high rates, Korean Americans of the second and third generations will not follow the paths of their parents. Instead, they will seek professional and white-collar wage employment in the mainstream American economy. Accordingly, as increasing numbers of them enter the U.S. labor market, self-employment rates among Korean Americans are expected to decline. In this sense, they are following the same path that Jewish Americans have already taken (Goldscheider and Kobrin 1980).

Korean Relations with Blacks and Latinos

The concentration of Korean immigrants in small businesses, particularly in minority neighborhoods, has caused racial tensions between Korean business owners and minority residents. While these owners regard

inner-city neighborhoods as the most affordable place to run their businesses, black residents view them as another wave of absentee owners
who drain resources out of the community without contributing to the
local economy. From this viewpoint, Koreans are not much different
from their Jewish and Italian predecessors, who were regarded as stealing
business opportunities from blacks.

The attitudes of inner-city blacks toward immigrants worsened during the 1980s, when their social and economic conditions deteriorated
as a result of plant closures in central cities and sharp cuts in public assistance programs for low-income and unemployed people. Massive job
losses in the heavy manufacturing sector, which used to pay black workers relatively high blue-collar wages, triggered a series of economic and
social problems in these inner-city neighborhoods, such as unemployment, poverty, and crime (Wilson, 1987). This, in turn, has lowered the
level of tolerance toward immigrants—particularly Latinos, who have
been gradually encroaching on black neighborhoods and competing for
residence, education, employment, and political representation. As a result, there has been a growing sense of frustration among blacks, who
feel that they have been constantly bypassed by immigrant groups in social and economic mobility and that the U.S. government provides pref-
erential assistance to refugees and immigrants over native-born blacks.

On top of these structural factors, prejudice, language barriers, cultural differences, and alleged incidents of shoplifting and mistreatment
of customers have precipitated numerous over-the-counter disputes between Korean store owners and black customers. These store-level disputes escalate into collective actions, such as boycotts, when black nationalist organizations intervene and mobilize individual blacks' bad
feelings toward individual Korean store owners into a broader notion
that Koreans are exploiting blacks. In this sense, the Korean–black conflict is not an economic competition or a cultural clash but an essentially
political phenomenon.

In comparison, Korean–Latino relations have been less violent and
hostile. This is partly because the two groups share a predominantly immigrant status and an "immigrant mentality." As such, neither group is
in a position to claim a nativistic sense of seniority over the other; instead, they feel emotionally and culturally close. As a result, Korean businesses have not experienced the same kind of rejection from the Latino
community as they have from the black community.

However, the future of Korean–Latino relations is not so bright.

Members of these two groups interact not only as merchants and customers (as do Koreans and blacks) but also as employers and employees. Latinos now represent the major workforce in many types of Korean businesses, such as restaurants, grocery markets, and garment manufacturers. In an important sense, these businesses survive and prosper at the expense of Latinos, who are perceived as cheap and docile labor. They are often paid less than the minimum wage, forced to work in hazardous environments, and even physically and sexually abused. Under these circumstances, there could be a conflict between the Korean petty bourgeoisie and the Latino proletariat in the future.

Research Agenda

Several issues merit further investigation in future research. First, more up-to-date information is needed on the ethnic succession of businesses in such inner-city neighborhoods as South Central Los Angeles. The destructive civil unrest in April 1992 expedited the out-migration of Korean businesses from South Central, opening up business opportunities there. It remains to be seen whether these opportunities will be seized by black entrepreneurs or by other immigrant groups such as the Vietnamese, who in recent years have been taking over Korean businesses in South Central in increasing numbers. As Korean business owners have become older, economically more secure, and sick and tired of crime and anti-Korean sentiment among black residents, they have become more willing to sell their businesses to such new immigrants, who are still aggressive and hungry enough to take these risks. If this trend continues in the future, conflicts between black residents and outsider immigrants will also continue.

Second, more research is needed on the role of export–import trade in the growth of immigrant and ethnic entrepreneurship. As explained in chapter 3, such trade between the United States and South Korea provided many Korean immigrants with initial business opportunities in minority areas. Several recent immigrant groups, such as the Chinese from Hong Kong and Taiwan and the ethnic Chinese from Vietnam, also participate on a large scale in the trade between the United States and their home countries (Kwong 1987; Gold 1994).

The import–export trade is one of the fastest growing business areas in the Asian American community. Its importance is likely to grow in the Pacific Rim era, in which commodities, capital, information, and people are exchanged across the Pacific Ocean at ever increasing rates. Furthermore, the cultural, social, and economic ties between Asian countries and their emigrants to the United States are becoming stronger with the advancement of communication and transportation. For these reasons, the capability of immigrant entrepreneurs to link overseas markets and capital with coethnic entrepreneurs in the United States will become increasingly important for the development of Asian immigrant entrepreneurship.

Finally, comparative research is needed on the role of black nationalism in the Korean–black conflict. As suggested in chapter 4, the intensity of this conflict seems to be strongly affected by the presence or absence of militant black nationalist organizations in a given city. For example, Korean–black relations have been less violent in Chicago and Atlanta than in New York City and Los Angeles, partly because in the former cities the Korean community has maintained good working relationships with national black leaders such as Jesse Jackson and Andrew Young. In Chicago, Operation PUSH and the Rainbow Coalition have intervened in many black boycotts of Korean businesses. In contrast, Korean–black relations in New York City and Los Angeles have been more violent and Korean businesses there have been subject to prolonged black boycotts, partly because of the active role of local organizations such as the December 12th Movement and the Brotherhood Crusade.

To date, there has been no research comparing Korean–black relations in more than three American cities. Thus, it is difficult to know how strongly and in what fashion black nationalism and nationalist organizations affect this relationship. Future research should focus on the varying effects of such organizations on Korean–black relations in different American cities.

Introduction

1. *Sa-I-Gu* was produced in 1993 by Christine Choy, Elaine Kim, and Dai Sil Kim-Gibson. Quotations from the interviews with Mrs. Lee are based on captions in the film.

2. In the 1970s, when Korean immigrants started entering the U.S. labor market, cleaning and sewing were the entry-level jobs for men and women, respectively. Koreans called this job pattern *Nam Ch'ŏng Yŏ Gong*, which translates as "men cleaning, women sewing."

3. The three-day event in Los Angeles is variously labeled a "riot," a "rebellion," or "civil unrest." These labels reveal important ideological, moral, and political differences among those who use them. People who call the event a riot highlight its destructive, senseless, and opportunistic aspects. Accordingly, they condemn people who participated in it as "rioters," "looters," and "arsonists" who took advantage of the vacuum in law enforcement for their selfish, materialistic interests. From this viewpoint, Korean store owners who lost their stores and other properties as a result are labeled "innocent victims" who were the wrong target in the wrong place at the wrong time. On the contrary, people who call the event a rebellion tend to justify the actions of the participants as an outbreak of frustration and anger accumulated over a long period of discrimination and injustice against racial minorities in a white-dominated society and judicial system. From this viewpoint, Korean store owners, who suffered enormous financial and psychological costs, are partly responsible for what they suffered because they had contributed to the unjust economic system of the United States as mediators between white capitalists and minority customers.

The label given to the event often depends on the race and political vision of the commentator. Most Koreans and whites call it simply "the L.A. riots," but many blacks—particularly left-wing intellectuals—prefer to call it "rebellion." Koreans find this label very annoying and irresponsible because they think they were unjustly victimized. In this book, I try to avoid using the terms "riots" and "rebellion" and instead use the more neutral label "civil unrest" because I want to examine the roles and predicament of Koreans and blacks as objectively as possible.

4. Survey data on public attitudes about the motives of the participants reveal clear cleavages between blacks and members of other races. According to public

opinion polls taken after the event (Bobo and et al. 1992), two-thirds of the black respondents thought that the participants were motivated by outrage and protest and less than one-third thought their motives were strictly acquisitive. In contrast, more than half of Asian, Latino, and white respondents understood their actions as strictly acquisitive and a minority saw them as a protest against social injustice.

5. Haengju San Sung is a mountain castle in the small town of Haengju. The word *haengju* has two meanings: one is the place-name, the other is "apron."

6. Koreans have a long tradition of naming an important historical event after the date on which it occurred. Although its social origin is not known, this practice has an important social function: it enables Koreans to remember the dates of important events more easily. To name a few, the March First Movement (in Korean, *Sam-Il Undong*), which unsuccessfully proclaimed the independence of Korea from Japanese colonial power, took place on March 1, 1919. The August Fifteenth Independence (*Pal-Il-O Kwangpok*) marked the restoration of independence and liberty to Korea on August 15, 1945, after the Japanese defeat in World War II. The June Twenty-Fifth Civil War, which is better known in the West as the Korean War, started on June 25, 1950, when North Korea invaded South Korea. The April Nineteenth Student Movement (*Sa-Il-Gu Haksaeng Undong*) was a large-scale student demonstration on April 19, 1959, against Syng Man Lee's corrupt and dictatorial government. The May Sixteenth Revolution (*O-Il-Yuk Hyŏkmyŏng*) was a military coup d'état led by General Park Chung Hee against the weak and unstable Chang Myŏn government on May 16, 1960. The May Eighteenth Kwangju Uprising (*O-Il-Pal Kwangju Hanggŏ*) was an armed uprising on May 18, 1981, by students and citizens of Kwangju against an emerging military regime. Because so many tragic and shocking events have occurred in the turbulent modern history of Korea, few dates on calendar are left without unique historic markers.

7. I have generally used the terms "Koreans," "blacks," and "Latinos" instead of "Korean Americans," "African Americans," and "Hispanic Americans" to highlight the racial dimension of intergroup relations. In fact, these are also the commonly used labels among members of the three groups.

Chapter One

1. A key factor differentiating ethnic groups from immigrant groups is the length of time they have been in a host country. Immigrant groups, which consist of foreign-born immigrants and their offspring, become ethnic groups when they persist over long enough periods to establish generational continuity of culture and identity. By the same token, immigrant entrepreneurship evolves into ethnic entrepreneurship when the members of the second, third, or later generations of an immigrant group are engaging in entrepreneurial activities.

2. The self-employment rate is the percentage of both employees of their own corporations and owners of unincorporated businesses among all employed persons 16 years of age and older. The self-employment rate for Korean Americans in 1990 was underestimated because it did not count employees of their own corporations as self-employed workers. The published tables of the 1990 census treated these individuals as private wage and salary workers. To correct this problem, I used data from the 5 percent Public Use Microdata Sample (PUMS) of the 1990

census. The adjusted self-employment rate for Korean Americans was 20.8 percent. If we include part-time entrepreneurs, the rate would be even higher.

3. A cohort consists of individuals who experienced the same significant demographic event during a specified period of time and who may be identified as a group at successive later dates on the basis of this common demographic experience (Shryock, Siegel, and Associates 1976, 550).

4. Historically, West Indian immigrants (blacks from English-speaking Caribbean countries such as Jamaica, Barbados, Trinidad and Tobago, Montserrat, the Virgin Islands, and Guyana) have been touted for their success in business (Haynes 1912; Glazer and Moynihan 1970; Sowell 1975), especially in comparison to American-born blacks, who have a dismal rate of business ownership. Scholars who compare these two groups of blacks in American cities emphasize such attitudinal and cultural traits of the immigrants as a strong work ethic, an emphasis on saving and education, an acute sense of financial management, an air of self-confidence, an exposure to the market economy, and a tradition of rotating credit associations, traits that are said to explain why West Indians are more successful in business and other social and economic spheres than American-born blacks. In this sense, West Indians are a "model minority" that proves the United States is still a land of opportunity where even the disadvantaged can "make it" if they work hard and believe in the American Dream. In the contemporary setting, Asian Americans have replaced West Indians as an example of how success or misfortune depends on the individual, not on society as a whole. However, recent empirical research (Modell 1991; Kasinitz 1992; Johnson 1995) reveals that West Indians do not differ significantly from African Americans in self-employment rates and that racism and discrimination against blacks hurt both groups in their attempts to form small businesses.

5. Because the U.S. Bureau of the Census is prohibited by law from collecting information on religion, the census does not have direct information on Jewish identity. However, researchers using census data have used ancestry and language spoken at home as proxy indicators of Jewish identity. For instance, Lieberson and Walters (1988) have found that a substantial segment of the population reporting Russian origins is Jewish. Using the NORC General Social Survey for the years 1972–85, they found that out of 250 people who identified themselves as Russians, 139 were raised as Jews (cited in Fairlie and Meyer 1994, 16). The question about the language spoken at home in the 1990 census also provides evidence for a close correspondence between Jewish identity and Russian ancestry. Among Russian Americans who reported a single ancestry, 15.3 percent spoke Yiddish (a combination of mostly German and Hebrew elements) and 9.4 percent spoke Spanish (a language used by Sephardic Jews) at home. The proportion of those who spoke Spanish at home was 10 percent among Lebanese, 7 percent among Syrians, 4 percent among Palestinians, and 5 percent among other Arab Americans. Five percent of Syrians also spoke Hebrew at home.

6. Several studies that examine the importance of start-up capital in self-employment decisions have reached different conclusions. Meyer (1990) argues that a person's assets play a small role in his or her decision to become self-employed. However, Evans and Leighton (1989), Blanchflower and Oswald (1990),

and Holtz-Eakin et al. (1993) have found assets to be of greater importance in this decision. As Fairlie and Meyer (1994) conclude, these differing results have yet to be reconciled.

7. Butler (1991) rejects the notion that black Americans lack a tradition of self-help and entrepreneurship. In particular, he opposes Light's cultural explanation, which attributes the underdevelopment of black capitalism to the absence of internal solidarity and rotating credit associations among blacks. As a counterexample, Butler uses evidence from Durham, North Carolina, in the 1770s to demonstrate the spirit of enterprise among blacks in the past. He also uses the case of Tulsa, Oklahoma, to show whites' resistance toward and discrimination against black businesses. The major culprits in the underdevelopment of black capitalism are, according to Butler, segregation and discrimination, which have prohibited black entrepreneurs from competing in the free, open market and instead forced them to do business in an uncompetitive, segregated market.

Because Butler uses a few isolated success stories as evidence for his argument, his generalizations are limited. Nonetheless, he makes a succinct point in regard to blacks' low rate of self-employment by saying that it is unfair to compare native-born blacks, who are already acculturated to American society, with immigrants who become self-employed to overcome language barriers and cultural differences. Bayard Rustin makes a similar point:

> If you want to raise the question about Koreans coming in, I want you to note something. Those Koreans open those shops at five o'clock in the morning, close them at eleven o'clock at night, the whole family works in the shop. And there was a time when we [African Americans] had extended families of that type. But there is not that kind of extended families in [black] America any longer. In other words, when people have been acculturated to a certain point, you cannot expect the same kind of behavior out of them that you can expect out of people who came yesterday. (Butler 1991, 290–91)

8. Gutman (1976) claims that the legacy of slavery for black families and social relations was not as destructive as Frazier thought and that blacks maintained vibrant traditions of family and culture. Contrary to the common belief that slavery shattered the immediate slave family, he says, the two-parent household was common among slaves and former slaves, marriage lasted long, exogamy was practiced, and kin networks were strongly maintained.

9. Light and Rosenstein (1995) call this approach reactive ethnicity theory in order to emphasize the emergent nature of ethnic solidarity.

10. Mavratsas (1995) explains the strong propensity for entrepreneurship among Greek immigrants in terms of their cultural capital, which includes strong family ties, an emphasis on individual mobility, and a commercial orientation. Cultural capital is different from assets and abilities that derive from one's social class, occupation, and training. It cannot be directly applied to the actual operation of an enterprise because it involves diffuse and generic skills and orientations, but it helps individuals learn quickly how to survive in business.

11. Yuengert (1989) examined the relationship between the self-employment rate of an ethnic group in the United States and that in the group's home

country. He found evidence that the latter rate has a positive and statistically significant effect on the probability that an individual immigrant is self-employed. His result was, however, questioned by Fairlie and Meyer (1994, 40–42), who argued that its significance was likely to be overstated because he did not allow for a group-level component of the error term in his individual-level equation. Fairlie and Meyer compared self-employment rates for thirty-one ethnic groups in the United States and in their home countries and found an insignificant correlation between the two rates. But their result is also subject to criticism because such an international comparison is difficult to make, partly because of different definitions of self-employment in each country. Moreover, their data for the home countries were generally from 1970, which may not be directly comparable to data for the United States in 1990.

12. Light and Bonacich are not consistent in their handling of middleman minority theory for Korean businesses. On pages 17 and 18 of their coauthored book, they state that this theory is too restrictive, partly because Korean businesses have arisen in a developed society rather than a traditional society that disdains commercial roles and partly because Koreans are not sojourners. For these reasons, they say that Korean business owners should be understood as immigrant entrepreneurs rather than middleman minorities. However, their position is not consistently maintained in chapter 15, in which they define Korean entrepreneurs in minority neighborhoods as middlemen between white capitalists and minority customers.

13. Disadvantage is an almost universal explanation of exceptional entrepreneurship among immigrants. In Britain, Pakistanis and East Indians are said to seek employment below their skill level or else create their own employment by forming small businesses because of native whites' prejudice and hostility (Aldrich et al. 1983, 8). Similarly, in the United States and Israel, Soviet immigrants are said to become entrepreneurs for lack of other employment options (Lubin 1985).

14. Light and Rosenstein (1995) distinguish simple disadvantage theory from resource-constraint disadvantage theory to emphasize that disadvantage alone cannot create entrepreneurs. They further distinguish between resource disadvantage and labor market disadvantage. People with the former, they say, are more disadvantaged than those with the latter.

15. P. Johnson (1981) found that disadvantages have different effects on workers of different socioeconomic levels. Faced with unemployment, one kind of disadvantage, nonmanual laborers are said to be more likely to become self-employed than manual laborers, and among the latter, skilled workers are more likely to become self-employed than unskilled workers. Similarly, Gold (1988), in his study of Vietnamese and Soviet Jewish immigrants in San Francisco, found that the underemployed, who hold jobs, are more successful in developing solid businesses than the unemployed, who cannot draw upon any resources. These findings vindicate the supposition that disadvantages combine with resources to promote self-employment.

16. In her most recent study of the garment industry in Los Angeles, Bonacich (1994) names manufacturers, retailers, and factors (as well as banks in general) as the players in the garment industry who make large sums of money. Contractors

and workers are viewed as victims who have to absorb reductions in profits and wages as a result of severe competition among subcontractors.

17. Ivan Light (1985) was the first to distinguish ethnic from class resources. His distinction, however, left us no way to classify resources from one's own family members, which I treat as a separate type of resource.

18. According to an estimate from the 5 percent PUMS of the 1990 U.S. census, more than a third of Korean immigrants had received four years of college education.

Chapter Two

1. Although Hong and Surh classify the upper class (mostly capitalists) and the upper-middle class separately at the conceptual level, they combine them into a single upper-middle class category in their empirical analysis.

2. Immigration from the Western Hemisphere—that is, Canada, Mexico, Central and South America, and the Caribbean—was not restricted until 1965.

3. At the risk of oversimplification, I have treated professional and white-collar workers as representatives of the middle class and nonwhite-collar workers as representatives of the lower class. There is no doubt that some of the latter have higher economic status than some professional and white-collar workers. Generally speaking, however, this distinction holds in South Korea.

4. The Gini Index measures the discrepancy between a perfectly equal income distribution and the actual distribution across various income categories. The concept of the Gini Index is best described through a diagram in which a perfectly equal distribution is illustrated by a diagonal straight line and the actual distribution is represented by a curve (the Lorenz curve) below this line. The greater the income inequality, the lower the curve will be, indicating that families in lower-income categories receive disproportionately small shares of the national wealth. The Gini Index ranges from 0 (a perfectly equal distribution) to 1 (perfect income inequality).

5. Several years ago, South Korean newspapers ran a series of articles about how difficult, miserable, and dangerous Korean immigrants' lives were in the United States. The series triggered vocal and angry protests from members of the Korean immigrant community, who claimed that the newspapers exaggerated and distorted their situations. Although many immigrants personally admit that their lives are difficult and unsatisfactory, they become resentful when others say so.

6. According to the 1990 U.S. census, Koreans accounted for 19.3 percent of the residents of Koreatown in Los Angeles, which was an 84 percent increase from 10.5 percent in 1980 (Min 1993, 189; U.S. Bureau of the Census 1993b, 1057–58).

Chapter Three

1. Korean businesses in Chicago's black areas are spatially concentrated in dozens of business districts located at the intersection of major streets. It is not difficult to distinguish Korean from non-Korean businesses in the KBCAs because they specialize in a limited range of products.

2. Although several KBCAs are residential areas for both blacks and Latinos, the majority of the residents are nonetheless black. Latinos tend to form their own

residential areas on the North Side of Chicago, near Lake Michigan. For this reason, the boundaries between black and Latino neighborhoods are more distinct in Chicago than in South Central Los Angeles, where the two groups account for an almost equal proportion of the local residents.

3. Chang (1990, 74) defined the core area of Koreatown as bounded by Vermont Avenue on the east, Western Avenue on the west, 8th Street on the north, and Olympic Avenue on the south. During the 1980s, according to Chang, the boundaries of Koreatown extended farther north along Vermont and Western Avenues up to Santa Monica Avenue, farther east to Hoover Street, farther west to Crenshaw Avenue, and farther south to Pico Boulevard.

4. A similar concentration of Korean businesses in minority neighborhoods is also evident in New York City and Los Angeles. According to Min (1992, 2–3), less than 10 percent of Koreans in New York City live in Brooklyn or the Bronx, but 30 percent and 25 percent of Korean businesses in New York City are located in these two boroughs, respectively. Those in Brooklyn, a heavily black borough, serve mainly black customers, whereas those in the Bronx serve mainly Latino customers. In Los Angeles, approximately 10,000 Koreans are engaged in indoor and outdoor swap meet businesses, and 80 percent of those are located in black and Latino neighborhoods of South Central and East Los Angeles. In addition, large numbers of Korean grocery, liquor, dry cleaning, auto repair, and gas station businesses are located in black and Latino neighborhoods.

5. Chang (1993, 18) has claimed that many Korean immigrants in Los Angeles purchased their stores from blacks, who in turn had bought them from Jewish owners after the Watts riots of 1965. Because these Jewish owners were anxious to sell their stores and leave the area, black buyers were able to acquire them at low prices and make huge profits by selling them to Korean immigrants in the mid-1970s. Chang mentioned this scenario very briefly in an endnote and did not provide any substantive evidence for his claims. More empirical data are needed to verify this view of the ethnic succession of businesses in South Central.

6. The exposure or lack of exposure to an urban economy is thought to be important in determining an immigrant group's level of business ownership in the United States. The comparison of Jewish and Italian immigrants illustrates the case. Stephen Steinberg (1981) says that Russian Jews who came to the United States in the early twentieth century were not peasants but urban people who had been engaged in manufacturing and commerce. Consequently, although they were poor, they were equipped with skills that would serve them well in an expanding industrial economy. When the U.S. economy later shifted from agriculture and manufacturing to services, Jews benefited from their background in trade and commerce (Marger 1991, 201). By comparison, Italians, particularly those from southern Italy and Sicily, were mainly agricultural peasants, and they remained laborers in the United States for a prolonged period. Because the economic rewards in this country have gone to entrepreneurs, not to laborers, the Jews have achieved more rapid economic mobility than the Italians (Glazer and Moynihan 1970).

7. With these figures, it is difficult to determine whether or not the North Korean refugees and their descendants are overrepresented among the L.A. respondents. According to Illsoo Kim (1981, 35), North Korean refugees and their

descendants in South Korea numbered approximately 5.1 million and constituted 14 percent of the South Korean population in 1977. Eui Yu (1983, 30) estimated that such refugees and their descendants supplied 22 percent of the Korean immigrants to Los Angeles.

8. In a predeparture survey of Korean immigrants conducted in Seoul in 1986, the average amount of money the respondents planned to take with them was $14,500 (Park et al. 1990, 66).

9. According to the predeparture survey conducted by Park et al. (1990, 86), 60.8 percent of the 1,834 respondents reported that they would go into business when they arrived in the United States.

10. There are three topics that Korean immigrants are not supposed to ask one another about: past occupation, current occupation, and level of education. Because of downward occupational mobility, the sense of status inconsistency is quite strong among many Korean immigrants.

11. Korean immigrant businesses suffer from high failure rates, but this does not weaken Koreans' determination to succeed. They remain in the self-employment sector despite repeated business failures rather than seek wage or salary employment. The low cost of failure that results from the small amount of initial capital usually invested is a major reason why Koreans continue to open new businesses after repeated failures. Also, although they initially open such businesses because they cannot find jobs in their original profession, they come to see business ownership as their preferred vocation. Such a tendency contrasts with that of Soviet Jewish and Vietnamese refugee entrepreneurs, who do leave businesses when desired wage or salary employment becomes available (Gold 1988, 419).

12. Lovell-Troy (1981) and Mavratsas (1995) note that Greek immigrant entrepreneurs usually start their careers in the United States by working in ethnic businesses of the type they plan to establish. In this sense, according to Ivan Light, an ethnic business is a school for entrepreneurs.

13. The job trajectory pattern of Korean business owners may be sharply different from that of wage and salary workers, among whom the intersectoral transition of employment is expected to be more frequent. No studies have been done on this issue.

14. The distinction between grocery and liquor stores is not clear because some grocery stores sell beer, wine, and/or liquor if they have Type 20 (off-premise beer and wine retail) or Type 21 (off-premise beer, wine, and liquor retail) licenses.

15. According to Min (1988), Korean immigrants in Atlanta, Georgia, prefer to own grocery stores located in black residential areas over those located in white residential areas because the former are known to be more lucrative. In his 1982 survey, 63 percent of Korean business owners in Atlanta believed that they would not be successful in a white area, and 24 percent said that it was absolutely impossible. Eui Young Yu (1990, 10) reaches a similar conclusion: Korean businesses serving Latinos and blacks are the best in terms of income. Sixty-three percent of those doing business mainly with Latinos make more than $50,000 a year. The corresponding figures are 50 percent with predominantly black customers, 42 percent with other Koreans, and 37 percent with whites. Yu cited white customers' discrimination against Korean store owners as well as competition from white businesses

as the major reasons for the lower income of Korean store owners whose clientele is mainly white.

16. As Light, Kwuon, and Zhong (1990) state, the distinction between personal savings and money from kyes is not clear-cut. Some people may save money earned from kyes and then use it later as part of their start-up capital. Similarly, some people may not personally participate in kyes yet do benefit from them through the participation of other family members, such as their wives. In both cases, the extent of kye participation and the proportion of kye money in the total start-up capital are likely to be greater than what is reported.

17. The internal solidarity and cooperation among members of district and surname associations often led to the exclusion of members of less powerful associations from lucrative businesses in Chinatown. For instance, by the 1890s, members of Sam Yup districts dominated the import–export trade, although they comprised only 10 percent of the Chinese population of San Francisco. When people from the more numerous but less powerful Sze Yup began to enter the trade, Sam Yup people opposed them. In retaliation, Sze Yup began a boycott of Sam Yup businesses, driving many of them into bankruptcy (Ma 1991, 154). Such conflicts permitted *tongs* (secret associations), which killed off business rivals and any people in the opposition, to emerge as powerful forces in Chinatown.

18. These findings are in sharp contrast to the results of earlier surveys, which downplayed the economic importance of kyes for business formation. H. Kim (1976) found that only 2 percent of the fifty-two respondents to his mail survey in four cities acknowledged that they had obtained all their capital from kyes. Young (1983) also found that only one of the forty respondents in his survey in New York City acknowledged that a kye had provided most of his start-up capital. Light and Bonacich (1988) reported that only one percent of their 213 respondents said that they had used kyes to finance their businesses. One exception to this negative viewpoint was the finding of Kim and Hurh (1985) that one-third of ninety-four respondents on Chicago's South Side accumulated some of their capital through kyes and one-third thought kyes were widely used among Korean business owners as a method of capital formation. See Light, Kwuon, and Zhong (1990) for an explanation of inconsistent survey results on this matter.

19. Women are also more active than men in the networks of West Indian rotating credit associations in Boston. Men contribute to these associations, but it is the women who handle and manage the money (Johnson 1995).

20. Such vertical integration of the ethnic economy also existed among Japanese immigrants before World War II. It evolved in the produce industry in Southern California, as Japanese growers sold their produce to Japanese wholesalers, who in turn sold to Japanese retailers (Bloom and Riemer 1949, 92–93). As Bonacich and Modell (1980, 50) put it, "Ethnic ties oiled this link." Although they comprised only 2 percent of the state population in 1920, Japanese immigrants produced almost 90 percent of California's celery, asparagus, onions, tomatoes, berries, and cantaloupes; more than 70 percent of its floricultural products; 50 percent of its seeds; 45 percent of its sugar beets; and 35 percent of its grapes (Chan 1991, 38). This suggests that one crucial factor in a successful ethnic business is the domination of one particular industry through vertical integration.

21. According to the U.S. Bureau of the Census's Survey of Minority-Owned Business Enterprises, by 1987 Korean Americans owned 69,304 businesses nationwide, whose total gross receipts were $7.683 million. Average gross receipts per business were $110,859, or less than 60 percent of the average receipts ($189,000) of businesses owned by white men. Of the 69,304 businesses, only 30 percent had paid employees, and the average number of such employees (excluding businesses without them) was 3.25. Ninety-four percent of Korean American businesses were owned by individual proprietors, and the owners and their family members were also the major operators.

22. Store rents in the L.A. garment district are extremely expensive. The average rent is between $6 and $15 per square foot, and Korean tenants pay on average $6,500 per month.

23. Some Korean business owners make generous political donations to influential black politicians simply to gain the opportunity to have their pictures taken with them. They then display these pictures in their stores to demonstrate to black customers their ties and friendship with black leaders. In Chicago, the picture of former mayor Harold Washington used to be the favorite among Korean business owners because of his wide popularity among blacks and his pro-Korean position during his mayoralty. His picture and those of other influential black political and spiritual leaders, such as Martin Luther King Jr., are hung in easily seen spots of the stores, as if they are charms to dispel evil spirits.

24. In 1980, blacks' probability of residential contact with Latinos was 0.380 in the Los Angeles–Long Beach Metropolitan Area and 0.038 in the Chicago Metropolitan Area (Massey and Denton 1987, 807). This means that blacks in Los Angeles–Long Beach were ten times more likely to have residential contact with Latinos than their counterparts in Chicago.

25. The division of labor between husband and wife in small business is almost universal in immigrant entrepreneurship. A study of Boston's ethnic entrepreneurs (including Greeks, Cambodians, and Jamaicans) shows that typically the husband is the sole proprietor and the wife works for the business, fulfilling such roles as cashier, salesclerk, bookkeeper, cook, or waitress (Halter 1995).

26. This style of election is not foreign to adult Korean immigrants who were used to single-candidate presidential elections during the Park Chung Hee and Chun Doo Hwan regimes. In this sense, the Korean immigrant community is an abridged version of South Korean society, in which prolonged dictatorship hinders people from practicing self-government and democracy.

27. Dearman (1982) conducted a survey of Korean churches in Los Angeles in 1979 and found that more than 90 percent of them belong to fundamentalist, conservative, neo-orthodox, evangelical, or pentecostal traditions, all of which are religiously conservative. Only one of the sixty-five ministers who responded to the questionnaire classified himself as a liberal. In New York City, Min (1992) conducted a survey of 185 Korean churches in 1989 and found that Presbyterian churches accounted for 49 percent and Methodist churches for 15 percent of the total.

28. Gold (1988, 426) states that the ethnic bonds that unite owners and workers are an important resource for Soviet Jewish and Vietnamese entrepreneurs in

San Francisco, but these bonds also oblige bosses to extend special privileges to workers. For this reason, some ethnic entrepreneurs avoid drawing on coethnic labor.

29. The once paternalistic relationship between Chinese bosses and workers has also weakened in contemporary Chinatowns of U.S. cities. Peter Kwong (1987, 32) notes that as the growth of the Chinese garment industry transformed Chinatown in New York from a small service-oriented economy into a community with manufacturers, these new industries no longer employed just family members or relatives; they hired dozens—sometimes hundreds—of women who were unrelated. He also observes that as capital became concentrated in the hands of a few, classes in the Chinese community became increasingly polarized and ethnicity lost its significance in employer–employee relations. In this context, such relationships became detached from traditional social norms and became more purely economic transactions between two parties with competing interests. In a similar vein, Nee, Sanders, and Sernau (1994, 857) claim that many workers express dissatisfaction with their positions in the ethnic economy. A Chinese immigrant worker in their ethnographic study bitterly complains:

Chinese bosses are very strict. They ask you to work long hours at low pay. The boss wants you to work without resting and he treats you like a working machine. . . . Chinese bosses are much stricter than American bosses.

30. Paul Siu wrote the best book on Chinese laundrymen, which was published in 1987. He himself was a Chinese laundry supply agent for two years and had many relatives and friends among Chicago's Chinese laundrymen, so he had an insider's view of their lives (Yu 1992, 2). His major contribution to the study of immigrant entrepreneurship was the concept of the sojourner, a stranger who spends many years of his life in a foreign country without being assimilated into it. The laundry business reinforces the sojourner mentality among the Chinese by depriving them of any meaningful chance of interacting with people outside the Chinese community.

31. Because of the smaller pool of Korean Americans and available capital, all Korean grocery stores in Koreatown of Chicago are still either small or medium in size.

32. This association is different from the Korean American Grocers' Association of Southern California, which represents Korean-owned, American-style grocery and liquor stores.

33. Gerald Suttles's concept of segmented social order helps me define Korean ethnic solidarity as an evolutionary phenomenon. In his ethnographic study of the Addams Area, a multiethnic neighborhood on Chicago's Near West Side, Suttles (1968) explains how primary ties based on the status distinctions of age, sex, and ethnicity, coupled with territorial segregation of blacks, Italians, Puerto Ricans, and Mexicans, provided a segmented social order in this slum. He explains:

The development of personal relations furnishes both a moral formula and a structural bridge between groups. Within each small, localized peer group, continuing face-to-face relations can eventually provide a personalistic order. Once these groups are established, a single personal relation between them can extend the range of such an order. With the acceptance of age grading and territorial usufruct, it becomes possible for slum neighborhoods to work out a moral order than includes most of their residents. (8)

Chapter Four

1. Heon Cheol Lee (1993) has presented the most comprehensive and systematic analysis of this black boycott in his Ph.D. dissertation, written at Columbia University, which focuses on the structural and political aspects of the Korean–black conflict rather than its psychological and cultural aspects. The description of the boycott in this section is based heavily on his analysis.

2. Throughout the news coverage of the civil unrest in April 1992, the Latasha Harlins tape was played repeatedly, second only to the Rodney King tape. During the unrest, images of the shooting were shown in conjunction with those of Korean Americans defending their stores. As one Korean American student subsequently stated in his term paper, these representations suggested that Korean Americans are hostile and reactionary (Gong 1994). These particular combinations of images have also proven to be damaging to Korean Americans because they sent a message to the public that Korean store owners deserved what they suffered. Through the media, Soon Ja Du's mentality has been associated with that of the owners who defended their businesses, and her crime has been viewed as representative of Korean Americans' behavior toward black Americans. However, such a representation can be seen as scapegoating, intended to redirect blacks' discontent toward whites against Korean Americans.

3. First-degree murder is a willful, deliberate, and premeditated killing, for which the sentence is twenty-five years to life in prison. Voluntary manslaughter is an unlawful killing without malice that occurs during a sudden quarrel or in the heat of passion, for which the maximum sentence is sixteen years in prison.

4. Within thirty-six blocks around the Empire Market, 336 serious crimes were reported to the police in 1990. Five of them were homicides and 184 were robberies. Du had once been shot by gang members, and because of gangs, she had closed her business for two weeks prior to the Harlins incident (*KTLA* 22 March 1991).

5. Anti-Asian bigotry and hate crimes began to receive national attention after the death of Vincent Chin, a 27-year-old Chinese American, in Detroit, Michigan, on June 19, 1982. He was assaulted by Ronald Ebens and Michael Nitz, two laid-off white automobile factory workers, who called him a "Jap" and blamed him for the loss of jobs in the industry. He was beaten to death by a baseball bat swung by Ebens. Seven years later, Jim Loo, a 24-year-old Chinese American, was killed by two white men in Raleigh, North Carolina, under similar circumstances. He was assaulted by Robert Piche and his brother Lloyd, who called him a "gook" and a "chink" and blamed him for American deaths in Vietnam. After they were expelled from the pool hall where the altercation took place, the brothers waited outside for Loo and his friends and then hit him on the head with a handgun. He fell onto a broken beer bottle, which pierced his eye and caused a bone fragment to enter his brain (U.S. Commission on Civil Rights 1992, ch. 2). In each case, the

victim was killed after being mistaken for or associated with Asians of other nationalities.

6. Park had experienced an armed robbery one and a half years earlier, but that time he had stopped the gunman with his bare hands and handed him over to the police. Since this incident, he had lived in fear of revenge.

7. Professor Edward Chang at California State Polytechnic University, Pomona (now an assistant professor in the Ethnic Studies Department of UC, Riverside), became the chair of this group, and Marcia Choo of the Asian Pacific American Dispute Resolution Center, Laura Chun of the Korean Health Information Center, Hak-Jae Jung of Asian Pacific Legal Counseling, Jerry Yu of the Korean American Coalition, and Pong-Hwan Kim of the Korean Youth and Community Center were the active members. Jerry Wang of the L.A. County Human Relations Commission and Yun-Hei Kim, the special aide to the mayor, were elected as the sponsors of the organization (*KTLA* 4 July 1991).

8. Majority–minority relations are not always the same as dominant–subordinated relations. Sometimes a group numerically in the minority can be a society's dominant group. For instance, whites in South Africa account for only 20 percent of the country's population, but they are dominant over blacks. In the United States, whites are not only the majority group (accounting for 75 percent of the population) but also the socially dominant group. As of 1990, blacks accounted for 12 percent, Hispanics 9 percent, Asians 3 percent, and native Americans 0.8 percent of the U.S. population.

9. The nature of Jewish–black relations is still a source of controversy among scholars. Some emphasize the historical alliance between the two groups because of their common historical experience of racial oppression. Others claim that the alliance between Jews and blacks is a myth and that relations between them have never been good. Weisbord and Stein (1970) have made the following balanced assessment: Jewish–black relations are a "bittersweet encounter" that has fluctuated between cooperation and conflict depending upon different historical and geographical circumstances. In the 1990s, a series of events such as the black riots against Jews in Crown Heights, Brooklyn, and the racist speeches of Louis Farrakhan of the Nation of Islam have turned this relationship sour and tense again.

10. Chang (1993, 12) claims that the Korean–black relationship is a relatively horizontal one, whereas the Jewish–black relationship is a vertical one, involving the economic, political, and social subordination of blacks to Jews. In contrast, blacks have political, social, and cultural advantages while Koreans have economic advantages. Chang speculates that Korean–black relations are potentially more explosive because members of each group view themselves as at least equal to if not better than the other.

11. Schermerhorn (1978, 12–13) defines the dominant group as the "collectivity within a society, which has preeminent authority to function both as guardians and sustainers of the controlling value system, and as prime allocators of rewards in the society."

12. John Higham ([1955] 1992, 4) defines nativism as "intense opposition to an internal minority on the grounds of its foreign (i.e., 'un-American') connections." By the 1840s, many Americans were making distinctions within the white race by opposing immigration from Ireland and Germany.

13. Disputes and clashes are distinguished here from conflicts. The former can occur because of personal and psychological factors, such as language barriers, cultural misunderstandings, and mistreatment of customers. In contrast, conflicts are direct, overt, enduring, and *collective* actions taken by blacks and Koreans against each other. Although frequent clashes are a necessary condition leading to Korean–black conflict, they do not automatically develop into conflicts.

14. The majority of Latinos with whom Koreans interact in Koreatown and South Central are Mexicans and immigrants from other Latin American countries.

15. As discussed in chapter 3, one of the frequent charges against Korean businesses in black neighborhoods is that they do not hire black employees. Koreans often respond to this charge by claiming that most of their businesses are family-owned and -operated, so they cannot afford paid employees. Their excuse cannot be justified, however, because the majority of those in black neighborhoods (73 percent) do hire employees (excluding family members), and the average number of employees is 4.4.

16. Min (1996) found similar hiring practices in Korean stores. According to his 1986 Los Angeles survey, Latinos constituted 48 percent of all workers, compared to less than 5 percent black workers. His more recent New York City survey in 1992 revealed that Latinos were still the most important group in the workforce, representing 42 percent of the total and followed by blacks (31 percent) and Koreans (23 percent).

17. Attitudes toward menial labor in immigrant businesses are found to be different between immigrant and native blacks. According to Green and Pryde (1991, 114), many native blacks do not find small businesses a meaningful route to upward mobility because of their long residence in and acculturation to American society. They are far less inclined than black immigrants from Caribbean countries to do what they consider "the dirty work" of making it up the ladder through mom-and-pop businesses.

18. I avoid using the term "superiority," since it is an emotionally and ideologically loaded term. "Seniority" may be a more appropriate and value-neutral term that reflects native-born blacks' widespread frustration at being bypassed by waves of immigrant groups (such as Jews, Koreans, Arabs, and Latinos) who have not been in the United States as long as they have been (Stengel 1985).

19. High rates of self-employment, of course, are part of this isolation. According to the estimates from the 1 percent B Sample of the 1990 PUMS, 24.3 percent of employed Korean Americans were self-employed in 1990, as compared to the national average of 10.2 percent. An additional 3.1 percent of employed Korean Americans engaged in small business as unpaid family workers, compared to the national average of 0.5 percent. In Los Angeles, 48 percent of adult Korean immigrants were self-employed and 28 percent worked in Korean-owned firms, leaving only 25 percent outside the Korean ethnic economy (Min 1996). In addition, 70 percent of Korean immigrants are reported to attend Korean Christian churches regularly.

20. See Park (1994) for a discussion of the political mobilization of the Korean American community during and after the Los Angeles civil unrest.

Abelmann, Nancy, and John Lie. 1995. *Blue Dreams: Korean Americans and the Los Angeles Riots.* Cambridge: Harvard University Press.

Aldrich, Howard, John Cater, Trevor Jones, and David McEvoy. 1983. "From Periphery to Peripheral: The South Asian Petite Bourgeoisie in England." *Research in Sociology of Work* 2:1–32.

Aldrich, Howard, Trevor Jones, and David McEvoy. 1984. "Ethnic Advantage and Minority Business Development." Chapter 11 in *Ethnic Communities in Business*, edited by Robin Ward and Richard Jenkins. New York: Cambridge University Press.

Aldrich, Howard, and Albert J. Reiss, Jr. 1970. "The Effects of Civil Disorders on Small Business in the Inner City." *Journal of Social Issues* 26:187–206.

———. 1976. "Continuities in the Study of Ecological Succession: Changes in the Race Composition of Neighborhoods and Their Businesses." *American Journal of Sociology* 81:846–66.

Baldwin, James. [1967] 1994. "Negroes Are Anti-Semitic Because They're Anti-White." In *Blacks and Jews: Alliances and Arguments*, edited by Paul Berman, 31–41. New York: Delacorte Press.

Bank of Korea. 1966, 1971, 1975, 1980, 1983. *Economic Statistics Yearbook (Kyongje T'onggye Yongam)*. Seoul, Korea.

———. 1981. *Korean Exchange Controls (Han'guk Oehwan Kwanri)*. Seoul, Korea.

Barringer, Herbert, Robert W. Gardner, and Michael J. Levin. 1993. *Asians and Pacific Islanders in the United States.* New York: Russell Sage Foundation.

Basch, Linda, Nina Glick Schiller, and Christina Szanton Blanc. 1994. *Nation Unbound: Transnational Projects, Postcolonial Predicaments, and Deterritorialized Nation-States.* Basel: Gordon and Breach Publishers.

Bates, Timothy. 1991. "Commercial Bank Financing of White and Black-Owned Small Business Startups." *Quarterly Review of Economics and Business* 31:64–80.

Bechhofer, Frank, and Brian Elliott, eds. 1985. "The Petite Bourgeoisie in Late Capitalism." *Annual Review of Sociology* 11:181–207.

Becker, Euguen. 1984. "Self-Employed Workers: An Update to 1983." *Monthly Labor Review* 107:14–18.

Becker, Howard. 1956. *Man in Reciprocity: Introductory Lectures on Culture, Society and Personality.* New York: Praeger.

Birch, David. 1981. "Who Creates Jobs?" *The Public Interest* 65:3–14.

———. 1987. *Job Creation in America: How Our Smallest Companies Put the Most People to Work.* New York: Free Press.

Blackistone, Kevin B. 1981. "Arab Entrepreneurs Take Over Inner City Grocery Stores." *Chicago Reporter* 10:1–5.

Blalock, Hurbert. 1967. *Toward a Theory of Minority-Group Relations.* New York: John Wiley & Sons.

Blanchflower, David G., and Andrew J. Oswald. 1990. "What Makes an Entrepreneur." Working Paper, Dartmouth College.

Bloom, Leonard, and Ruth Riemer. 1949. *Removal and Return: The Socio-Economic Effects of the War on Japanese Americans.* Berkeley and Los Angeles: University of California Press.

Bobo, Lawrence, and James R. Kluegel. 1991. "Modern American Prejudice: Stereotypes, Social Distance, and Perceptions of Discrimination toward Blacks, Hispanics, and Asians." Paper presented at the annual meeting of the American Sociological Association, Cincinnati, Ohio, August 23–27.

Bobo, Lawrence, James Johnson, Melvin Oliver, J. Sidanius, and C. Zubrinsky. 1992. *Public Opinion before and after a Spring of Discontent: A Preliminary Report on the 1992 Los Angeles County Social Survey.* Occasional working paper series, vol. 3, no. 1, UCLA Center for the Study of Urban Poverty.

Boissevain, Jeremy. 1984. "Small Entrepreneurs in Contemporary Europe." In *Ethnic Communities in Business*, edited by Robin Ward and Richard Jenkins, 20–38. New York: Cambridge University Press.

Bonacich, Edna. 1972. "A Theory of Ethnic Antagonism: The Split Labor Market." *American Sociological Review* 37:547–59.

———. 1973. "A Theory of Middleman Minorities." *American Sociological Review* 38:583–94.

———. 1984. "Some Basic Facts: Patterns of Asian Immigration and Exclusion." In *Labor Immigration under Capitalism: Asian Workers in the United States before World War II*, edited by Lucie Cheng and Edna Bonacich, 60–78. Berkeley and Los Angeles: University of California Press.

———. 1988. "The Social Costs of Immigrant Entrepreneurship." *Amerasia Journal* 14:119–28.

———. 1994. "Asians in the Los Angeles Garment Industry." In *The New Asian Immigration in Los Angeles and Global Restructuring*, edited by Paul Ong, Edna Bonacich, and Lucie Cheng, 137–63. Philadelphia: Temple University Press.

Bonacich, Edna, Ivan Light, and Charles Choy Wong. 1980. "Korean Immigrant Small Business in Los Angeles." In *Sourcebook on the New Immigration*, edited by Roy Simon Bryce-Laporte, 167–84. New Brunswick, N.J.: Transaction Books.

Bonacich, Edna, and John Modell. 1980. *The Economic Basis of Ethnic Solidarity.* Berkeley and Los Angeles: University of California Press.

Boswell, Terry E. 1986. "Split Labor Market Analysis of Discrimination against Immigrants, 1850–1882." *American Sociological Review* 51:352–71.

Bottomore, Tom B. 1966. *Classes in Modern Society.* New York: Pantheon.

Braverman, Harry. 1974. *Labor and Monopoly Capital: The Degradation of Work in the Twentieth Century.* New York: Monthly Review Press.

Bregger, John E. 1963. "Self-Employment in the U.S., 1948–62." *Monthly Labor Review* 86 (Jan.): 37–43.

Butler, John Sibley. 1991. *Entrepreneurship and Self-Help among Black Americans: A Reconsideration of Race and Economics*. Albany, N.Y.: State University of New York Press.

CACI Marketing Systems. 1991. *The Sourcebook of Zip Code Demographics*, Census Edition, vol. 1. Arlington, Va.: CACI Marketing Systems.

———. 1992. *The Sourcebook of Zip Code Demographics*, Census Edition, vol. 2. Arlington, Va.: CACI Marketing Systems.

Caplovitz, David. 1973. *The Merchants of Harlem*. Beverly Hills, Calif.: Sage Publications.

Cator, W. L. 1936. *The Economic Position of the Chinese in the Netherlands Indies*. Chicago: University of Chicago Press.

Central Daily News of Chicago (Jung Ang Ilbo). 1991. *1991 Korean Business Directory (1991 Hanin Opsorok)*. Chicago: Central Daily News of Chicago.

Chan, Sucheng. 1986. *This Bittersweet Soil: The Chinese in California Agriculture, 1860–1910*. Berkeley and Los Angeles: University of California Press.

———. 1991. *Asian Americans: An Interpretive History*. Boston: Twayne Publishers.

Chang, Edward Tea. 1990. "New Urban Crisis: Korean–Black Conflict in Los Angeles." Ph.D. dissertation, University of California, Berkeley.

———. 1993. "Jewish and Korean Merchants in African American Neighborhoods: A Comparative Perspective." *Amerasia Journal* 19 (2):5–21.

Cheng, Lucie, and Yen Espiritu. 1989. "Korean Business in Black and Hispanic Neighborhoods: A Study of Intergroup Relations." *Sociological Perspectives* 32:521–34.

Cherry, Robert. 1990. "Middleman Minority Theories: Their Implications for Black–Jewish Relations." *Journal of Ethnic Studies* 17 (4):117–38.

Chin, Ku-Sup, In-Jin Yoon, and David Smith. 1996. "Immigrant Small Business and International Economic Linkage: A Case of the Korean Wig Industry in Los Angeles, 1968–1977." *International Migration Review* 30:485–510.

Chiswick, Barry C. 1982. "The Economic Progress of Immigrants: Some Universal Patterns." In *The Gateway: U.S. Immigration Issues and Policies*, edited by Barry R. Chiswick, 119–58. Washington, D.C.: American Enterprise Institute.

Cho, Yun-Song. 1991a. "Leaders of the Korean and Black Communities Made a Unified Statement." *Korea Times Los Angeles*, March 20.

———. 1991b. "The Public Opinion Calls for Reconsidering the Tae Sam Park Case." *Korea Times Los Angeles*, September 10.

Choi, Ki-Duk. 1996. "The Korean Immigrant Community—Abridged Version of Korean Society." In *United States—Superpower's Light and Darkness (Miguk-Ch'ogandguk ui Pitkwa Kunul)*, supplement to *Singdonga* January: 524–29.

Choldin, Harvey M. 1973. "Kinship Networks in the Migration Process." *International Migration Review* 7:163–76.

Choy, Bong-Youn. 1979. *Koreans in America*. Chicago: Nelson-Hall.

Christian Institute for the Study of Justice and Development (CISJD). 1986. *Social Justice Indicators in Korea (Han'guk ui Sahoe Jungui Jipyo)*. Seoul, Korea: Minjungsa.

Chung, Joseph S. 1979. "Small Ethnic Business as a Form of Disguised Unemployment and Cheap Labor." In *United States on Civil Rights. Civil Rights Issues of Asian and Pacific Americans: Myths and Realities*, 509–17. Washington, D.C.: Government Printing Office.

Coleman, James. 1988. "Social Capital in the Creation of Human Capital." *American Journal of Sociology* 94:95–120.

Cresce, Arthur R., Susan J. Lapam, and Stanley J. Rolark. 1992. "Preliminary Evaluation of Data from the Race and Ethnic Origin Questions in the 1990 Census." Paper presented at the annual meeting of the American Statistical Association.

Curry, Tom, and Jeanne McDowell. 1992. "Lessons of Los Angeles." *Time*, May 18, 38–39.

Dearman, Marion. 1982. "Structure and Function of Religion in the Los Angeles Korean Community: Some Aspects." In *Koreans in Los Angeles: Prospects and Promises*, edited by Eui-Young Yu, Earl Phillips, and Eun Sik Yang, 165–83. Los Angeles: Koryo Research Institute, Center for Korean-American and Korean Studies, California State University, Los Angeles.

Doeringer, Peter, and Michael Piore. 1971. *Internal Labor Markets and Manpower Analysis*. Lexington, Mass.: Heath.

Edwards, Richard, Michael Reich, and David Gordon, eds. 1975. *Labor Market Segmentation*. Lexington, Mass.: D.C. Heath and Company.

Espiritu, Yen Le. 1992. *Asian American Panethnicity: Bridging Institutions and Identities*. Philadelphia: Temple University Press.

Evans, David, and Linda Leighton. 1989. "Some Empirical Aspects of Entrepreneurship." *American Economic Review* 79:519–35.

Fadragas, Angela M. 1984. "Lake View." In *Local Community Fact Book: Chicago Metropolitan Area Based on the 1970 and 1980 Censuses*, edited by Chicago Fact Book Consortium, 14–17. Chicago: Chicago Review Press.

Fain, Scott. 1980. "Self-Employed Americans: Their Number Has Increased." *Monthly Labor Review* 93:33–40.

Fairlie, Robert W. 1994. "The Absence of the African-American Owned Business: An Analysis of the Dynamics of Self-Employment." Working paper no. 94–9, Center for Urban Affairs and Policy Research, Northwestern University.

Fairlie, Robert W., and Bruce M. Meyer. 1994. "The Ethnic and Racial Character of Self-Employment." Working paper no. 94–8, Center for Urban Affairs and Policy Research, Northwestern University.

Frazier, Franklin. 1957. *Black Bourgeoisie*. New York: Free Press.

Freedman, Marrice. 1959. "The Handling of Money: A Note on the Background to the Economic Sophistication of the Overseas Chinese." *Man* 59:64–65.

Fuchs, Lawrence H. 1990. "The Reactions of Black Americans to Immigration." In *Immigration Reconsidered: History, Sociology, and Politics*, edited by Virginia Yans-McLaughlin, 293–314. New York: Oxford University Press.

Furnivall, J. S. 1956. *Colonial Policy and Practice: A Comparative Study of Burma and Netherlands India*. New York: New York University Press.

Gibbs, Geoffrey T. 1991. "Can African-Americans Now Truly Believe in Judicial Fairness?" *Los Angeles Times*, November 24.

Glazer, Nathan, and Daniel P. Moynihan. 1970. *Beyond the Melting Pot: The Negroes,*

Puerto Ricans, Jews, Italians, and Irish on New York City. Cambridge: MIT Press.

Gold, Steven J. 1988. "Refugees and Small Business: The Case of Soviet Jews and Vietnamese." *Ethnic and Racial Studies* 11:411–38.

———. 1994. "Chinese–Vietnamese Entrepreneurs in California." In *The New Asian Immigration in Los Angeles and Global Restructuring,* edited by Paul Ong, Edna Bonacich, and Lucie Cheng, 196–226. Philadelphia: Temple University Press.

Goldscheider, Calvin, and Rances Kobrin. 1980. "Ethnic Continuity and the Process of Self-Employment." *Ethnicity* 7:256–78.

Gong, William. 1994. "Korean Americans and the 1992 Los Angeles Riots: Ethnic Tension in the Inner-City." Student paper for AS AM 104 (Korean American Experience), University of California, Santa Barbara.

Green, Shelley, and Paul Pryde. 1991. *Black Entrepreneurship in America.* New Brunswick, N.J.: Transaction Publishers.

Grown, Caren, and Timothy Bates. 1992. "Commercial Bank Lending Practices and the Development of Black-Owned Construction Companies." *Journal of Urban Affairs* 14:25–41.

Gutman, Herbert G. 1976. *The Black Family in Slavery and Freedom, 1750–1925.* New York: Pantheon.

Haber, Sheldon, Enrique J. Lamas, and Jules H. Lichtenstein. 1987. "On Their Own: The Self-Employed and Others in Private Business." *Monthly Labor Review* 110:17–23.

Hager, Philip. 1992. "Justices Uphold Karlin's Ruling in Slaying of Latasha Harlins." *Los Angeles Times,* July 13.

Halter, Marilyn, ed. 1995. *New Migrants in the Marketplace: Boston's Ethnic Entrepreneurs.* Amherst: University of Massachusetts Press.

Han, Bae-Jin. 1977. "Out-Migration of Rural Labor Force and Labor Market." Master's thesis, Seoul National University.

Hansis, Dick. 1984. "West Garfield Park." In *Local Community Fact Book: Chicago Metropolitan Area Based on the 1970 and 1980 Censuses,* edited by Chicago Fact Book Consortium, 70–72. Chicago: Chicago Review Press.

Haynes, Edmund. 1912. *The Negro at Work in New York City.* New York: Arno Press.

Higham, John. [1955] 1992. *Strangers in the Land: Patterns of American Nativism, 1860–1925.* New Brunswick, N.J.: Rutgers University Press.

Hilton, Mike. 1979. "The Split Labor Market and Chinese Immigration, 1848–1882." *Journal of Ethnic Studies* 6:99–108.

Holtz-Eakin, Douglas, David Joulfaian, and Harvey Rosen. 1993. "Entrepreneurial Decisions and Liquidity Constraints." Working paper no. 4526, National Bureau of Economic Research.

Hong, Doo-Seung, and Kwan-Mo Surh. 1985. "The Current Status of Korean Class and Problems with Conceptual Reconstruction." In *Studies of Korean Class (Han'guk Sahoe Kyech'ung Yon'gu),* vol. 1, edited by Jin-Kyun Kim, 11–24. Seoul, Korea: Hanul.

Hong, Sa-Un. 1979. *A Study of Korean Emigration (Han'guk Haeoe Imin Yongu).* Seoul: Korean Development Institute.

Horvat, Branko. 1982. *The Political Economy of Socialism*. Armonk, N.Y.: M. E. Sharpe.

Houchins, Lee, and Chang-Su Houchins. 1974. "The Korean Experience in America, 1903–1924." *Pacific Historical Review* 43:548–75.

Hsia, Jayjia. 1988. *Asian Americans in Higher Education and at Work*. Hillsdale, N.J.: Lawrence Erlbaum Associates, Publishers.

Hurh, Won Moo, and Kwang Chung Kim. 1984. *Korean Immigrants in America: A Structural Analysis of Ethnic Confinement and Adhesive Adaptation*. Madison, N.J.: Fairleigh Dickinson University Press.

Hwang, Dong-Hee. 1995a. "All Merchants in Jobber Market Protest High Store Rents." *Korea Times Los Angeles*, February 10.

———. 1995b. "Meeting between Landlords and Tenants Was Canceled." *Korea Times Los Angeles*, February 16.

———. 1995c. "Another Demonstration in Jobber Market." *Korea Times Los Angeles*, February 17.

Hwang, Dong-Hee, and Ho Yeol Ki. 1993. "Farewell America, Good-bye Shattered Dream: Owner of John's Market Returns to Korea to Escape 'War Zone.'" *Korea Times Los Angeles (English Edition)*, March 31.

Institute of Social Sciences, Seoul National University. (ISS) 1987. *Korean Society in Transition (Chonhwan'gi ui Han'guk Sahoe)*. Seoul, Korea: Korea Times Publishing Office.

Jenkins, Craig. 1977. "Push/Pull in Recent Mexican Migration to the U.S." *International Migration Review* 11:178–89.

Jo, Moon H. 1992. "Korean Merchants in the Black Community: Prejudice among the Victims of Prejudice." *Ethnic and Racial Studies* 15 (3):395–411.

Johnson, James, and Melvin Oliver. 1989. "Interethnic Minority Conflict in Urban America: The Effects of Economic and Social Dislocation." *Urban Geography* 10:425–33.

Johnson, Peter. 1981. "Unemployment and Self-Employment: A Survey." *Industrial Relations Journal* 12:5–15.

Johnson, Violet. 1995. "Culture, Economic Stability, and Entrepreneurship: The Case of British West Indians in Boston." In *New Migrants in the Marketplace: Boston's Ethnic Entrepreneurs*, edited by Marilyn Halter, 59–80. Amherst: University of Massachusetts Press.

Joravsky, Ben. 1987. "Koreans Sell, Blacks Buy: A Clash of Cultures at the 63rd Street Mall." *Reader*, February 13:3.

Jung, Gyung-Gyun, et al. 1991. "Sociology of Medical Insurance." In *Medical Sociology (Pogon Sahoehak)*, 388–428. Seoul, Korea: Seoul National University.

Jung, Sok-Chang. 1991. "Another Big Black Demonstration in Front of John's Market." *Korea Times Los Angeles*, September 11.

KAGRO (Korean-American Grocers Association of Southern California). 1990. "Understanding Korean-American Retailers: Sensitivity Training Program for Sales and Marketing Professionals." Unpublished paper, Los Angeles, Calif., June 8.

Kang, Connie. 1992. "Visions of Darkness and Hope." *Los Angeles Times*, December 18.

———. 1993. "Shooting of Grocer Rekindles Fear among Korean Merchants." *Los Angeles Times*, October 26.

Kasinitz, Philip. 1992. *Caribbean New York: Black Immigrants and the Politics of Race.* Ithaca: Cornell University Press.

Katz, Jesse, and Stephanie Chavez. 1991. "Blacks Seek to Channel Anger over Sentence." *Los Angeles Times*, November 17.

Katz, Jesse, and Frank Clifford. 1991. "Many Find Verdict Fair, but There Is Still Outrage." *Los Angeles Times*, October 12.

Kim, Bok-Lim C. 1978. "Pioneers in Intermarriage: Korean Women in the United States." In *Korean Women in a Struggle for Humanization*, edited by Harold Hakueon Sunoo and Dong Soo Kim, 59–95. Memphis: Association of Korean Christian Scholars in North America.

Kim, Hyung-Chan. 1976. "Ethnic Enterprises among Korean Emigrants in America." *Journal of Korean Affairs* 6:40–58.

———. 1980. "Koreans." In *Harvard Encyclopedia of American Ethnic Groups*, edited by Stephan Therstorm, 601–6. Cambridge: Belknap Press of Harvard University Press.

Kim, Illsoo. 1981. *New Urban Immigrants: The Korean Community in New York.* Princeton: Princeton University Press.

———. 1987. "Korea and East Asia: Pre-emigration Factors and U.S. Immigration Policy." In *Pacific Bridges: The New Immigration from Asia and the Pacific Islands*, edited by James Fawcett and Benjamin Carino, 327–45. Staten Island: Center for Migration Studies.

Kim, Jin-Kyun. 1986. "The Class Structure and the Working Class in Contemporary Korea." In *Social Changes in South Korea (Han'guk Sahoe ui Pyondong)*, edited by Social Science Institute, 55–83. Seoul, Korea: Songgyunkwan University Press.

Kim, Jung-Sup. 1991a. "Tae Sam Park Proved Innocent." *Korea Times Los Angeles*, June 8.

———. 1991b. "Agreement to Suspend the Boycott Temporarily." *Korea Times Los Angeles*, October 5.

Kim, Kwang Chung, and Won Moo Hurh. 1983. "Korean Americans and the Success Image: A Critique." *Amerasia* 10:3–21.

———. 1985. "Ethnic Resource Utilization of Korean Immigrant Entrepreneurs in the Chicago Minority Area." *International Migration Review* 19:82–111.

Kim, Kwang Chung, Won Moo Hurh, and Marilyn Fernandez. 1989. "Intra-Group Differences in Business Participation: Three Asian Immigrant Groups." *International Migration Review* 23:73–95.

Kim, Kyung-Keun. 1990. "Schooling and Married Women's Work in a Developing Country: The Case of the Republic of Korea." Ph.D. dissertation, University of Chicago.

Kim, Sung-Hwan. 1991a. "Various Approaches to the Conflict." *Korea Times Los Angeles*, September 26.

———. 1991b. "Demonstration against Judge Karlin." *Korea Times Los Angeles*, November 23.

Kim, Tong-Il. 1983. "Urbanization and Rural Development." In *Future Directions of Korean Society (Han'guk Sahoe Odiro Kana)*, edited by Korean Sociological Association, 159–77. Seoul, Korea: Institute of Modern Society.

Kim, Warren. 1971. *Koreans in America.* Seoul, Korea: Po Chin Chai Printing Co.

Kirschenman, Joleen, and Kathryn Neckerman. 1991. "We'd Love to Hire Them, but . . . : The Meaning of Race for Employers." In *The Urban Underclass,* edited by Christopher Jenks and Paul Peterson, 203–34. Washington, D.C.: Brookings Institution.

KIWA. 1994. "KIWA Program Update." *KIWA News* 1 (summer).

Koo, Hagen. 1984. "The Political Economy of Income Distribution in South Korea: The Impact of the State's Industrialization Policies." *World Development* 12 (10): 1029–37.

———. 1987. "The Interplay of State, Social Class, and World System in East Asian Development: The Cases of South Korea and Taiwan." In *The Political Economy of the New Asian Industrialism,* edited by Frederic C. Deyo, 165–81. Ithaca: Cornell University Press.

———. 1990. "From Farm to Factory: Proletarianization in Korea." *American Sociological Review* 55 (3):669–81.

Koos, David. 1982. "South Asians in the Garment Industry: A Preliminary Study." *South Asia Bulletin* 2:59–67.

Korea Exchange Bank. 1987. *Exchange Controls Law and Order of Its Implementation (Oehwan kwanribop kwa Sihaengryong).* Seoul, Korea.

Korea Times of Chicago. 1991. *1991 Korean Business Directory (1991 Hanin Opsorok).* Chicago: Korea Times of Chicago.

Korean Economic Planning Board (KEPB). 1962. *1960 Population and Housing Census Report (1960 Ingu mit Jutaek Sensosu Pogo).* Seoul, Korea.

———. 1965, 1970, 1975, 1980, 1985, 1990, 1992. *Annual Report on the Economically Active Population (Kyongje hwaldong Ingu Yon'gam).* Seoul, Korea.

———. 1983. *Major Statistics of Korean Economy (Kyongje Chuyo Jip-yo).* Seoul, Korea.

———. 1987. *Social Indicators of Korea (Han'guk ui Sahoe Chip'yo).* Seoul, Korea.

Korean Ministry of Education. 1965–90. *Statistical Yearbook of Education (Kyoyuk Tonggye Yon'gam).* Seoul, Korea.

Korean Ministry of Labor. 1975, 1980, 1985, 1988, 1989. *Yearbook of Labour Statistics (Nodong T'onggye Yon'gam).* Seoul, Korea.

———. 1985. *Report on Occupational Wage Survey (Chikoppyol Imgumsiltae Chosapogo).* Seoul, Korea.

Korean Overseas Information Service (KOIS), Ministry of Culture and Information. 1983. *A Handbook of Korea.* Seoul, Korea.

Kourvetaris, Yorgos A. 1988. "The Greeks of Asia Minor and Egypt as Middleman Economic Minorities during the Late 19th and 20th Centuries." *Ethnic Groups* 7:85–111.

Kwong, Peter. 1987. *The New Chinatown.* New York: Noonday Press.

Lai, Him Mark. 1980. "Chinese." In *Harvard Encyclopedia of American Ethnic Groups,* edited by Stephan Therstrom, 222–34. Cambridge: Belknap Press of Harvard University Press.

Lee, Everett. 1966. "A Theory of Migration." *Demography* 3:47–57.

Lee, Heon Cheol. 1993. "Black–Korean Conflict in New York City: A Sociological Analysis." Ph.D. dissertation, Columbia University.

Lee, Hoon. 1994. "4.29 Displaced Workers Justice Campaign." *KIWA News* 1 (winter):6–13.

Lenski, Gerhard. 1966. *Power and Privilege: A Theory of Social Stratification.* New York: McGraw-Hill.

Leslie, Annie R. 1984. "Englewood." In *Local Community Fact Book: Chicago Metropolitan Area Based on the 1970 and 1980 Censuses,* edited by Chicago Fact Book Consortium. Chicago: Chicago Review Press.

Li, Angelina Hoo-Yee. 1980. "Labor Utilization and the Assimilation of Asian Americans." Ph.D. dissertation, University of Chicago.

Lieberson, Stanley, and Mary C. Walters. 1988. *From Many Strands: Ethnic and Racial Groups in Contemporary America.* New York: Russell Sage Foundation.

Light, Ivan. 1972. *Ethnic Enterprises in America: Business and Welfare among Chinese, Japanese, and Blacks.* Berkeley and Los Angeles: University of California Press.

———. 1980. "Asian Enterprise in America: Chinese, Japanese and Koreans in Small Business." In *Self-Help in Urban America,* edited by Scott Cummings, 33–57. Port Washington: Kinnikat Press.

———. 1984. "Immigrant and Ethnic Enterprise in North America." *Ethnic and Racial Studies* 7:195–216.

———. 1985. "Immigrant Entrepreneurs in America: Koreans in Los Angeles." In *Clamor at the Gates,* edited by Nathan Glazer, 161–78. San Francisco: Institute for Contemporary Studies Press.

Light, Ivan, and Edna Bonacich. 1988. *Immigrant Entrepreneurs: Koreans in Los Angeles, 1965–1982.* Berkeley and Los Angeles: University of California Press.

Light, Ivan, Hadas Har-Chvi, and Kenneth Kan. 1994. "Black/Korean Conflict in Los Angeles." In *Managing Divided Cities,* edited by Seamus Dunn, 72–87. London: Ryburn Publishing.

Light, Ivan, Im Jung Kwuon, and Deng Zhong. 1990. "Korean Rotating Credit Associations in Los Angeles." *Amerasia Journal* 16(1):35–54.

Light, Ivan, Georges Sabagh, Mehdi Bozorgmehr, and Caludia Der-Martirosian. 1993. "Internal Ethnicity in the Ethnic Economy." *Ethnic and Racial Studies* 16:581–98.

Light, Ivan, and Angel Sanchez. 1987. "Immigrant Entrepreneurs in 272 SMSAs." *Sociological Perspectives* 30:373–99.

Light, Ivan, and Carolyn Rosenstein. 1995. *Race, Ethnicity, and Entrepreneurship in Urban America.* New York: Aldine de Gruyter.

Litwark, Eugene. 1960. "Occupational Mobility and Extended Family Cohesion." *American Sociological Review* 25:9–21.

Liu, John, and Lucie Cheng. 1994. "Pacific Rim Development and the Duality of Post-1965 Asian Immigration to the United States." In *The New Asian Immigration in Los Angeles and Global Restructuring,* edited by Paul Ong, Edna Bonacich, and Lucie Cheng, 74–99. Philadelphia: Temple University Press.

Loewen, James W. 1971. *The Mississippi Chinese—Between Black and White.* Cambridge: Harvard University Press.

Longworth, R. C. 1992. "On One Street, Two Different Paths of Success." *Chicago Tribune*, September 17, section 7.

Los Angeles Times. 1993. "Asians in the Southland." August 20.

Lovell-Troy, Lawrence. 1981. "Ethnic Occupational Structure: Greeks in the Pizza Business." *Ethnicity* 8:82–95.

Lubin, Nancy. 1985. "Small Business Owners." Chapter 7 in *New Lives: The Adjustment of Soviet and Jewish Immigrants in the U.S. and Israel*, edited by Rita J. Simon. Lexington, Mass.: Lexington Books.

Ma, Eve Armentrout. 1984. "The Big-Business Ventures of Chinese in North America, 1850–1930." In *The Chinese American Experience*, edited by Genny Lim, 101–12. San Francisco: Chinese Historical Society of America and Chinese Culture Foundation of San Francisco.

———. 1991. "Chinatown Organizations and the Anti-Chinese Movement, 1882–1914." In *Entry Denied: Exclusion and the Chinese Community in America, 1882–1943*, edited by Sucheng Chan, 147–69. Philadelphia: Temple University Press.

Marger, Martin N. 1991. *Race and Ethnic Relations: American and Global Perspectives*. Belmont, Calif.: Wadsworth Publishing Company.

Marger, Martin N., and Constance A. Hoffman. 1994. "Intended Immigrant Entrepreneurs in Ontario: Expanding the Concept of Immigrant Entrepreneurs." Paper presented at the 89th annual meeting of the American Sociological Association, Los Angeles, August 5.

Marx, Karl. [1867] 1977. *Capital*, Vol. 1. New York: Vintage.

Mason, Edward, M. J. Kim, D. H. Perkins, K. S. Kim, and D. C. Cole. 1980. *The Economic and Social Modernization of the Republic of Korea*. Cambridge: Harvard University Press.

Massey, Douglas, and Nancy Denton. 1987. "Trends in the Residential Segregation of Blacks, Hispanics, and Asians: 1970–1980." *American Sociological Review* 52:802–25.

Mavratsas, Caesar. 1995. "Greek-American Economic Culture: The Intensification of Economic Life and a Parallel Process of Puritanization." In *New Migrants in the Marketplace: Boston's Ethnic Entrepreneurs*, edited by Marilyn Halter, 97–119. Amherst: University of Massachusetts Press.

McGinn, Noel, et al. 1980. *Education and Development in Korea*. Cambridge: Harvard University Press.

McKenney, Nampeo R., and Arthur R. Cresce. 1990. "The Identification of Ethnicity in the United States: The Census Bureau Experience." Paper presented at the annual meeting of the Population Association of America.

Meyer, Bruce. 1990. "Why Are There So Few Black Entrepreneurs?" Working paper no. 3537, National Bureau of Economic Research.

Meyer, Michael. 1992. "Los Angeles Will Save Itself." *Newsweek*, May 18.

Mills, C. Wright. 1951. *White Collar: The American Middle Classes*. New York: Oxford University Press.

Min, Pyong Gap. 1984. "From White-Collar Occupations to Small Business: Korean Immigrants' Occupational Adjustment." *Sociological Quarterly* 25:333–52.

———. 1988. *Ethnic Business Enterprise: Korean Small Business in Atlanta*. New York: Center for Migration Studies.

————. 1990. "Problems of Korean Immigrant Entrepreneurs." *International Migration Review* 24:436–55.

————. 1992. "The Structure and Social Functions of Korean Immigrant Churches in the United States." *International Migration Review* 26 (4):1370–95.

————. 1993. "Korean Immigrants in Los Angeles." Chapter 9 in *Immigration and Entrepreneurship*, edited by Ivan Light and Bhachu Parmmole. New Brunswick, N.J.: Transaction Publications.

————. 1996. *Caught in the middle: Korean merchants in America's multiethnic cities.* Berkeley and Los Angeles: University of California Press.

Min, Pyong Gap, and Charles Jaret. 1984. "Ethnic Business Success: The Case of Korean Small Business in Atlanta." *Sociology and Social Research* 69:412–35.

Mitchell, Marsha. 1991. "Black Man Killed by Korean Merchant; No Charges Filed." *Los Angeles Sentinel*, June 13.

Modell , Susanne. 1991. "Caribbean Immigrants: A Black Success Story?" *International Migration Review* 14: 248–76.

Moon, Tae-Gi. 1991a. "A Korean Female Store Owner Killed a Black Teenage Girl: Killing or Self-Defense?" *Korea Times Los Angeles*, March 19.

————. 1991b. "Black Demonstration in Front of Ms. Du's Market." *Korea Times Los Angeles*, March 22.

————. 1991c. "The Store That Killed a Black." *Korea Times Los Angeles*, March 23.

————. 1991d. "Blacks Will Purchase Stores Unkind to Blacks." *Korea Times Los Angeles*, March 28.

————. 1991e. "One Hundred Blacks Held a Violent Demonstration in Front of a Korean Store." *Korea Times Los Angeles*, March 24.

————. 1991f. "Interview with a Friend of Mitchell." *Korea Times Los Angeles*, June 4.

————. 1991g. "Arson on Two Korean Markets Involved in the Killing of Black Customers." *Korea Times Los Angeles*, August 19.

————. 1991h. "Interview with Rev. Edgar Boyd." *Korea Times Los Angeles*, August 29.

————. 1991i. "The John's Market Returned to the Starting Point." September 13.

Mydans, Seth. 1991. "Korean Grocer Convicted in Shooting." *New York Times*, October 12.

National Opinion Research Center (NORC). 1991. *General Social Surveys, 1972–1991: Cumulative Codebook.* Chicago: NORC, University of Chicago.

Navarro, Armando. 1993. "The South Central Los Angeles Eruption: A Latino Perspective." *Amerasia Journal* 19:69–86.

Nee, Victor, Jimy Sanders, and Scott Sernau. 1994. "Job Transition in an Immigrant Metropolis: Ethnic Boundaries and the Mixed Economy." *American Sociological Review* 59 (6):849–72.

Nishi, Setsuko M. 1979. "Asian American Employment Issues: Myths and Realities." In *United States Commission on Civil Rights. Civil Rights Issues of Asian and Pacific Americans: Myths and Realities.* Washington, D.C.: Government Printing Office.

O'Brien, David, and Stephen S. Fugita. 1982. "Middleman Minority Concept: Its Explanatory Value in the Case of the Japanese in California Agriculture." *Pacific Sociological Review* 25:185–204.

O'Connor, James. 1973. *The Fiscal Crisis of the State.* New York: St. Martin's Press.

Oh, Angela. 1991. "Move Past the Anger." *Los Angeles Times,* November 5.

O'Hare, William. 1987. "Best Metros for Black Businesses." *American Demographics* (July): 38–41.

Oliver, Melvin, and James Johnson. 1984. "Interethnic Conflict in an Urban Ghetto: The Case of blacks and Latinos in Los Angeles." *Research in Social Movements, Conflict, and Change* 6:57–94.

Omi, Michael, and Howard Winant. 1986. *Racial Formation in the United States: From the 1960s to the 1980s.* New York: Routledge & Kegan Paul.

Ong, Paul M. 1989. "Introduction." Chapter 1 in *The Widening Divide: Income Inequality and Poverty in Los Angeles.* Research group, Eulalio Castellanos . . . ; project director, Paul M. Ong. Los Angeles: The Research Group on the Los Angeles Economy.

Ong, Paul, Edna Bonacich, and Lucie Cheng. 1994. "The Political Economy of Capitalist Restructuring and the New Asian Immigration." In *The New Asian Immigration in Los Angeles and Global Restructuring,* edited by Paul Ong, Edna Bonacich, and Lucie Cheng, 3–35. Philadelphia: Temple University Press.

Ong, Paul, and Suzanne Hee. 1993. *Losses in the Los Angeles Civil Unrest April 29–May 1, 1992.* Los Angeles: UCLA Center for Pacific Rim Studies.

Ong, Paul, and John Liu. 1994. "U.S. Immigration Policies and Asian Immigration." In *The New Asian Immigration in Los Angeles and Global Restructuring,* edited by Paul Ong, Edna Bonacich, and Lucie Cheng, 45–73. Philadelphia: Temple University Press.

Ong, Paul, Kye Young Park, and Yasmin Tong. 1994. "The Korean–Black Conflict and the State." In *The New Asian Immigration in Los Angeles and Global Restructuring,* edited by Paul Ong, Edna Bonacich, and Lucie Cheng, 264–94. Philadelphia: Temple University Press.

Paik, Seung-Hwan. 1991. "Fruitless Compromise Conforming Fully to Blacks' Demands." *Korea Times Los Angeles,* September 5.

Park, Insook Han, James T. Fawcett, Fred Arnold, and Robert W. Gardner. 1990. "Korean Immigrants and U.S. Immigration Policy: A Predeparture Perspective." *Papers of the East–West Population Institute* 114 (March).

Park, Winnie. 1994. "Political Mobilization of the Korean American Community." In *Community in Crisis: The Korean American Community after the Los Angeles Civil Unrest of April 1992,* edited by George Totten III and Eric Schockman, 109–220. Center for Multiethnic and Transnational Studies, University of Southern California.

Patterson, Wayne. 1976. "Upward Social Mobility of the Koreans in Hawaii." *Korean Studies* 3:81–92.

———. 1988. *The Korean Frontier in America: Immigration to Hawaii, 1896–1910.* Honolulu: University of Hawaii Press.

Perez-Pena, Richard. 1991. "Unusual Threat for a Judge in a Bitter Slaying Trial." *Los Angeles Times,* November 22.

Piore, Michael. 1979. *Birds of Passage: Migrant Labor in Industrial Societies.* New York: Cambridge University Press.

Pomerantz, Linda. 1984. "The Background of Korean Emigration." In *Labor Immigration under Capitalism: Asian Workers in the United States before World War II*, edited by Lucie Cheng and Edna Bonacich, 277–315. Berkeley and Los Angeles: University of California Press.

Population and Development Studies Center. 1988. "The Seoul National University: History, Organization, and Activities." Paper presented at the University of California at Los Angeles International Workshop on the Movement of Highly Educated Labor in the Pacific Rim, Los Angeles, August 29–September 2.

Portes, Alejandro, and Robert L. Bach. 1985. *Latin Journey: Cuban and Mexican Immigrants in the United States*. Berkeley and Los Angeles: University of California Press.

Portes, Alejandro, and Robert D. Manning. 1986. "The Immigrant Enclave: Theory and Empirical Examples." In *Competitive Ethnic Relations*, edited by Susan Olzak and Joane Nagel, 47–68. San Diego: Academic Press.

Portes, Alejandro, and Alex Stepick. 1993. *City on the Edge: The Transformation of Miami*. Berkeley and Los Angeles: University of California Press.

Portes, Alejandro, and John Walton. 1981. *Labor, Class, and the International System*. New York: Academic Press.

Portes, Alejandro, and Min Zhou. 1992. "Gaining the Upper Hand: Economic Mobility among Immigrant and Domestic Minorities." *Ethnic and Racial Studies* 15:491–522.

Ray, Robert N. 1975. "A Report on Self-Employed Americans in 1973." *Monthly Labor Review* 98:49–54.

Regalado, James A. 1994. "Creating Multicultural Harmony? A Critical Perspective on Coalition-Building Efforts in Los Angeles." In *Community in Crisis: The Korean American Community after the Los Angeles Civil Unrest of April 1992*, 221–35. Los Angeles: Center for Multiethnic and Transnational Studies, University of Southern California.

Rieder, Jonathan. 1985. *Canarsie: The Jews and Italians of Brooklyn against Liberalism*. Cambridge: Harvard University Press.

Rinder, Irwin D. 1958–59. "Strangers in the Land: Social Relations in the Status Gap." *Social Problems* 6:253–60.

Royer, Ariela. 1984. "Albany Park." In *Local Community Fact Book: Chicago Metropolitan Area Based on the 1970 and 1980 Censuses*, edited by Chicago Fact Book Consortium, 35–37. Chicago: Chicago Review Press.

Ryu, Tongsik. 1988. *A History of Christ Methodist Church, 1903–1988 (Hawaii ui Hanin kwa Kyohoe)*. Hawaii: Christ Methodist Church.

Sahagun, Louis. 1991. "Blacks Won't End Korean Store Boycott." *Los Angeles Times*, August 31.

Schaefer, Richard. 1988. *Racial and Ethnic Groups*. Glenview, IL: Scott, Foresman and Company.

Schermerhorn, Richard. 1978. *Comparative Ethnic Relations: A Framework for Theory and Research*. Chicago: University of Chicago Press.

Schimek, Paul. 1989. "Earnings Polarization and the Proliferation of Low-Wage Work." Chapter 2 in *The Widening Divide: Income Inequality and Poverty in Los Angeles*. Research group, Eulalio Castellanos . . . ; project director, Paul

M. Ong. Los Angeles: The Research Group on the Los Angeles Economy.

Schmidt, William E. 1990. "Ideas & Trends: For Immigrants, Tough Customers." *New York Times*, November 25.

Schoenberger, Karl. 1992. "Moving between Two Worlds: Koreans in the U.S." *Los Angeles Times*, July 12.

Shin, Eui Hang, and Kyung-Sup Chang. 1988. "Peripherization of Immigrant Professionals: Korean Physicians in the United States." *International Migration Review* 22 (4):609–26.

Shin, Linda. 1971. "Koreans in America, 1903–1945." *Amerasia Journal* 1:32–39.

Shryock, Henry S., Jacob S. Siegel, and Associates. 1976. *The Methods and Materials of Demography*. Condensed edition by Edward G. Stockwell. Orlando, Fla.: Academic Press, Inc.

Silverstein, Stuart, and Nancy Brooks. 1991. "Shoppers in Need of Stores." *Los Angeles Times*, November 24.

Siu, Paul. 1987. *The Chinese Laundroman: A Study of Social Isolation*. New York: New York University Press.

Soja, Edward, Rebecca Morales, and Goetz Wolff. 1983. "Urban Restructuring: An Analysis of Social and Spatial Change in Los Angeles." *Economic Geography* 58:221–35.

Sokolove, Michael. 1994. "Helping Korean Shops as Guard—and Guide." *Philadelphia Inquirer*, November 15: A18.

Solomon, Steven. 1986. *Small Business USA: The Role of Small Companies in Sparking America's Economic Transformation*. New York: Crown Publishers.

Sowell, Thomas. 1975. *Race and Economics*. New York: David McKay Co., Inc.

Steinberg, Stephen. 1981. *The Ethnic Myth: Race, Ethnicity and Class in America*. New York: Atheneum.

Steinmetz, George, and Erik O. Wright. 1989. "The Fall and Rise of the Petty Bourgeoisie: Changing Patterns of Self-Employment in the Postwar United States." *American Journal of Sociology* 95:973–1018.

Stengel, Richard. 1985. "Blacks: Resentment Tinged with Envy." *Time*, July 8, 42–43.

Stolberg, Sheryl, and Frederick Muir. 1992. "Judge Karlin's Win Baffles Black Leaders." *Los Angeles Times*, June 4.

Stryker, Sheldon. 1958. "Social Structure and Prejudice." *Social Problems* 6:340–54.

Sung, Betty Lee. 1976. *A Survey of Chinese-American Manpower and Employment*. New York: Praeger Publishers.

Suttles, Gerald. 1968. *The Social Order of the Slum*. Chicago: University of Chicago Press.

Sway, Marlene. 1980. "Simmel's Concept of the Stranger and the Gypsies." *Social Science Journal* 18:41–50.

Takami, David. 1988. "Can Asian Americans Influence the Election?" *AsiAm* (January):23–45.

Takaki, Ronald. 1989. *Strangers from a Different Shore: A History of Asian Americans*. Boston: Little, Brown.

Thompson, Virginia, and Richard Adloff. 1955. *Minority Problems in Southeast Asia.* Boston: Beacon Press.

Time. 1988. "Do-It-Yourself Financing: To Immigrants Short on Credit, Loan Clubs Offer Cash and Dream." *Time*, July 25, 62.

Uhlaner, Carole. 1991. "Perceived Discrimination and Prejudice and the Coalition Prospects of Blacks, Latinos, and Asian Americans." In *Racial and Ethnic Politics in California*, edited by Byron Jackson and Michael Preston, 339–71. Berkeley: Institute of Governmental Studies.

U.S. Bureau of the Census, U.S. Department of Commerce. 1982. *1980 Census of Population*, General Population Characteristics. Washington, D.C.: Government Printing Office.

———. 1983. *1980 Census of Population*, Vol. 1: Characteristics of the Population, Chapter C: General Social and Economic Characteristics, Part 1: United States Summary. Washington, D.C.: Government Printing Office.

———. 1984. *1980 Census of Population*, Vol. 1: Characteristics of the Population, Chapter D: Detailed Population Characteristics, Part 1: United States Summary. Washington, D.C.: Government Printing Office.

———. 1985. *1982 Survey of Minority-Owned Business Enterprises.* Washington, D.C.: U.S. Government Printing Office.

———. 1988. *Statistical Abstract of the United States: 1989* (109th edition). Washington, D.C.: Government Printing Office.

———. 1991. *1987 Survey of Minority-Owned Business Enterprises.* Washington, D.C.: U.S. Government Printing Office.

———. 1992. *1990 Census of Population*, General Population Characteristics, United States. Washington, D.C.: Government Printing Office.

———. 1993a. *1990 Census of Population*, Social and Economic Characteristics, United States. Washington, D.C.: Government Printing Office.

———. 1993b. *1990 Census of Population and Housing, Population and Housing Characteristics for Census Tracts and Block Numbering Areas*, Los Angeles–Long Beach, CA PMSA Section 2 of 7, Table 8, 1057–58.

U.S. Bureau of Labor Statistics. 1948–1992. *Employment and Earnings.* Washington, D.C.: Government Printing Office Monthly.

———. 1988. *Labor Statistics Derived from the Current Population Survey, 1948–87.* Washington, D.C.: Government Printing Office.

———. 1989. *Handbook of Labor Statistics.* Washington, D.C.: Government Printing Office.

U.S. Commission on Civil Rights. 1988. *The Economic Status of Americans of Asian Descent: An Exploratory Investigation.* Washington, D.C.: Government Printing Office.

———. 1992. *Civil Rights Issues Facing Asian Americans in the 1990s.* Washington, D.C.: Government Printing Office.

U.S. Immigration and Naturalization Service. 1966–1977. *The Annual Reports of the U.S. Immigration and Naturalization Service.* Washington, D.C.: Government Printing Office.

———. 1978–1990. *The Statistical Yearbook of the U.S. Immigration and Naturalization Service.* Washington, D.C.: Government Printing Office.

Vialet, Joyce C., and Larry M. Eig. 1991. "Immigration Act of 1990 (P.L. 101–649)." *Migration World* 14 (1):32–42.

Waldinger, Roger. 1986. *Through the Eye of the Needle: Immigrants and Enterprise in New York's Garment Trades.* New York: New York University Press.

———. 1989. "Structural Opportunity or Ethnic Advantage?: Immigrant Business Development in New York." *International Migration Review* 23:48–72.

Waldinger, Roger, Howard Aldrich, and Robin Ward. 1990. *Ethnic Entrepreneurship: Immigrant Business in Industrial Societies.* Newbury Park: Sage Publications.

Wang, L. Ling-Chi. 1991. "The Politics of Ethnic Identity and Empowerment: The Asian American Community Since the 1960s." *Asian American Policy Review* 2:43–56.

Warren, Robert. 1980. "Volume and Composition of U.S. Immigration and Emigration." In *Sourcebook on the New Immigration,* edited by Roy Simon Bryce-Laporte, 1–14. New Brunswick, N.J.: Transaction Books.

Weisbord, Robert, and Arthur Stein. 1970. *Bitter Sweet Encounter: The Afro-American and the American Jews.* Westport: Negro University Press.

Wilkinson, Tracy, and Frank Clifford. 1991. "Korean Grocer Who Killed Black Teen Gets Probation." *Los Angeles Times,* November 16.

Willmott, W. E. 1966. "The Chinese in Southeast Asia." *Australian Outlook* 20:252–62.

Wilson, Kenneth L., and Alejandro Portes. 1980. "Immigrant Enclaves: An Analysis of the Labor Market Experiences of Cubans in Miami." *American Journal of Sociology* 86:295–319.

Wilson, William. 1978. *The Declining Significance of Race.* Chicago: University of Chicago Press.

———. 1987. *The Truly Disadvantaged: The Inner City, The Underclass, and Public Policy.* Chicago: University of Chicago Press.

Wong, Bernard. 1987. "The Chinese: New Immigrants in New York's Chinatown." In *New Immigrants in New York,* edited by Nancy Foner, 243–71. New York: Columbia University Press.

Wong, Eugene F. 1985. "Asian American Middleman Minority Theory: The Framework of an American Myth." *Journal of Ethnic Studies* 13:51–88.

Wong, Morrison G. 1982. "The Cost of Being Chinese, Japanese, and Filipino in the United States: 1960, 1970, and 1976." *Pacific Sociological Review* 25:58–78.

Yancy, Robert J. 1974. *Federal Government Policy and Black Business Enterprise.* Cambridge: Ballinger Publishing Company.

Yee, Jaeyeol. 1990. "The Formation and Reproduction of Self-Employment in a Developing Economy: Analysis of Job Shift Rates in South Korean Urban Labor Market." Paper presented at the 85th annual meeting of the American Sociological Association, Washington, D.C., August 11–15.

Yim, Sun Bin. 1985. "Social Networks among Korean Immigrants in the United States." Ph.D. dissertation, University of California, Los Angeles.

Yochum, Gilbert, and Vinod Agarwal. 1988. "Permanent Labor Certification for Alien Professionals, 1975–1982." *International Migration Review* 22:265–319.

Yonsei University. 1990. *Yonsei University (Yonse Taehak)* Seoul, Korea.

Yoon, In-Jin. 1991a. "The Changing Significance of Ethnic and Class Resources in Immigrant Businesses: The Case of Korean Immigrant Businesses in Chicago." *International Migration Review* 25:303–32.

———. 1991b. "Self-Employment in Business: Chinese-, Japanese-, Korean-Americans, Blacks, and Whites." Ph.D. dissertation, University of Chicago.

———. 1995. "The Growth of Korean Immigrant Entrepreneurship in Chicago." *Ethnic and Racial Studies* 18 (2):315–35.

———. 1996. "Self-Employment in Business among U.S. Ethnic Groups." *Korea Journal of Population and Development* 25:123–54.

Young, Philip K. 1983. "Family Labor, Sacrifice, and Competition: Korean Greengrocers in New York City." *Amerasia* 10:53–71.

Yu, Eui Young. 1983. "Korean Communities in America: Past, Present, and Future." *Amerasia Journal* 10:23–51.

———. 1990. *Korean Community Profile: Life and Consumer Pattern.* Los Angeles: The Korea Times.

Yu, Renqiu. 1992. *To Save China, To Save Ourselves: The Chinese Hand Laundry Alliance of New York.* Philadelphia: Temple University Press.

Yuengert, Andrew M. 1989. "Self-Employment and the Earnings of Male Immigrants in the U.S." Discussion paper no. 581, Economic Growth Center, Yale University.

Zhou, Min. 1992. *Chinatown: The Socioeconomic Potential of an Urban Enclave.* Philadelphia: Temple University Press.

Korean-Language Newspapers

Korea Times of Chicago (KTC; *Han'guk Ilbo Chicago P'an*). 12/4/1980. "Albany Park Developed as the Center of Koreatown."

———. 8/4/1981. "Concern over Excessive Competition among Koreans."

———. 8/7/1981. "Black Merchants on 47th Street Plan to Boycott a Korean Store."

———. 8/10/1981. "Black Boycott on 47th Street."

———. 8/11/1981. "Arson on a Korean Store on 47th Street."

———. 8/20/1981. "Jo Kim Negotiates Terms of Withdrawal."

———. 2/14/1983. "First Korean Businesses on Clark Street Are Moving."

———. 11/8/1983. "Tenth Anniversary of Dong Woo Club: Foundation of Korean Businesses and Churches in Chicago."

———. 11/14/1983. "Koreans Are the Cornerstone of Lawrence Avenue."

———. 1/19/1985. "Cash Transactions and Tax Evasion in Korean Business."

———. 9/30–12/16/1986. "Visiting the Korean Business Concentration Areas on the South Side of Chicago."

———. 7/22/1987. "Shoe Repair Business."

———. 9/2/1988. "Racial Dispute in the 87th Street Business District."

———. 11/21/1989. "Korean Investment in Real Estate on Lawrence Avenue Tripled in Ten Years."

———. 7/13/1990. "The Korean–Black Dispute in Roseland Was Settled."

———. 7/14/1990. "Koreans Own 2,000 Laundry and Dry Cleaners in Chicago."

———. 11/8/1990. "Current Status of Korean Laundry and Dry Cleaning Businesses in Chicago."

———. 3/21/1991. "Dong Woo Club, Frontier of Korean Immigration to Chicago."

———. 6/16/1992. "Let's Keep the Frontier with Courage: Visiting the Site of the Bulls Riots."

———. 6/18/1992. "Damage Compensation Hearing Will Open Soon."

Korea Times Los Angeles (KTLA; *Han'guk Ilbo Los Angeles P'an*). 3/22/1991. "Korean Liquor Stores in South Central Became the Target of Black Retaliation."

———. 3/23/1991. "Learn a Lesson from the Korean Community of Chicago."

———. 3/24/1991. "Mayor Bradley Intervened in the Racial Dispute over the Killing of Harlins."

———. 3/30/1991. "Blacks' Retaliation against Korean Stores Increases."

———. 6/6/1991. "I'm Not Lonely (1): Tae Sam Park's Diary."

———. 7/4/1991. "Let's Prevent the Second John's Market."

———. 8/6/1991. "Another Misconduct of the Black Boycotters at Tae Sam Park's John's Market."

———. 8/31/1991. "Mayor Bradley Intervened in the Korean–Black Conflict."

———. 9/12/1991. "The KARE Decided to Terminate Its Financial Assistance to John's Market."

———. 11/17/1991. "Black Community Expressed Dissatisfaction with the Verdict."

———. 11/27/1991. "Five Molotov Cocktails Thrown into a Korean Liquor Store."

———. 12/20/1991. "Baseball Batting Incident: Asian Rage Spreads."

Korea Times Los Angeles (English Edition) (KTLAEE). 3/31/1993. "A Hired Gunn: Investigator Assists KA Merchants in Improving Customer Relations."